THE STORY OF
HMS *REVENGE*

THE STORY OF HMS *REVENGE*

A Ship in Time

Alexander Stilwell

Pen & Sword
MARITIME

For Sarah, William, Olivia and Philippa

First published in Great Britain in 2009 by
Pen & Sword Maritime
an imprint of
Pen & Sword Books Ltd
47 Church Street
Barnsley
South Yorkshire
S70 2AS

Copyright © Alexander Stilwell, 2009

ISBN: 978-1-84415-981-9

Typeset in 11/13pt Sabon by
Concept, Huddersfield, West Yorkshire

Printed by the MPG Books Group
in the UK

Pen & Sword Books Ltd incorporates the Imprints of Pen & Sword
Aviation, Pen & Sword Maritime, Pen & Sword Military, Wharncliffe
Local History, Pen & Sword Select, Pen & Sword Military Classics,
Leo Cooper, Remember When, Seaforth Publishing and
Frontline Publishing.

For a complete list of Pen & Sword titles please contact
PEN & SWORD BOOKS LIMITED
47 Church Street, Barnsley, South Yorkshire, S70 2AS, England
E-mail: enquiries@pen-and-sword.co.uk
Website: www.pen-and-sword.co.uk

Contents

Acknowledgements

I would like to thank the family of the late John Winton and Constable & Robinson Ltd for allowing me to draw on his research for the Smerwick operation, Armada and part of the Dutch wars.

I am grateful to Brigadier Henry Wilson for taking this book on at Pen & Sword Maritime. I would like to thank Bobby Gainher for his careful editing.

The staff of the Royal Naval Museum, Imperial War Museum and National Maritime Museum have been helpful with identifying illustrations.

Chapter 1

Scene – A Ship at Sea: an Island

When *Revenge* was laid down at Deptford in 1575, it was only five years after Pope Pius V had issued a Bull of Excommunication against Elizabeth I (1558–1603), which proved to be the warning bell for the inevitable squaring up of Protestant England and Catholic Spain.

While Puritans in England kicked at the traces of Elizabeth's Anglican Church settlement, Catholic Jesuit priests trained on the Continent landed in England to try to bring about a Catholic revival, their hopes centred on Mary Queen of Scots.

In the Netherlands, the Protestant movement was growing in the wake of the depredations of the Spanish Duke of Alba, and English emissaries and spies did their best to foment resistance. In France religious wars raged, to England's convenience, leaving Spain as her deadliest enemy.

Whereas Englishmen had sallied forth onto the 'vasty fields of France' under King Henry V, now Continental Europe was a fortress impregnable to more than the occasional expeditionary force to help the Dutch. Without sufficiently powerful land forces to make a real difference in European affairs, Englishmen focused more and more on the possibilities offered by the sea. Unable to tackle the enemy head on, they nipped at its ankles like jackals teasing a lumbering elephant.

The spirit of the Elizabethan age lent itself to adventure. A nation without formidable military resources is more likely to rely on wit and cunning than brute force for survival, and there was plenty of wit in Elizabethan England. The monarch herself was a feisty redhead who drew on all her female guile to survive in a world dominated by men. Playwrights such as Kyd, Marlowe and Shakespeare, authors

1

of the Revenge tragedies, drew on their resources of wit to entertain exacting audiences, who would throw rotten vegetables rather than endure a slow play. In an environment where English trade was not yet established, sea captains lived on their wits in order to survive.

There was little to restrain the inspirations of adventurers: initiative, inventiveness, and derring-do ruled the waves before cumbersome administrative machinery had had time to take over. The Queen gave her captains a loose rein, tugging the bridle only when their greed or audacity got the better of them. Thus English adventurers roamed the seas to plunder, to trade and to find new lands that would harbour the explosive energies of the Elizabethans.

Although England may now have become the most adventurous maritime nation, it would be a long time before Britannia ruled the waves. The English were tantamount to thieves and condemned men, stealing through the streets of a world city largely divided between Spain and Portugal and, after Portugal was annexed by Spain in 1580, dominated by Spain.

Drake's rounding of Cape Cod and circumnavigation of the globe in the *Golden Hind* showed that not only were the English daring but also tenacious. It also proved that small ships made from English oak could withstand the worst the world's seven seas could throw at them.

Elizabeth knighted her captain at Deptford while Walsingham plotted to trap the Catholic Queen-in-waiting, Mary Queen of Scots, and get her head on the block. It seemed to be only a matter of time before the Spanish nemesis would be visited on England.

Revenge was a suitable name for a ship sailed by such bold, brazen mariners. The galleon had the look of a weapon, with spare, sleek lines leading to a sharp, beaked prow. She was suited to the purposes of her country – designed for fast attack and manoeuvrability, and dispensing with the capacity of larger and more cumbersome ships to hold stores for long voyages: 'English galleons were more or less pure men-of-war, whose fast underwater lines made them fast, handy and weatherly. As a result they lacked stowage; they were ill-fitted to carry bulk cargoes, or indeed to stow victuals and water to carry large forces over any long distance.'[1]

Revenge was notable for its low profile, a departure from the broad, high-sided designs of many contemporary ships inspired by the earlier carracks.[2] Her spiritual ancestors were the Portuguese caravels, the fast, light, lateen-sailed craft that had been used by Henry the Navigator to explore the coast of Africa. Sir Francis Drake himself considered her a masterpiece of naval construction and Sir William Monson described her as a 'race ship', 'low and snug in the water like a galliasse'.

Like the caravels, which Sir Walter Raleigh remembered 'swarming about us like butterflies', *Revenge* was more 'weatherly' than her predecessors and able to close up to windward of 'high-charged' ships.

Revenge compared with some of her peers in the Navy Royal

Ship	Date	Tons	Keel/beam	Depth/beam
Foresight	1570	294	2.90	0.519
Bull	1570	193	3.64	0.500
Tiger	1570	149	2.17	0.565
Dreadnought	1573	405	3.00	0.500
Swiftsure	1573	288	2.64	0.506
Revenge	1577	471	2.88	0.500
Scout	1577	132	3.00	0.550

The only danger was that the English might have exceeded themselves in their quest to find the perfect proportions. *Revenge* was ideal but later designs were thought to be less so:

From about the mid-sixteenth century to the Armada, it seems quite evident that the English shipbuilders were constantly experimenting, seeking the perfect shape for their ships.

Starting with short, shallow vessels, they began lengthening and deepening them. During the early Elizabethan years, they almost achieved the perfection they sought, but did not know it. So they continued changing until they were past the ideal proportions.[3]

Revenge was built at Deptford dockyard, which had been established by Henry VIII in 1513 as close as possible to the Royal Armouries. The main construction would have been of seasoned oak, a strong and durable wood that was less likely to splinter under gunfire. It was part of the shipwright's art to select straight trees for long planks and bent ones for the deck supports and other fittings.

The main body of the ship would have been sourced from English forests, such as the Forest of Dean or the New Forest, while masts were often made from fir trees imported from the Baltic.

The building of the ship required long-term planning, since the proper seasoning of the wood involved years of storage, soaking in water in specially constructed pools and intervals in the construction to allow the timbers of the frame and hull to settle. Ships built in a hurry would cause their makers to repent at leisure, although this was not a problem faced by the Navy Royal, since English ships were built with an emphasis on quality over speed of construction. The quality of the *Revenge*'s build was such that during her last battle in 1591, she survived the attacks of no less than fifteen Spanish warships.

Revenge would have been equipped with canvas sails cut and sewn specifically to fit her dimensions, with sailmaking and the spinning of hem for ropes being carried out on site.

Revenge was designed by one of the Royal shipwrights, Peter Pett or Matthew Baker, who would also have overseen the building work on the ship. The design would have been approved by Sir John Hawkins, the Treasurer of the Navy, who was a prime mover in the new type of ship design. Not only was *Revenge* a sleek design, ideal for speed and quick manoeuvre, she was also comparatively heavily gunned for her size. Her firepower was four times greater than *The Great Bark*, also of 500 tons, launched in 1540 and she had considerably more firepower for her size than her Spanish counterparts.[4]

Measurements of the galleon HMS *Revenge*

Keel	92 feet
Maximum beam	32 feet
Depth of hold	16 feet
Fore rake	32 feet
Stern rake	5 feet, 6 inches
Weight	500 tons

Guns

By the time *Revenge* was built, England had perhaps the most efficient gun manufacture and supply system in Europe. By 1548 there were fifty-three furnaces, forgeries and bloomeries in The

Weald, with the muzzle-loading manufacture being overseen by men such as the French gun-founder Pierre Baude, the King's 'gunstone maker' William Lovett and local ironmaster Ralph Hogg. By 1573, seven furnaces were casting 300–400 tons of guns and shot every year. Bronze guns were a development of the principles used in founding bronze bells. Each gun was different, since the mould had to be broken after each casting.

Iron guns were more dangerous to the user than bronze guns, since they were liable to explode if there was a flaw in them, whereas bronze guns just tended to crack. But iron was relatively cheap and plentiful. Despite these advances in iron-gun manufacture, however, the Navy in Elizabeth's reign, including *Revenge*, was still largely equipped with bronze cannon.

Revenge's main armament consisted of culverins, the heavy build of which made them less likely to fail and their weight reduced the amount of recoil on firing. The bronze culverins were reliable and as accurate as could be expected of a smooth-bore gun. English guns were mounted on wooden trucks designed specifically for use on a ship, whereas the Spanish guns tended to be mounted on carriages reminiscent of an army field gun. The English system gave their gunners an advantage by reducing recoil and making it easier to reload.

Typical armaments on *Revenge*

Number	Type of Gun
2	6.5in to 7in 30-pounder muzzle-loading (ML) demi-cannon, *c.*10ft long
4	6in ML 24-pounder cannon periers
10	5–5.5in ML 7-pounder culverins, *c.*13ft long
6	4.5in ML 9-pounder demi-culverins, *c.*12ft long
10	3in ML 5-pounder sakers, *c.*11ft long
2	2.5in ML 3-pounder falcons, *c.*7ft long
2	5.5in breech-loading (BL) port pieces with 3.5in chambers, 16in long
4	4in BL fowlers
or	
6	1¼in BL bases (light battery guns)
Total:	
40–42 guns	

Ordnance report, 1588, for *Revenge*

Number	Type of Gun
2	Cannon
6	Demi-cannon
12	Culverins
2	Demi-culverins
4	Minions (3in ML 4-pounders, *c.* 8ft)
11	Small pieces
Total:	
37 guns	

Revenge was classified as a 'Second Rate' of 500 to 800 tons (First Rates such as *Triumph* and *Victory* were 800 tons and above), and her complement was 150 seamen, 24 gunners and 76 soldiers, totalling 250. Apart from the Captain or Admiral, the crew included: a master, responsible for navigation, and his mate; a boatswain; a quartermaster; a coxswain; a cook; a steward; a master carpenter and master gunner, and their mates. There was also a surgeon, a trumpeter and a pilot. The crew's pay varied from £2.00 per month for the Master to ten shillings for a seaman, although this sometimes depended on the available cash resources.

With the rapid expansion of the Navy to face the growing threat from Spain, the standard of entry into it had to be continually lowered in order to attract sufficient men or, by the use of press gang, to force them to join.

As their own clothes wore out, the crew had no option but to buy replacements from the purser, paid for out of their own pockets, though they would be given a pay advance to do so. Typical of the kind of material required was a 1580 order of canvas for breeches and doublets, cotton for linings and petticoats, stockings, caps, shoes and shirts. Pipe Office accounts for 1595 listed a supply of calico for 200 suits of apparel, 400 shirts, woollen and worsted stockings, linen breeches and 'Monmouth' caps.

With the huge increase in the time spent at sea, as Tudor sailors embarked on longer and longer voyages, the provision and storage of food developed into a major problem. The staple diet for the Tudor sailor at sea was salt beef, salt fish, biscuit and cheese. These were the only foods that would remain edible for long periods, provided they were in a reasonable condition when first brought aboard. This, however, was not always the case as the tight-fisted Queen drove hard bargains with the civilian contractors who supplied the Navy's food. The contractors for their part maximized their profits by providing the cheapest parts of carcases, fish past its sell-by date, mouldy biscuits and stale cheese.

In 1565, the agent victualler was paid 4½ pence per day per man and 5 pence per day per man at sea. By 1587 these sums had only risen to 6½ pence and 7 pence, despite the fact that the cost of living had doubled. Even so, the Queen had a clause inserted in the contract specifying that these sums were to be paid only 'untill it shall please Almightie God to send such plentie as the heigh prises and rates of victuall shalbe diminished'.

Lord Charles Howard reported:

That both our drink, fish and beef is so corrupt as it will destroy all the men we have, and if they feed on it but a few days, in very truth we should not be able to keep the seas, what necessity soever did require the same, unless some new provision be made, for as the companies in general refuse to feed on it, so we cannot in reason or conscience constrain them.[5]

The effect of poor food was aggravated by the rule of 'six upon four' on long voyages, whereby six men had to subsist on the rations normally issued to four men.

Fresh water, which was stored on board in wooden casks, became foetid in a few days and the sailor made up his liquid allowance with his entitlement of a gallon of beer a day. Brewed without hops, such beer quickly went sour and was a likely cause of the 'infectione' (probably a form of gastroenteritis) so often mentioned in voyage reports.

Short rations, decayed or putrefying food, sour beer, poor or non-existent ventilation below decks, overcrowding (partly to allow for the expected mortality during a long voyage, but also to provide sufficient manning for the new tactics of fast attack and withdrawal), the constant stink from foul bilges and hogsheads of urine kept on deck (for fire-fighting purposes), all made the Tudor sailor particularly vulnerable to disease, especially scurvy. It would be not for another two centuries that the properties of lemon juice as an anti-scorbutic against scurvy were discovered. Sir Richard Hawkins, writing in 1622, estimated that in twenty years of Elizabeth's reign at least 10,000 men died from scurvy alone.

In view of these conditions, it does not seem surprising that the majority of sailors in the Navy at the time were little better than pirates, ever ready to mutiny if discontented or thwarted in their expectations of spoil. It is even less surprising when one considers that the interest in spoil was often exceeded by their captains.

Yet, for all his faults, his greed and his brutality, on occasion and with the right leadership, the Elizabethan sailor was capable of acts of sublime bravery, as the war with Spain was about to show.

Navigation

Elizabethan mariners used a number of navigational devices which helped them to determine their latitude, including the astrolabe, cross staff, back staff, quadrant and magnetic compass as well as charts. They could not, however, determine longitude at sea since they did not have accurate enough time pieces aboard to compare local time, measured by a celestial body, with the time at a reference location kept by a clock. The navigators on ships like *Revenge* would therefore have needed to use dead reckoning to supplement their readings for latitude – this involved the measurement of the heading and speed of the ship, the speeds of the ocean currents and the drift of the ship, and the time spent on each heading.

No less than six of the navigational and other mathematical instruments made by Humfrey Cole (*c*.1530–91) are dated 1575, the year of the launch of *Revenge*. This coincidence underlines the adventurous spirit of the day, as well as the fact that long expeditions, whether for privateering, service of the Crown or discovery, required accurate instruments, lest time, provisions and even lives should be wasted.

The astrolabe was as ubiquitous in the sixteenth century as Global Positioning System (GPS) instruments are now. It was a multi-functional instrument that could be used for telling the time during the day and at night, surveying, determining latitude and even casting horoscopes. The mariner's astrolabe dispensed with the optional extras found on the planispheric astrolabe.

Although some of the embryonic work in astronomy and geography was inaccurate, instruments such as the astrolabe embodied the staggering achievements of men like Hipparchus and Ptolemy who discovered the alterations of the measured positions of the stars. The accuracy of these discoveries enabled early mathematicians to construct precise instruments that became widely used, for example by the captains sent out by Prince Henry the Navigator of Portugal to discover the route to India via the Cape of Good Hope. The instrument gave the Portuguese a tremendous advantage over mariners from other nations who did not possess them. Columbus, Magellan and Drake were among the great seafarers who used the astrolabe on epic voyages of discovery.

The astrolabe consists of a celestial part (rete), terrestrial parts (plates), a thick brass plate with a rim (the mater) and index for the front (the rule), and another one for the back with additional sights (the alidade). The user holds the instrument by a loop at the top, allowing it to dangle like a plummet, and sights a star with the sighting rule. He then reads the altitude off the scale engraved on the ring, thus determining his latitude. The astrolabe and its use was described by Geoffrey Chaucer to his son in the first scientific work written in English:

2. To knowe the altitude of the sonne or of othre celestial bodies.

Put the ryng of thyn Astrelabie upon thy right thombe, and turne thi lift syde ageyn the light of the sonne; and remewe thy rewle up and doun til that the stremes of the sonne shine thorugh bothe holes of thi rewle. Loke than how many degrees thy rule is areised fro the litel crois upon thin est lyne, and tak there the altitude of thi sonne. And in this same wise maist thow knowe by night the alti- tude of the mone or of brighte sterres.[6]

The cross staff may have been even more widely used by Elizabethan mariners than the astrolabe. It consists of a yardstick with a perpendicular cross stick that can be slid up and down. By using a tangent table, the user could work out the angle created by the positioning of the perpendicular slide. The back staff was similar, except that the user stood with his back to the sun and measured its shadow.

The quadrant was even more straightforward than the cross staff. Made of wood or brass, it was a 45° angle piece with a peephole for sighting. The instrument was suspended from a ring and a reading was taken by holding a plumb line over the appropriate angle.

The nautical compass had been used by the Chinese in the fourth century and it was regularly used by Elizabethan navigators, bearing in mind the fact that other navigational instruments required visible celestial bodies. The navigators of the time would have been aware that the compass does not always indicate true north, but the location of the North Star over the North Pole would have allowed them to calculate the difference. *Revenge* would have carried a compass mounted on a binnacle, in much the same manner as the one discovered on the *Mary Rose*. The compass was suspended on concentric rings in order to maintain a horizontal position despite the movements of the ship.

By 1569, Gerardus Mercator had published a map of the world, which included the Mercator projection, on which parallel and meridians on maps were drawn uniformly at 90°. This system was particularly useful for navigation, since compass courses could be drawn as straight lines. Although not very accurate at the time, due to the difficulty of determining longitude, the charts of the Elizabethan navigator would at least have allowed him to plot past and present positions, and to determine where he was going.

Irish Insurrection
Before playing a starring role in the defeat of the Armada, *Revenge* earned her spurs in an operation against the insurrection of 1579/80 in Munster, in the south-west of Ireland. The rising was led by James Fitzgerald, known as Fitzmaurice, assisted by an English priest, Nicholas Sander, who had connections at the Vatican and in Madrid.

Buoyed by the promise of Spanish reinforcements, Fitzmaurice sailed for Ireland in the spring of 1579 and was spotted off the Cornish coast in June with one large and two smaller ships. As an indication of his determination, he captured a ship from Bristol and threw the entire crew into the sea, about which the Spanish Ambassador, Mendoza, commented on 20 June that this 'appears to have given them [in London] a fright'.

When the news of Fitzmaurice's arrival in Dingle Bay in July finally reached London on 9 August, Lord Burghley proposed that a naval task force should be sent to intercept him and on 29 August five Royal ships, *Revenge, Dreadnaught, Swiftsure, Foresight* and *Achates*, sailed from the Thames, commanded by Sir John Perrot in *Revenge*.

For this adventure, *Revenge* would most likely have been commanded by Sir William Winter, but he was otherwise engaged on a confidential assignment, escorting the Queen's potential paramour, Prince Francis of Anjou-Alençon, from England to Boulogne.

Perrot, reputed to be the son of Henry VIII, was a professional soldier who had a fearsome reputation for suppressing a riot when President of Munster by killing or hanging 800 rebels. A Welsh grandee, he was a councillor of the Marches, Vice-Admiral of the Welsh seas and commissioner for piracy in Pembrokeshire.

Revenge was on station between 14 September and mid-October when she returned to England. On the return journey, Perrot chased and captured a pirate called Deryfold off the Flemish coast. She was briefly grounded on the Kentish Knocks before reaching Harwich.

In Ireland, Fitzmaurice was joined by his kinsman, the Earl of Desmond, and by 1580 most of Munster was in a state of open rebellion. The English responded by assembling an army under the loyal Irish Earl of Ormonde who, along with the acting Lord Deputy Sir William Pelham, advanced into Desmond's country, devastating the countryside as they went.

At this point Sir William Winter returned to Ireland in *Revenge* along with three other Royal ships, *Swallow, Foresight* and *Merlin*. Winter sailed up the Shannon to land guns, ammunition and powder which enabled Pelham to take Desmond's stronghold at Carragfoyle as well as two other forts. Winter then moved to Dingle Bay where he destroyed Fitzmaurice's ships. After this the rebellion soon collapsed.

This operation demonstrated the effectiveness of naval forces in support of land forces, an early forerunner of the modern task force.

After a brief spell back in England, Winter returned in *Revenge* after news was received that the Spanish Admiral Don Martín de Recaldi had arrived at Smerwick bay and offloaded supplies and troops before returning to Spain. This time Winter's squadron consisted of nine ships, one of which was the *Foresight* under the famous navigator and explorer Martin Frobisher.

The engagement of the English ships with the fort, known as Dun an Oir, is immortalized in a map drawn up under Winter's directions after the event. Known as the Smerwick map, it shows

Revenge in a gaudy livery, anchored in the bay pounding the fort with her bow guns, with the *Swiftsure* and *Aid* doing the same. The three smaller ships are seen operating in a kind of carousel, passing nearer to the fort and firing at it with bow, broadside and stern guns when appropriate. Guns have been landed by the ships to help with the siege of the fort.

The Spaniards were quickly overwhelmed by these tactics and called for a truce on 9 November before surrendering on the 10th. The English treated them without mercy, slaughtering all but a handful of officers and men. Even pregnant women were hanged.

Iberian patrol

The next major operation involving *Revenge* was in 1586, when Sir John Hawkins sailed in her, leading a squadron of nineteen other ships, of which five were Queen's ships and the rest financed by the Crown. Hawkins cruised off the Portuguese coast from August until October to shadow French shipping and to intercept the incoming silver convoys. Although this aspect of his mission was comparatively successful, he took four prizes. Maintaining a presence offshore for so long so far from base was an achievement in itself and one which seriously disconcerted the Spanish.

By the Treaty of Nonsuch in 1585 England had agreed to support the Dutch against the Duke of Parma. In May of the same year, Philip of Spain ordered English ships importing grain to be seized. The English retaliated with a series of attacks on the Cape Verde islands in November 1585, on Santo Domingo in January 1586 and on Carthagena in March. A note of triumph was sounded in a later account of the voyage: 'Thus we departed from them, passing hard by Carthagena, in the sight of all the fleet, with a flag of Saint George in the maintop of our frigate, with silk streamers and ancients down to the water, sailing forward with a large wind.'[7]

Philip now set about in earnest with his Catholic duty of planning to wipe the exasperating English heathen off the face of the seas and to bring their heretic Queen to heel, and in January he formally ordered plans for the invasion of England.

The Duke of Parma had suggested that he could use his army in the Netherlands to invade England. Apart from the Channel, the Navy Royal was the only thing preventing him from doing so. All he required was for a Spanish fleet to crush the English fleet and the way would be clear.

The threat to England was all the greater after Spain's acquisition of the Portuguese throne in 1580. This gave Spain the use of Lisbon at the mouth of the Tagus, one of the most spacious and important Atlantic ports, with its favourable trade winds and amenable current, as well as a fleet of some of the best-designed, best-armed and best-manned galleons afloat.

The Portuguese squadron was to play a central role in the Armada and it was accompanied by several others, including the Biscay Squadron, the Levant Squadron, the Castile Squadron and the Andalucía Squadron. But although some of these squadrons, like the Portuguese, were sailed by competent mariners, much of the Armada seems to have consisted of little more than bulk to give force to a battering ram.

Despite its tactical weaknesses, the Armada was a force to be reckoned with, and if its battering ram should succeed in breaking through the wooden walls of England, the game would be over for Protestant England.

John Hawkins, in a letter to Sir Francis Walsingham, bears witness to the frustration of the English seamen, whose personalities did not lend themselves to patiently awaiting their fate, and also throws an interesting light on the inherent tension between the desire for war and the Christian duty to seek peace:

My duty humbly remembered unto your Honour: ... I do therefore now utter my mind particularly to your Honour how I do conceive some good to be done at last. I do see we are desirous to have peace, as it becometh good Christians, which is best for all men; and I wish it might anyway be brought to that pass; but in my poor judgement the right way is not taken.

If we stand at this point in a mammering and at a stay, we consume, and our Commonwealth doth utterly decay. I shall not need to speak of our estate, for that your Honour knoweth it far better than I do: neither need I to rehearse how dead and uncertain our troffies are; most men in poverty and discontented, and especially the poorer sort; our navigation not set on work; but the French and Scots eat us up, and grow in wealth and freights, and not assured to us in friendship. Our treasure doth consume infinitely with those uncertain wars, and nothing assured to us but new and continual change. We have to choose either a dishonourable and uncertain peace, or to put on virtuous and valiant minds, to make a way through with such a settled war as may bring forth and command a quiet peace ...

Therefore, in my mind, our profit and best assurance is to seek our peace by a determined and resolute war, which no doubt would be both less charge, more assurance of safety, and would best discern our friends from our foes both abroad and at home, and satisfy the people generally thoughout the whole realm ... By open wars all the subjects of this realm should know what to do. They would not only be satisfied in conscience, but they would, every man that loveth God, the Queen and his country, contribute, set forward, fight, devise, and do somewhat for the liberty and freedom of this country ... Many things more might be said to the preferring of open war before a dissembled peace, which God doth best allow, and the well affected people of the realm do desire, even to the spending of a great portion of their substance. And therefore I conclude that with God's blessing and a lawful open war, the Lord shall bring us a most honourable and quiet peace, to the glory of His church and to the honour of Her Majesty and this realm of England; which God for His mercy's sake grant. And so I leave to trouble your Honour.

From aboard the Bonaventure, the first of February 1587.

Your Honour's humbly to command,

John Hawkyns[8]

The Singeing

Fully aware of the force being assembled to sail against them, it was not in the character of the Elizabethan sea dogs, least of all Sir Francis Drake, to stay at home in tremulous expectation. Drake was assigned to get England's retaliation in early and in April 1587 he set sail with twenty-three ships, arriving off Cadiz on 19 April.

As Drake's ships began to enter the bay, Don Pedro de Acuña, the commander of some galleys that had recently put into port, positioned his vessels across the entrance of the harbour to block the advancing English ships. A galley that was sent out to reconnoitre and to ascertain whether the approaching fleet was friendly or not soon got an answer in the form of various cannon balls.[9] At this point panic ensued in the town and the local citizens ran for refuge in the castle.

Although the Spanish galleys had sharp teeth – apart from a wicked battering ram, they also bristled with small-calibre cannon – these would make little impression on the English oak of Drake's sailing ships, if ever they should contrive to get close enough to fire at them. English broadsides kept the galleys at bay and eventually drove them off, leaving the port exposed and particularly the shipping that had come there from various directions before heading off to various places, some of them bound for Lisbon to reinforce the Armada. One ship that unwisely decided to fire at the English ships was soon sunk by combined broadsides. The remainder were like lambs for the slaughter. Despite occasional forays by the Spanish galleys, Drake set about sorting out the prizes in a businesslike manner.

Apart from the trading barques in the port, there was a new Spanish galleon in the upper bay which, once it had been fitted with its guns, would no doubt be one of the lead fighting ships in the Armada. Drake sailed up and duly set fire to her.

While the local citizenry gazed in horror at the English depredations they were at least consoled by the fact that while the English were busy with the shipping in the bay they would not have time to land and cause mayhem on shore. They were even more consoled when reinforcements began to arrive and the Spanish soldiery now assembling in the town would make a landing by the English a very dicey adventure indeed.

The Spaniards had also been busy manoeuvring some of the massive shore cannon into places from whence they could start firing on any English ships in range. The *Golden Lion* proved a suitable target and a lucky shot pierced her hull. Several jackals in the form of galleys then came out to nip at the heels of the injured *Lion* but skilful seamanship by the *Lion*'s crew succeeded in getting her out of the immediate danger.

If Drake had ever been welcome, it would have been obvious by now that he was overstaying it. The Spaniards were becoming bolder and it would not be too long before some form of reinforcements arrived by sea. Having satisfied his desire for both booty and a prestigious naval target, Drake had no desire to hang around but for several hours the English ships were becalmed while the Spaniards continued to hurl cannon balls and also attempted to sail some fireships in their direction, all of which were skilfully fended off by adroit small-boat handling. At length the wind began to blow again and the English moved off, with the Spanish galleys at a safe distance behind, now more relieved to see the back of Drake than with any hope of vengeance.

The English had sunk about thirty ships at Cadiz, one of them a major galleon, and the expedition delayed Armada preparations. Spain, however, had the resources to make up the loss and the great project moved inexorably forward. Drake had indeed singed the King of Spain's beard but had done no harm to his person.

Drake was in no hurry to go home and the next port of call was Lagos in the Portuguese Algarve, originally named Al Gharb Al Andalus, or The West of Iberia, by the Moors. Here Drake unwisely decided to land and to tramp about in the heat so sought after by holidaymakers centuries later. The Portuguese, meanwhile, brave but realistic about their chances against a well-formed and well-armed English force, watched for their chances both on horseback and on foot, making occasional cavalry sorties and firing from long range among the olive groves.

Having achieved nothing, Drake's men went back to the ships and moved on down the coast to Sagres near Cape St Vincent where his assault was more determined. He besieged the castle which in due course surrendered and caused as much damage as he could. This act of vandalism was singularly inappropriate for various reasons and perhaps reveals the complexity of the man.

The castle at Sagres was the castle of Prince Henry the Navigator (1394–1460), the man responsible perhaps more than any other for the great European voyages of discovery. The mother of Henry the Navigator was the English princess Philippa of Lancaster, the daughter of John of Gaunt. Prince Henry is reputed to have embodied many Christian virtues, including calm judgement mixed with determination. His vision inspired the Portuguese and later other nations to go further than any others had gone before. He embodied also the natural alliance between England and Portugal which had been underwritten by the Anglo-Portuguese Alliance of 1373, the longest-lasting alliance between any two nations in world history. What is even more peculiar is that there is evidence that Drake himself was well able to distinguish between the Portuguese and his natural enemies, the Spaniards:

May 17, 1587

Right Honourable,

There hath happened between the Spaniards, Portingals, and ourselves divers combats, in the which it hath pleased God that we have taken forts, ships, barks, carvels, and divers other vessels more than a hundred, most laden, some with oars for galleys, planks and timber for ships and pinnaces, hoops and pipe-staves for cask, with many other provisions for this great army ...

The Portingals I have always commanded to be used well, and set them ashore without the wanting of any of their apparel, and have made them to know that it was unto me a great grief that I was driven to hurt of theirs to the value of one real or plate, but that I found them employed for the Spaniards' services, which we hold to be our mortal enemies, and gave some Portingals some money in their purses and put them aland in divers places, upon which usage, if we stay here any time, the Spaniards which are here in Portugal, if they come under our hands, will become all Portingals and play as Peter did – forswear their master rather than to be sold as slaves. I assure your honour this hath bred a great fear in the Spaniard ...

As long as it shall please God to give us provisions to eat and drink, and that our ships and wind and weather will permit us, you shall surely hear of us near this Cape of St Vincent, where we do and will expect daily what her Majesty and your honours will further command.[10]

Prince Henry was responsible for both the vision and the development and deployment of the technology, including the astrolabe, that would enable seafarers such as Drake himself to set off on extraordinary voyages of discovery and to create new nations across the seas. As he gazed out to sea from the glorious promontory of Cape St Vincent and sought the inspiration that would drive the human spirit into the unknown, little did Prince Henry know that an English Protestant corsair would one day ship up on his shore and burn his library.

Having completed his act of vandalism, Drake departed, though only temporarily, for Lisbon where he took pleasure in putting the wind up the Spanish masters of the place, though he did not care to try his luck against the forts at Cascais or St Julian, or attempt to enter the mouth of the Tagus and harry Lisbon itself. His presence was enough to cause commanders to send soldiers such as were available scurrying hither and yon in case the English should decide to land.

Born in relatively humble circumstances near Tavistock in Devon in 1542, Francis Drake was a star among a firmament of West Countrymen who were to have a profound influence on English naval history. They included Walter Raleigh, John Hawkins and Richard Grenville. Drake was brought up at a time when the conflict between Catholics and Protestants in England was still fresh in the memory, especially after the excesses of Bloody Mary, and the young Francis is likely to have been steeped in the desire for vengeance, largely inherited from his father, Edmund, who hated Catholics.

For such a man the opportunity to defend his country against a Catholic monarch might have seemed like an answer to prayer, but this would probably be an overstatement. Drake was reputed to have been tolerant to Catholic captives, allowing them to take time to say the rosary or making arrangements for them to eat fish on a Friday. Drake's fierce Protestantism, however, underlines the extraordinary nature of the English reformation and the reason for the Armada, for England had only become a 'Protestant' country about fifty years previous to the Armada, whereas it had not only been a Catholic country for 900 years previous to that but also perhaps the most Catholic of all the European nations. The shrine of Walsingham in Norfolk was one of the principle shrines in the European pilgrimage itinerary, outshining even Santiago de Compostela. The reverence to Mary in England, in virtue of her Son, was such that England was described as the dowry of Mary. The abbeys of England, the architectural embodiment of the Christian virtues, were so numerous that it required a veritable holocaust for Henry VIII to rid himself of them.

The Catholic Church had created the parish system and was the source of English law. King Alfred the Great had made great inroads into unifying England in the name of Catholic Christianity. Under the tutelage of the Church the great universities of Oxford and Cambridge sprang up along with schools such as that of Our Lady of Eton. The common law of England was nurtured under its wings and the great cries for freedom underwritten by habeas corpus and Magna Carta reflected the Christian principles of the freedom and dignity of the individual which the Church bequeathed to Western civilization. All twenty-five medieval cathedrals in England had been built by the Catholic Church and would be lovingly preserved for posterity by the Anglican Church after the Reformation. There had been no revolts against the Church in England and none planned. The Old Faith was part and parcel of daily life. In view of the speed of communications, or lack of it, in medieval and renaissance England, the very idea that England was centrally controlled by a foreign religious potentate was a nonsense, and it also contradicted Catholic principles of subsidiarity. In England, communities were centred on their locality, not on Rome. Their community, their church, their abbey or their cathedral was the centre of worship, although these were linked in spirit to the universal Church. The liturgy heard by the English would in due course be heard by every nation on the planet. This was therefore a brotherhood of belief, not a hegemony.

Catholic Christian principles married very neatly with English instincts and the Anglo-Saxon heritage. The thrust of European hegemony which the English would repeatedly resist for centuries beyond the Armada was a post-Christian phenomenon – Napoleon, Hitler and the European Union all had in common their rejection of a Christian God. England, with its wooden walls, including HMS *Revenge*, successfully resisted the first two, but feats of arms would not be equal to the sinuous advances of the last.

It was the misfortune of the Catholic Church that the Armada strengthened the English notion that the Catholic Church comprised a threat from abroad and an assault on their homeland and possessions. It strengthened the hand of Queen Elizabeth who had of late ordered the murder of her cousin Mary Queen of Scots while pretending she had nothing to do with it. While Elizabeth played her hand skilfully, the Catholic Church blundered and effectively set a seal on the English Reformation for ages hence. The Spanish Catholic Church blundered in particular by instituting the Inquisition and by planning to bring it to England to 'convert' the English. They might have known better. Even English Catholic recusants would have rejected that idea. It was the genius of the Anglican Church that it would tread a fine line between the Old Faith and the new and effectively preserve those characteristics which were peculiar to English Christianity. As such, Englishmen continued to value their 'entailed inheritance', as Edmund Burke put it, against all comers and defended Christian civilization while so-called Catholic nations were torn apart by revolutions and *pronunciamentos*, given false visions of *liberté*, *égalité* and *fraternité* and were patronized and bullied by fascist dictators. Set in amber in a silver sea, the 'scepter'd isle' maintained the inheritance of the Old Faith – the genuine and precious Christian liberty for which Englishman down the centuries would continue to give their lives and to extend around the globe.

Henry VIII, if he should be remembered for anything, should be remembered for a feat of propaganda unrivalled in world history and such as might make Joseph Goebbels himself turn in his grave for envy. In order to satisfy his immediate marital requirements and urges and to make up for financial deficits consequent upon misguided foreign ventures, Henry VIII, who himself had as a young man gone barefoot on pilgrimage from Ely to Walsingham, succeeded in not only turning a nation against its own faith but also in shaping the thoughts of every Englishman and woman for centuries to come. Goebbels might have been comforted to think that Henry's campaign against the Old Faith of England was most neatly summarized by his own adage: 'If you tell a lie big enough and keep repeating it, people will eventually come to believe it.' The ruins of the old abbeys of England, however, continued to bear eloquent testimony to the fact that 'at the length truth will out.'

Let the judgement on these events come from a Protestant author, William Cobbett:

> No Englishman worthy of that name, worthy of a name which carries along with it sincerity and a love of justice; no real Englishman can have contemplated the foul deeds, the base hypocrisy, the flagrant injustice, exposed in the foregoing pages [concerning the English Reformation], without blushing for his country. What man with an honourable sentiment in his mind is there who does not almost wish to be a foreigner, rather than be the countryman of Cranmer and Henry VIII?[11]

In another letter, Drake left to posterity a memorable phrase about perseverance, while perhaps revealing that he was now in two minds about remaining off the Iberian coast:

> There must be a beginning of any great matter, but the continuing unto the end until it be thoroughly finished yields the

true glory. If Hannibal had followed his victories, it is thought of many, he had never been taken by Scipio. God make us all thankful again and again that we have, although it be little, made a beginning upon the coast of Spain.[12]

His privateering instinct was to some extent balanced by his sense of duty to his country:

If we can thoroughly believe that this which we do is in the defence of our religion and country, no doubt but our merciful God, for His Christ our Saviour's sake, is able and will give us victory, although our sins be red. God give us grace, we may fear Him, and daily to call upon Him. So shall neither Satan nor his ministers prevail against us. Although God permit Job to be touched in body, yet the Lord will hold his mind pure.

Your Honour's most ready to be commanded,

Francis Drake[13]

More than perhaps any other of the Elizabethan captains, Drake embodied the conflicting demands of privateer and servant of the Crown. His freelance activities in distant parts of the globe earned him a mixture of admiration, opprobrium and hate, depending on which activity he happened to be engaged in. His abilities as a commander made him one of the most effective captains in the service of the Crown; his circumnavigation of the globe placed him among a pantheon of navigators that includes Magellan, Vasco da Gama and Columbus; but Sir Francis Drake never escaped from his loyalty to money, to a fat prize ship and the rewards that could be gained from her.

At the end of May, Drake decided, despite his philosophical musings on perseverance, to leave the Portuguese coast and head west into the Atlantic. The latest intelligence reports told him that a Portuguese carrack, the *São Felipe*, was sailing towards the Azores. Although his squadron was split up by a storm, after which some of the ships decided to head for home, Drake hung on and, with six of his ships, eventually tracked down the *São Felipe* and forced her to surrender. She turned out to be the richest of all rich pickings and was worth more than three times as much as all the ships Drake had taken at Cadiz.

Drake had every reason to be satisfied with his expedition. Apart from the overall success of the raid on Cadiz and the disruption he had caused both there and around the Portuguese coast, he had also sunk a major new Spanish fighting galleon and captured one of the richest prize ships that had ever sailed from the Americas. His disruption of the preparations for the Armada were propitious because they contributed to the fateful appointment with destiny that would drive the Armada away from English shores the following year.

As the Duke of Parma made ready in the Low Countries, and as Philip of Spain continued to build up his forces in Lisbon, the critical moment approached when all these preparations and energies must be unleashed.

The Dutch adventurer Emanuel van Meteeren marvelled at the size of the Spanish fleet and its appendages in his account of the Armada:

All the ships appertaining to this navy amounted unto the sum of 150. The number of mariners were above 8000 of slaves 2088 of soldiers 20000 (besides noblemen and gentlemen voluntaries) of great cast pieces 2650. The foresaid ships were of an huge and incredible capacity. The whole fleet was large enough to contain the burden of 60 thousand tons.

The galleons were 64 in number, being of an huge bigness, and very stately built, of marvellous force also, and so high, that they resembled great castles, most fit to defend themselves and to withstand any assault, but far inferior unto the English and Dutch ships, which any with great dexterity wield and turn themselves. The upper work of the said galleons was of thickness and strength sufficient to bear off musket shot. The lower work and the timbers thereof were cut of measure strong, being framed of planks and ribs four or five foot in thickness, insomuch that no bullets could pierce them, but such as were discharged hard at hand: which afterward proved true, for a great number of bullets were found to stick fast within the massy substance of those thick planks.

The galleasses were rowed with great oars, there being in each one of them 300 slaves for the same purpose, and were able to do great service with the force of their ordnance. All these together with the residue aforenamed were furnished and beautified with trumpets, steamers, banners, warlike ensigns, and other such like ornaments.

Their pieces of brazen ordnance were 1600 and of iron 1000. The bullets thereto belonging were 120 thousand. Item of gunpowder 5600 quintals. Of match 1200 quintals.

Moreover they had great store of cannons, double cannons culverins and field pieces for land services.

They had in like sort great store of mules and horses, and whatsoever else was requisite for a land-army. They were so well stored of biscuit, that for the space of half a year, they might allow each person in the whole fleet half a quintal every month; whereof the whole sum amounteth unto an hundred thousand quintals.

Likewise of wine they had 147 thousand pipes, sufficient also for half a year's expedition. Of bacon 6500 quintals. Of cheese three thousand quintals. To be short, they brought all things expedient either for a fleet by sea, or for an army by land.

There were in the said navy five tercios of Spaniards, (which tercios the Frenchmen call regiments) under the command of five governors termed by the Spaniards, masters of the field, and amongst the rest there were many old and expert soldiers chosen out of the garrisons of Sicily, Naples and Tercera. Besides the which companies there were many bands also of Castilians and Portuguese.[14]

Despite its impressive size, the reality was that a certain amount of it at least was padding: 'Of his 130 ships only about 30, mainly from the squadrons of Portugal and Biscay, were properly armed warships. Guns had been a constant problem; neither Spanish gunfounding nor powder manufacture being equal to the demands being placed upon them.'[15] Moreover the guns were 'handled by soldiers with no experience of sea fighting, and a deeply rooted reluctance to pay any attention to seamen'.[16]

The English fleet had put to sea before Christmas 1587 but it proved to be a false alarm. After that they were more or less stood down on skeleton crews in order to save money, prevent wear and tear to the ships and to keep the crews relatively fresh.

The English fleet in the Channel at its greatest extent was under 100 ships, about forty of which were first-rank fighting warships. These were, however, first-rate galleons, like the *Revenge*, and well armed, whereas a large proportion of the Spanish ships were unwieldy merchantmen.

Then came the *Revenge* of 1575–7, 450 tons, very moderate in size, yet a hard hitter, as her end in '91 was to prove. Drake thought her the perfect galleon of his time, and chose her of all the fleet as his ship for the Armada fight. She became the type on which all the new battleships were built after Hawkins took charge in 1577.[17]

The hitting power of the Navy Royal was proportionately greater than that of the Spanish fleet. The Master of Naval Ordnance, William Winter, had taken care to equip the English galleons, including the *Revenge* on which he had sailed to Ireland during the Insurrection, with ship-destroying guns with which the Navy Royal could stand off from its enemy and pound them from a distance. The brass guns on HMS *Revenge* were among 264 such guns distributed throughout the fleet and supplemented by another forty-eight iron guns.

Guns were the essential element in the new navies, as the Spanish would discover to their cost:

In world-history the defeat of the Armada is no mole-hill and in the history of that defeat the Gun is a mountain, a feature of the view which cannot possibly be overlooked. Why? Because (save for two minor incidents, one an act of sabotage, the other a tactical blunder which should never have happened) every scrap of damage inflicted by man on man, or by man on ship, was done by gunfire alone: because, in fact, for the first time in human history we are assisting at a fleet-action which was a gun duel and nothing else. Moreover, the gun had come to stay with a vengeance. From the Armada fight to (say) Cape Matapan, every considerable naval action was essentially a gun duel.[18]

And moving from the general to the particular ship under discussion, *Revenge* was arguably the most powerful galleon deployed against the Armada by the Navy Royal:

If both numbers and weights are correct, and if we are reckoning here on the particular pound weight which corresponds with the English pound ... then was the *Revenge* far more formidably armed than any other ship of the whole period: for all forty-three guns would be demi-culverins or upwards. Even if we allow sakers to be included – and, strictly speaking, they should not be, for the average saker weighed only 1750lb – she still remains more heavily armed than any known Elizabethan ship of any period of the reign.[19]

Of the ships available to fight the Armada, thirty-four were Queen's ships; fifty-three had been taken up the Lord Admiral and paid for by the Queen; twenty-three were coasters financed by the Queen; thirty were paid for by the City of London; and thirty-four were provided by nobles or merchants. This Navy Royal was somewhat different from the fully fledged Royal Navy that would confront Napoleon and Hitler:

The emergence of the royal navy as a professional fighting fleet distinct from the irregular sea-forces of the nation as a whole had hardly begun, and the crowd of shipping that gathered in the Channel in 1588 had little in common with Nelson's navy, or even with Blake's. The commanders had little experience in the handling of large fleets and only the most primitive notions of strategy and tactics.[20]

The performance of *Revenge* and the Navy Royal would not only decide the fate of England but of Holland as well. Alexander Farnese (1545–92), Duke of Parma (1586–92) and Governor of the Spanish Netherlands (1578–92) had an army of about 30,000 ready to embark for England. Such had been Parma's success in subduing the Netherlands – Tournai, Maastricht, Breda, Bruges and Ghent had fallen like dominoes under his advance – and Antwerp, Ostend and Sluys followed in due course, despite attempts by the English to reinforce the Dutch resistance.

Militarily, therefore, Philip II seemed to have a very strong hand indeed but he and Alexander Farnese were now faced with a problem that would also be faced by Napoleon and Hitler in future years: how to get across that comparatively narrow band of sea called the Channel and gain a foothold on English soil. The barges could be found to transport the troops but how to deal with the Navy Royal?

Philip II was wise enough to have foreseen – as Napoleon and Hitler would in their turn – that, one way or another, the English navy would have to be defeated or so overwhelmed as to be unable to intervene effectively to stop the transport of troops and supplies. The reputation of the Navy Royal was such, however – even the mention of the name El Draque would send a shiver down Spanish spines – that Philip also knew that the fleet he assembled would have to be like no other.

Philip could count upon the collaboration in this expedition of those who were natural enemies of the Spanish and who had much more in common with the English, namely the Portuguese. Philip had been wise enough not to wield too heavy a hand in Portugal: he allowed them to maintain their traditional laws and customs and their own coinage, and the Portuguese merchant class were happy to go along with the Spaniards as long as it was economically advantageous to them.

Religious Context

The Armada had been the brainchild of the Marquis of Santa Cruz and its purpose not so much a crusade against the Protestant English as to bring to heel the recalcitrant Dutch. The Jesuits and others quickly jumped on the bandwagon, giving the Armada the appearance of a religious crusade. There were also attempts to make the offensive seem like a 'just war' and an act of 'self-defence':

> Every conceivable pretext for a just and holy war is to be found in this campaign ... This is a defensive, not an offensive, war: one in which we are defending our sacred religion and our most holy Roman Catholic faith; one in which we are defending the high reputation of our King and lord, and of our nation; defending, too, the land and property of all the kingdoms of Spain, and simultaneously our peace, tranquillity and repose.[21]

It was not surprising that a Spanish Jesuit priest should rail against the Protestant English. The Jesuits were the flower and the foot soldiers of the counter-reformation. They would not be found nursing flagons of wine or sitting over feasts, as Protestant propaganda would have it – they would fight enemy wherever and whenever they found it.

As the cause against the infidel – with whom it was possible to negotiate and make peace – weakened, the spirit of religious militancy embodied in the concept of a crusade – 'the only enterprise generally accepted and shared in the West'[22] – far from losing its strength, was transferred with all its inspiration and force to other political conflicts. Only now there was a different enemy – heresy – and the war was in a more distant setting – the north of Europe. The heretic and the schismatic became the new common enemy; his religious dissent spelt disloyalty towards the monarch – as in the case of the Netherlands rebels – and he represented the constant threat of foreign aggression – as in the case of England. It was imperative to maintain a united and solid front against this dual danger; as a result, religious unity became the corner-stone of the political structure.[23]

The English Jesuits, however, had a different perspective on the matter. Their mission was purely to serve the needs of the remaining English Catholic community. Edmund Campion, an English Jesuit priest, had already been martyred in England in 1581, while on a mission to his native country. Strangely enough, this fervent English Jesuit had been educated at Christ's Hospital school, an institution set up under Edward VI to replace the 'hospitals', namely the Abbeys, that had been destroyed by Henry VIII in the English Reformation. It continues to provide an excellent education to this day. Campion was a dazzling scholar at Oxford and impressed Queen Elizabeth when she visited the University with his eloquence. During his studies, however, he came to have doubts about the Church of England and decided to become a Catholic. He went to Douai in France, where many English Catholics were trained before returning to England to face almost certain death. In the small kingdom which pitted itself against the Catholic Goliath of Spain, the few English Catholic priests pitted themselves against the might of the English Protestant State and its master of spies, Francis Walsingham.

Sure enough, in due course, Campion was captured, having had the opportunity to travel around his native country while,

> the scars of the Tudor revolution were still fresh and livid; the great houses of the new ruling class were building ... the village churches were empty shells, their altars torn out and their ornaments defaced ... the old monasteries, their roofs stripped of lead and their walls a quarry for the new contractors. The ruins were not yet picturesque.[24]

Campion was given a show trial, thrown in the Tower and tortured. A Protestant preacher said of Campion, 'This man, having departed the realm hath joined himself to the man of Rome, our common enemy, Antichrist, and now hath returned again unto the realm.'[25] Campion was, he said, 'an unnatural man to his country, degenerate from an Englishman, an apostate in religion, a fugitive from this realm, unloyal to his Prince.'[26] While his accuser practised a religion merely 50 years old in England, however, Campion practised one of 900 years in England and 1,500 all told. Campion was dragged to Tyburn on a hurdle and then hung, drawn and quartered on 1 December 1581. Campion had told his judges and executioners: 'In condemning us, you condemn all your own ancestors – all the ancient priests, bishops and kings – all that was once the glory of England, the island of saints, and the most devoted child of the See of Peter.'[27]

The point that Campion's accusers were confused over was the division between the temporal and spiritual leadership in England. Henry VIII had decided it was convenient to have both: the remaining English Catholics argued, mostly on their way to the gallows, that the spiritual leadership belonged to the successor of Saint Peter on whose shoulders Jesus Christ had placed that responsibility. When he was sentenced to death in 1535, Sir Thomas More also made that distinction:

> Seeing that I see ye are determined to condemn me (God knoweth how) I will now in discharge of my conscience speak my own mind plainly and freely touching my indictment and your Statute withal.
>
> And forasmuch as this indictment is grounded upon an Act of Parliament directly repugnant to the laws of God and his

holy Church, the supreme government of which, or of any part whereof, may no temporal prince presume by any law to take upon him, as rightfully belonging to the See of Rome, a spiritual pre-eminence by the mouth of our Saviour himself, personally present upon earth, only to St Peter and his successors, bishops of the same see, by special prerogative granted; it is therefore in law, amongst Christian men insufficient to charge any Christian man.[28]

Thomas More embodied the loyalty of the pre-Reformation English: loyal to their sovereign within the land they loved but loyal to Jesus Christ and his Church in all matters pertaining to the spiritual realm that knew no national boundaries. The first clause of Magna Carta, the Charter of freedom for Englishman and for many others by association, stated that the Church in England should be free:

Quod Anglicana ecclesia libera sit, et habeat jura sua integra et libertates suas illaesas ... quam et nos observabimus et ab heredibus nostris in perpetuum bona fide volumes observari. (That the English Church shall be free, and should have its rights undiminished and its liberties unimpaired ... This freedom we shall observe ourselves and desire to be observed in good faith by our heirs in perpetuity.)

Magna Carta was underwritten by Pope Innocent III.

If the '*Anglicana ecclesia*', meaning the English Catholic Church, was free under Magna Carta, what would be the case if it were set free from that freedom? Two pluses generally make a negative. According to More: 'Your law [The Act of Supremacy] has dissolved the unity, the peace and the concord of the Church, although the Church is, as all know, a body which is one, universal, whole and undivided, and therefore in matters of religion, nothing can be decided without the general consent of the whole.'[29] He added the significant point regarding Henry: 'Yet I know full well what has been the chief cause of my condemnation: it is that I would never give my approval to this new marriage.'[30]

Three of the panel gathered in Westminster Hall to condemn him were close relations of Anne Boleyn.

Henry VIII would not be the first to discover that the laws of the Christian Church did not suit his personal preferences. The decline of Christianity in England into the twenty-first century could probably be explained in the same light.

Another member of the English Catholic 'special forces' was the poet Robert Southwell. At his trial, Southwell, like so many of his companions and predecessors, insisted on the distinction between his continued loyalty to his English sovereign and his loyalty to the Catholic Church:

> I confess that I was born in England, a subject to the Queen's Majesty, and that by authority derived from God I have been promoted to the sacred order of priesthood in the Roman Church, for which I return most hearty thanks to his Divine Majesty. I confess also that I was at Uxenden, in Middlesex, at that time when, being sent for thither by trick and deceit, I fell into your hands, as it is well known; but that I never entertained any designs or plots against the Queen or kingdom. I call God to witness, the revenger of perjury; neither had I any other design in returning home to my native country than to administer the sacraments according to the rite of the Catholic Church to such as desired them.[31]

Unfortunately for Southwell, his accusers were unable to make a distinction between the universal realm of Jesus Christ and the realm of England, and Southwell was condemned to the savage execution reserved for those who had committed treason.

That Southwell was able to answer his accusers at all was remarkable in itself as over the preceding years in the Tower he had been subjected to various tortures, including the infamous 'wall torture', which had also been used against the Carthusian monks who had joined More and Fisher in opposing both the Act of Supremacy and the Act of Succession.

An account of 'wall torture' was left by another Jesuit, John Gerard, who managed to escape from the Tower by abseiling down into a waiting boat:

> They took me to a big upright pillar, one of the wooden posts which held the roof of this huge underground chamber. Driven in to the top of it were iron staples for supporting heavy

weights. Then they put my wrists into iron gauntlets and ordered me to climb two or three wicker steps. My arms were then lifted up and an iron bar passed through the rings of the gauntlet, then through the staple and rings of the second gauntlet. This done, they fastened the bar with a pin to prevent it slipping, and then, removing the wicker steps one by one from under my feet, they left me hanging by my hands and arms fastened above my head ... such a gripping pain came over me. It was worst in my chest and belly, my hands and arms. All the blood in my body seemed to rush up into my arms and hands and I thought that blood was oozing out from the ends of my fingers and the pores of my skin ... The pain was so intense that I thought I could not possibly endure it.[32]

If left long enough in this position, the victim would eventually die from internal injuries and/or suffocation. Robert Southwell was tortured on the wall at least ten times for periods of up to ten hours at a time. As the injury was internal, the victim would appear to have no visible injuries.

At the end of July the massive crescent of the Spanish Armada was spotted from Saint Michael's Mount in Cornwall. The beacons were fired all the way up the coast as well as inland and the *Golden Hind* sailed under Captain Thomas Fleming to take the news to Plymouth.

It is easy to imagine a breathless Fleming hurrying into the presence of Drake and Howard as they played bowls. Here the privateer, the English sea dog, displayed the calm insouciance that was to become a prerequisite of the national character in times of crisis. There was time, he said, to finish the game and defeat the Spanish.

He was indeed correct, for at that moment the wind was blowing in the wrong direction and the English fleet could not sail in any case.

Chapter 2

The Spanish Tragedy

The sailors who first spotted the Spanish Armada from the tops of their ships in the light of the setting sun on 30 July must have experienced a similar sense of awe and apprehension to that experienced 356 years later, on 6 June 1944, by German gunners on the coast of Normandy. The crowd of masts, sails and rigging would have made it difficult to count the 130 ships that were present, with brightly coloured banners flying to represent the provinces of Spain, and each ship carrying the Burgundian red saltire. The fact that the fleet carried vast numbers of guns, 8,000 seamen, 18,000 soldiers, five regiments of infantry, thirty-two companies of light troops and 2,000 Portuguese would have been of little consequence to the amazed onlookers as the huge fleet moved steadily onwards in its crescent formation.

That morning, Howard, the Lord High Admiral, had led his squadron of fifty-four ships across and ahead of the Armada's line of approach, aiming to work to windward of the Spanish fleet. Drake in the *Revenge* had led his squadron of eight ships to the west. Although the main current on an ebb tide would set eastwards up the Channel, as a local Plymouth man, Drake knew that there would also be an inshore back current setting westward around Rame Head. This current would take Drake's ships almost to Looe in Cornwall. He wrote to Lord Henry Seymour to inform him of his movements:

Right Honourable and My Very Good Lord,

I am commanded by my good Lord, the Lord Admiral, to send you the Caravel in haste with this letter, giving your Lordship to understand that the army of Spain arrived upon our coast the

20th of this present, the 21st we had them in chase; and so coming up into them there hath passed some common shot between some of our fleet and some of theirs; and as far as we perceive they are determined to sell their lives with blows. Whereupon his Lordship hath commanded me to write unto your Lordship and Sir William Wynter, that those ships serving under your charge should be put into the best and strongest manner you may, and ready to assist his Lordship for the better encountering of them in those parts where you now are ...

Written aboard her Majesty's good ship the Revenge off Start, this 21st, late in the evening, 1588.

Your good Lordships

poor friend ready to be commanded,

FRA: Drake

This letter, my honourable good Lord, is sent in haste; the fleet of Spaniards is somewhat about a hundred sails; many great ships, but truly I think not half of them men of war, haste, your Lordships, assured.

To the Right Honourable

the Lord Henry Seymour,

Admiral of her Majesty's Navy in the narrow sea, or, in absence, to Sir William Wynter, knight, give these with speed – haste, haste, haste.[1]

The Spanish, for their part, had held a council of war at which it was decided that they would not sail further than the Isle of Wight until they had received word that the Duke of Parma's troops were ready to embark. To attack Plymouth, although they had an opportunity to do so, would have been against the King's orders.

The Spaniards' fidelity to their orders and a high degree of seamanship by the English enabled the Navy Royal to get to windward of the Armada by first light on Sunday, 31 July, having taken advantage of a south-west wind that had blown up in the night.

Far from being penned in to Plymouth harbour, the English were now away to the south-west of the Armada, with the weather gauge in their favour. Howard could now set the terms of the battle and the Spaniards would have to contend with a loose lion rather than a caged one.

Despite the new threat, the huge Spanish crescent sailed inexorably onwards, maintaining its tight formation of three divisions, a vanguard, main battle squadron and rearguard. 'The Spanish crescent, maintained with remarkable discipline, awed and baffled the English adversaries all the way up the Channel.'[2]

The van contained twenty ships of the Levant and Guipuzcoan squadrons, commanded by Don Alonso de Leiva, with Martín de Bertendona and Oquendo as divisional commanders. The main battle squadron was led by Medina Sidonia in the *San Martín*, with the Portuguese squadron, and the Indian Guard and galleons of Castile, commanded by Don Flores de Valdés. The rearguard consisted of twenty ships of the Biscayan and Andalucian squadrons, led by Juan de Martinez Recalde. In the centre of the crescent were the troop-carrying transports.

Having first sent the aptly named pinnace *Disdain* to lay down the gauntlet by firing a shot into the hull of the *San Martín*, Howard led his squadron in the *Ark Royal* to attack the southern, starboard tip of the crescent horn. They engaged with Don Alonso de Leiva's 820-ton Levant ship, the *La Rata Coronado*.

Don Alonso's ship, as well as the rest of the Levant squadron, turned northwards, while Howard's ships, instead of closing in as the Spaniards expected them to, continued to sail on a parallel course, firing from a range of about 400 yards. Damage and casualties were light on both sides.

Similar tactics were adopted by Drake in the *Revenge*, who led his squadron against the Biscayan ships on the northern, port side of the crescent. These were commanded by Recalde in his 1,050-ton fifty-gun *San Juan de Portugal*. Recalde peeled off to challenge Drake but the rest of his squadron sailed on regardless, leaving their commander to the tender mercies of the *Revenge*, *Victory* and *Triumph*.

Again, instead of taking the opportunity to close on the stranded ship, the English stood off at about 400 yards, firing continuous broadsides into the *San Juan de Portugal* and into the Spanish reinforcements when they eventually arrived.

The Spaniards would no doubt have welcomed the opportunity to close the range with the English and to involve them in a mêlée with grappling hooks, short-range, ship-smashing guns and boarders. This would have effectively cancelled out the two major tactical advantages that the English possessed – their superior gunnery as well as their agility and freedom of manoeuvre. If any of the English ships had been tempted to close with the *San Juan de Portugal* they might not have been able to get away when the Spanish reinforcements arrived.

Revenge thus skipped away, having severely damaged Recalde's ship but not crippled her. This raised a large question for the English: if they could not even sink a Spanish galleon that had been separated from the main body of the Armada, how could they hope to stop the inexorable advance of the colossus itself?

In pondering this conundrum, they would at least have been cheered by the series of setbacks that plagued the Spaniards that day. The 1,150-ton *Nuestra Señora del Rosario* (Our Lady of the Rosary), flagship of Don Pedro de Valdés, collided first with one of the Biscayan ships and then with the 730-ton *Santa Catalina*. As a result, she lost her bowsprit and her foremast mainstay. Thus crippled, she was to be the centre of a curious incident involving *Revenge* later that night. In mid-afternoon the 960-ton urca *San Salvador* blew up, killing 200 men, wrecking the upper deck and blowing out the stern. The ship carried the Paymaster General and several chests full of gold, and the whole Armada was brought to a halt while boats were sent to take off the precious cargo and the surviving crew.

What the English could not achieve with their whole navy had been instantly brought about as if by Divine Providence. Nor was this the only time the Armada would be stopped. When the *Rosario*'s foremast finally gave way, the Armada had to be halted a second time while a tow was passed. The tow parted and the *Rosario* was left wallowing in the rough sea, to the consternation of the Armada captains.

At a council of war on *Ark Royal* that evening the English had few tactical options at their disposal. Although they could congratulate themselves on their seamanship, more damage had been inflicted on the Armada by accident than by English design. They had little choice but to follow in the wake of the colossus, watching for signs of weakness, like jackals judging their chances behind a lumbering herd. It was thought likely the Spanish would attempt to occupy the Isle of Wight and a number of other possible anchorages were discussed, including Weymouth and Poole.

In the meantime, at this hour of mounting national peril, *Revenge* was given the honour of leading the English fleet, the great lantern in her stern providing a beacon for the English captains in the encircling gloom. Behind *Revenge* was the Lord High Admiral himself in *Ark Royal*. One can imagine the lookout in *Ark Royal* straining his eyes and perhaps wondering whether a thick mist had enveloped *Revenge*, for, after a while, the light in her stern disappeared into the gloom. Confusion spread quickly through the fleet, with some ships backing their sails and coming to a halt while others shortened sail and continued tentatively on the same course. Howard himself persevered, with *White Bear* and *Mary Rose* in close touch.

Some time later, the *Ark Royal* detected a faint light far away to leeward and, despite the fact that *Ark Royal* was one of the swiftest vessels in the fleet, Howard assumed Drake had somehow managed to outsail him and he therefore headed for the light.

When dawn broke, Howard discovered to his consternation that the light he had followed belonged not to *Revenge* but to a Spanish galleon and that he was now about a gunshot away from the rear of the Spanish crescent, with his own ships several miles away to windward. Howard rapidly hauled round and beat a hasty retreat.

The mystery of the disappearing *Revenge* began to resolve itself during the course of the day. First, Captain John Fisher of the 200-ton armed merchantman *Margaret and John*, from London, appeared alongside *Ark Royal*. Fisher told Howard that he had come across the *Rosario* the previous evening, accompanied by a galleon, a galleasse and a pinnace, all three of which sheared off when they saw the *Margaret and John* approaching.

The *Rosario* was as quiet as a grave, with no lights and no sails hoisted. Although Fisher sent a boat alongside, rough seas and the *Rosario*'s sheer bulk precluded boarding. Only when Fisher ordered some muskets to be fired did the Spaniards show any signs of life: 'Presently they gave us two great shot whereupon we let fire with our broadside through her doing her some hurt. After this we cast about our ship and kept close by the Spaniard until midnight, sometime hearing a voice in Spanish calling us.'

At about midnight, Fisher said he saw the *Ark Royal* in the moonlight and 'fearing his Lordship's displeasure if we should stay behind the fleet, we made all the sail we could and followed my Lord to overtake him, leaving the *Rosario* to her own devices.'

As Fisher requested permission to go back and take his prize, a pinnace arrived alongside *Ark Royal* with a messenger from Drake. There was to be no humble apology to his Admiral from the scourge of the Spanish empire. Drake's explanation for his behaviour the previous night was, if nothing else, imaginative. Soon after midnight, he claimed, he saw unfamiliar sails passing to seaward and he assumed they must be Spanish ships slipping back down the Channel in order to get behind the English fleet. He therefore set off to intercept the interlopers, accompanied by the *Roebuck* and two pinnaces. Since he did not want the whole fleet to follow him, he extinguished the lantern in the *Revenge*'s stern.

When he caught up with the strange ships, he discovered that they were German merchantmen, so he called off the chase. While striving to catch up with the English fleet (who were depending upon him as a guide), he came upon a large enemy ship which proved, on closer inspection, to be the *Rosario*. Hailing the ship, Drake demanded her surrender, saying he was not 'at leisure to make any long parley'. In view of the fact that the *Rosario* had 300 men on board as well as forty-six guns, this was a confident line to take. Perhaps impressed by his manner, and not considering it a dishonour to submit to El Draque himself, Don Pedro de Valdés agreed to surrender.

The *Rosario* was sent into Tor Bay under captain Whiddon, while Valdés and forty officers and gentlemen were taken on board *Revenge*.

Despite the tension and disappointment of their capture, the Spaniards may also have felt a sense of relief that they were no longer wallowing helplessly and ignominiously in the Channel, and that they had not been sunk. There is likely to have been a restrained mutual respect between the officers of the two great seafaring nations, which on the English side included the captain of the *Revenge*, Lieutenant Jonas Bodenham; the purser, Martin Jeffrey; and the boatswain, Richard Derrick. Nicholas Oaseley, not a regular member of the ship's complement but a merchant who had been one of Sir Francis Walsingham's agents in Spain, was also present.

Oaseley engaged Don Pedro in conversation and discovered that the Spanish captain, annoyed no doubt that he had been abandoned by his countrymen, was prepared to talk in some detail about Spanish plans. Don Pedro was to remain a gentleman prisoner of Drake's until he was ransomed for £3,000 some years later.

It would not have taken Howard very long to sift the fact and the fiction from Drake's tale. No other English ships in the fleet had seen Drake's mystery sails to seaward and in any case it was not up to Drake to decide to disregard his orders so as to set off on a wild goose chase. If he considered there really had been a danger to the fleet he could have dispatched another ship to investigate or sent a pinnace to inform the Admiral.

It seems therefore that in a moment of dire national peril, Francis Drake had dumped the English fleet, the nation's only real source of protection, in mid-Channel, in order to sail away after some rich financial pickings. Not only that, he had also placed the Lord High Admiral along with three capital ships in extreme danger, for it would have been highly possible for the Spaniards to have sent galleasses and galleons out from the rear of the Armada to intercept the English ships as Howard sailed unwittingly towards its mortal embrace. If Howard had been unable to make the clean escape that he did, it is unlikely that he would have let Drake off so lightly.

Drake's detour in pursuit of the Spanish galleon *Rosario* at the height of the battle against the Armada is an immortal reminder of this conflict of loyalties. As it was, the only censure Drake had to face was from those captains, such as Frobisher, who envied him his prize:

> He hath done good service indede, for he took don Pedro, for after he had seen her [the *Rosario*] in the evening, that she had spent her masts, then lyke a cowarde, he kept by her all nyght, because he would have the spoyle. He thinketh to cossen us of our shares of XC thousande duckatts, but we will have our shares, or I will make hym spend the best blood in hys belly, for he hath had enowgh of these cossenyng cheats already.

Martin Frobisher, partly one would guess because he had an eye on the booty himself, was particularly astringent about this episode. It seems it was not only for Francis Drake that duty was secondary to booty.

On Monday, 22 July, Medina Sidonia reorganized his formation, maintaining the crescent formation which had proved an effective defence, but strengthening the rearguard in order to provide an added deterrent to English attacks.

Having been becalmed on Monday night, the two fleets were stirred into action on the Tuesday morning by a brisk north-east wind, which gave Medina Sidonia the weather gauge. Howard attempted to lead his ships, close-hauled, towards the north-west, in order to round the landward tip of the crescent and gain the weather gauge but Medina Sidonia intercepted him and forced him to retrace his steps. This time he tried to get round the seaward tip of the crescent.

There was a fierce battle as Howard's ship crossed the reinforced rearguard of the Armada, with the *Ark Royal*, *Elizabeth Jones*, *Leicester*, *Golden Lion*, *Victory*, *Mary Rose*, *Dreadnought* and *Swallow* forming a kind of ragged line-ahead formation, and each discharging a broadside as they passed the *San Martín* before turning and coming back for a second pass. Almost unwittingly they had performed the 'line of battle' tactic which was to be a staple of naval tactics for centuries to come.

> The most stunning and original tactic was the initial use by the English of what the Spaniards called an attack *en ala*, that is, line ahead ... Although they retained the initiative throughout this period, and frustrated any intention which Medina Sidonia may have had to enter the Solent, the English again failed to inflict any significant damage on the Spanish ships, or to disrupt their formation.[3]

Frobisher meanwhile had been forced to anchor near Portland Bill. Having tried unsuccessfully to cut the Spaniards off, he found himself at the mercy of unpredictable inshore tides and currents. Seeing his plight, the Spanish set upon him with four galleases and galleons to back them up. Before the highly manoeuvrable galleases could do any damage, however, *Triumph* raked them with gunfire, which sent them limping off for shelter.

In the afternoon, *Revenge* and the other ships under Drake's command launched a surprise attack on the seaward edge of the crescent, Drake having correctly judged the change in the wind. The attack may have caught the Spaniards off their guard but it still failed to make a serious impression on the Armada.

On Wednesday, 24 July, *Revenge* was back in the thick of the action. The Spanish 650-ton urca *Gran Grifón* began to lag behind the rest of the fleet and, like a young lion upon a straggling ox, *Revenge* was upon her. Drake's attack on the *Gran Grifón* was merciless. First he fired a broadside into her, then went ahead and turned round for another broadside. After this he crossed the *Grifón*'s stern and raked her upper deck with musket shot. By this time Recalde had ordered reinforcements to come to the *Gran Grifón*'s aid, while more English ships also appeared. Soon there was a general engagement with the Spanish right wing, during which *Gran Grifón*, no longer fit to sail on her own, was towed by a galleass back to the main body of ships while other galleasses engaged *Revenge*.

Medina Sidonia soon appeared in the *San Martín*, along with some other ships, but the English once again refused to become embroiled in a general engagement and withdrew to long-culverin range.

In the afternoon, both fleets were becalmed off the Needles, with a throng of spectators lining the cliffs of the Isle of Wight, as if at some giant theatre.

The free-lance activities of *Revenge*, whether discreditable as with the *Rosario*, or laudable, as with the *Gran Grifón*, underlined the lack of central control in the English fleet. Howard, for example, having at one point chased his second-in-command's spectre fruitlessly through the night, was also unaware that *Revenge* had gone into action against *Gran Grifón* and precipitated what could have developed into a major engagement.

Fortunately for England, rather than indulging in squabbles over control, it was agreed among the captains at the council of war that the fleet should be divided into four squadrons, each of about twenty-five ships, led by Frobisher in the *Triumph*, Lord Howard in the *Ark Royal*, Hawkins in the *Victory* and Drake in the *Revenge*.

Under pressure of circumstances, the commanders of the Navy Royal had quickly established a system that was to prove a major advance in naval tactics.

On this Wednesday, small craft plied to and from port to the Navy Royal ships, carrying round shot, powder, victuals and fresh water. They also brought young blood in the shape of the sons of noblemen who yearned to share in the hour of glory.

The gateway to England now seemed to be the Solent and in order to pre-empt a Spanish attempt in this direction, Howard planned to deploy Frobisher's squadron forward to the landward side of the Armada.

As dawn broke on Thursday the 25th, the Armada's commanders seemed to have read Howard's mind and they proceeded up the Channel keeping as close inshore as possible. The English crowded behind, looking for an opportunity to overtake on the inside and block the entrance to the Solent.

The *Santa Ana* and *San Luís* struggled astern of the Armada and were engaged by Hawkins and Hood. Medina Sidonia in the *San Martín*, along with some other ships, came back to help them and the *San Martín* was in turn attacked by Frobisher in the *Triumph*. A change in the wind left *Triumph* cut off in the lee of the Armada and the Spaniards duly bore down on her like hounds on a stag. Fortunately the wind changed again just in time and *Triumph* skipped away.

Later in the morning, Drake and Hawkins, positioned out to seaward, attacked the right wing of the Armada, concentrating on the Portuguese galleon *Sâo Mateus* and the 52-gun *Florencia*. *Revenge* and her companions sent the two Spanish warships staggering back into the ranks of the supply ships they were supposed to protect. This action, along with the movements of wind and tide, contributed to manoeuvring the Armada into a position beyond the entrance to the Solent. This was a success in itself, but there seems to have been more to the intentions of Drake and Hawkins than this: they intended to drive the Spanish ships on to the dangerous shoals and rocks of the Owers Bank, stretching out from Selsey Bill.

As indicated in Medina Sidonia's *Relation*, which he enclosed in a letter to the King, Medina Sidonia recognized the danger in time: 'The Duke seeing that in the proposed assault the advantage was no longer with us, and that we were now near the Isle of Wight, discharged a piece and proceeded on his course, the rest of the Armada following in very good order, the enemy remaining a long way astern.' The decorous tone of this account disguises what was most likely a sense of panic as the ships came nearer to the shoals and as they became aware of the real significance of the opportunity that had just been lost. The Spanish Armada had failed to penetrate the wooden walls of England and was now entirely dependent for the success of its mission on Parma being at the right place at the right time for transport across the Channel.

It was not surprising, therefore, as the next two days, Friday and Saturday, passed without incident, that the English became more and more celebratory or that by the end of Friday, Hawkins, Frobisher, Lord Thomas Howard and Lord Edmund Sheffield had all been knighted.

By Saturday the 27th, the Armada had been forced to lope off to Calais and, though undefeated and still almost as formidable as it was when it was first sighted of Land's End, it had suffered a moral defeat. In order to raise morale, things would now need to work smoothly with Parma. He must embark his army and the walls of England must then be staved in as the Armada sailed towards its inevitable invincible destiny.

Once again, the English had other plans. Rather than rest on their laurels for even one night, they set about harassing the anchored Spanish fleet almost as soon as they arrived off Calais on Sunday night. The results were to be beyond their wildest expectations.

Medina Sidonia had already received bad news from Parma. The Duke's army was nowhere near ready and it could be up to a fortnight before it was fully assembled. Medina Sidonia must have looked on with increased foreboding as Lord Henry Seymour's squadron joined the main English force from the north.

The Spanish had every reason for trepidation. Federigo Gianibelli, designer of a particularly fiendish variety of exploding fireship, known to the Spaniards as a *máquina de minas*, was known to be in England – the anchored Armada presented the perfect target for such a device.

Sure enough, without even bothering to send for fireships from home, the English torched eight ships from their fleet and sent them down on the tide with loaded guns, towards the Spanish ships. The tide was flowing at nearly 3 knots, backed up by an extra three quarters of a knot of North Sea current. The distance to be covered was about a mile and a half. The Spaniards therefore had about thirty minutes in which to take evasive action.

Although the pinnaces sent out to windward by Medina Sidonia managed to tow two fireships clear, the remainder continued to bear down on the Spaniards like the hounds of hell. The flames set off guns and there were shattering detonations. Calais had become Gehenna.

Two [fireships] were successfully intercepted and towed aside, but the remaining six got through, and it was at that point that the hitherto excellent discipline of the Spanish fleet cracked. Only the flagship and four of its immediate neighbours successfully executed the planned manoeuvre and remained on station. The remainder cut their cables and scattered in panic, to the Admiral's rage and chagrin.[4]

The Spaniards needed no further evidence that Gianibelli was upon them. With the flaming spectres bearing down, lighting up sky and sea, panic spread throughout the Armada. All of a sudden, the indomitable formation that had been held all the way up the Channel, defying English attempts to penetrate it, had been broken.

In the light of dawn, *Revenge* and the rest of the English fleet gave chase. *Revenge* herself came within a hundred yards of the *San Martín* and fired her bow guns at her before turning to fire a broadside that raked the upper deck. Then she sailed out of range, but not without receiving some damage in return.

One Spanish account relates that *Revenge* was 'pierced through by cannon balls of all sizes above forty times' and that Drake's 'very cabeen was twise shot thorow'. Drake himself used to tell the story of how 'the bedde of a certain gentleman lying weary thereupon was taken quite from under him with the force of a bullet.' The breathless exultation of the English can be sensed in another letter written by Drake from *Revenge*:

Drake to Walsingham

July 29, 1588

Right Honourable:- This bearer came aboard the ship I was in in a wonderful good time, and brought with him as good knowledge as we could wish. His carefulness therein is worthy recompense, for that God hath given us so good a day in forcing the enemy so far to leeward as I hope in God the Prince of Parma and the Duke of Sidonia shall not shake hands this few days; and whensoever they shall meet, I believe neither of them will greatly rejoice of this day's service. The town of Calais hath seen some part thereof, whose Mayor her Majesty is beholden unto.

Business commands me to end. God bless her Majesty, our gracious Sovereign, and give us all grace to live in His fear. I assure your Honour this day's service hath much appalled the enemy, and no doubt but encouraged our army.

From aboard her Majesty's good ship the *Revenge*, this 29th of July, 1588.

Your Honour's most ready to be commanded,

FRA. Drake

There must be great care taken to send us munition and victual withersoever the enemy goeth.

Yours,

Fra. Drake[5]

Howard pursued the remains of the Spanish Armada as far as Newcastle before turning back, leaving the Spaniards to continue on that agonizing voyage round the top of Scotland and down the Irish coast, losing no less than sixty ships on the way. Medina Sidonia returned to Spain a broken man, both physically and morally, his closed litter being pelted with stones on the way back to his home near Cadiz.

The English commanders, by contrast, were fêted but, although God had appeared to indicate whose side He was on, a virulent disease sweeping through the English fleet seriously marred the celebrations and seemed to suggest that Divine punishments were not the monopoly of the other side.

Despite the apparent success of the campaign against the Armada, which had been left to break itself to pieces on the rocks of the British Isles, revenge was still in the minds of the English sea captains. The Armada had been shepherded away from the English coast by dint of masterly English seamanship, but the captains of the Navy Royal could not claim to have defeated it entirely through tactical genius or firepower. The elements had played a large part.

Drake himself seemed to acknowledge this sense of anticlimax when he stated rather lamely in a letter to Lord Howard:

August 11, 1588

Most Honourable,

The sudden sending for of my very good, my Lord Admiral, hath caused me to scribble these few lines, first, most humbly beseeching your honour to deliver this letter unto her Majesty as a testification of my Lord Admiral's most honourable usage of me in this action, where it hath pleased his good Lordship to accept of that which I have sometimes spoken, and commanded that little service which I was able to deserve – wherein if I have not performed as much as was looked for, yet I persuade myself his good Lordship will confess I have been dutiful.

Your Honour's faithfully

to be commanded,

Fra: Drake[6]

Perhaps in order to help reinstate his dashing and offensive reputation, together with Sir John Norreys, Drake presented the Queen in September with a plan for a counter-attack against Lisbon. Drake had chosen his partner well, for Norreys had built a formidable reputation as a military commander against the Duke of Parma, and he had badly dented the aura of invincibility maintained at that time by Spanish military arms. He had been brought back to serve as Leicester's chief of staff during the Armada invasion scare.

As was to be expected, the expedition was not all about Queen and country. Drake and Norreys planned to place the Portuguese pretender Dom Antonio on the Portuguese throne and thereafter make the most of the access to the lucrative trade to the Far East that had been opened up by the Portuguese.

The plan was to finance the expedition through Royal funds and private venture. The City of London raised £10,000, topped up by £5,000 from Drake. The Queen provided £20,000 along with six naval vessels, two pinnaces, a siege train, arms and armour and three months' victuals. Norreys managed to raise from the States-General of Holland 600 English cavalry, thirteen companies of

English foot soldiers and ten companies of Walloons. When the Queen found herself in too deep for comfort, Parliament voted extra funds.

The fleet sailed in March 1589 and Drake even managed to persuade sixty Dutch flyboats that they met on the way to join in. When he pulled in to Plymouth, more ships joined, along with a host of young gentlemen volunteers seeking glory and a fortune. The final tally was eight Queen's ships, seventy-seven armed merchantmen and the sixty Dutch flyboats. There were about 3,000 English and 900 Dutch sailors, along with 11,000 soldiers. The soldiers were formed into 115 companies in fifteen regiments.

The ships were organized in five squadrons, each composed of about fifteen English merchantmen and fifteen Dutch flyboats, each commanded by a 'Colonel of the Squadron'. Drake flew his flag in the *Revenge*. His officers included Lieutenant Thomas Drake, Corporal Yonge, Captain of the Watch Webbe and Chief Master Thomas West. The other colonels of squadrons were: Sir John Norreys in the *Nonpareil*; Vice Admiral Thomas Fenner in the *Dreadnought*; Sir Roger Williams in the *Swiftsure*; and Sir Edward Norreys in the *Foresight*. Captain William Fenner in the *Aid* had a roving duty to ensure that 'all the squadrons observe their prescribed orders'. The pinnaces formed a separate light division under a 'Master of the Discoveries', the equivalent of a Chief Intelligence Officer, with the rank of 'Lieutenant-Colonel of the Pinnaces'.

After a delay of a fortnight due to contrary winds, which caused further expense for the Queen, the fleet sailed on 18 April 1589. They were short of food, though Drake pinned some hope on a good harvest in Spain and Portugal. He wrote to the Government:

> By the end of the month, harvest will begin both in Spain and Portugal, which doth put us in good hope of relief, yet twenty thousand persons are not satisfied with small means. Upon my credit with your lordship there never was army in better order than this, nor greater hope of good, if God grant relief of victual, which I distrust not. The might of God is as great as Himself.[7]

His orders were that: 'Before you shall attempt either Portugal or the Azores, our express pleasure and commandment is that you distress the ships of war in Guipuzcoa, Biscay and Galicia.'[8]

Drake arrived in Corunna Bay, six days after leaving Plymouth. Although, as the port of embarkation of the Armada, Corunna was a good place to exact revenge, the presence of the *San Juan* and two galleys provided him with little opportunity. He turned his attention, therefore, to the town itself, with boat parties being sent to seize landing points on the beaches across the bay from the town, while Sir John Norreys led an expedition to secure the approaches to the town itself.

At midnight an attack on the lower town was launched, 500 of its defenders were killed and the military commander, Don Juan de Luma, was captured.

The English scoured the countryside around for food and then got drunk on the contents of a wine store. The attack on the higher town was unsuccessful and what had begun as an incisive raid began to look like a time-wasting distraction. The English set light to the lower town and then set sail with their loot, including 3,000 pikes and fifty bronze cannon.

Santander was another potential target, 350 miles to the east, with about forty Armada ships, but it was heavily fortified and the assault would involve running the gauntlet up a narrow channel overlooked by guns.

On 9 May 1589, the fleet sailed to rendezvous at the Berlengas arquipelago, some 50 miles north of Lisbon, though some ships were deterred by a strong westerly wind. On the way, Drake was met by the Earl of Essex, sailing in *Swiftsure*, and Sir Roger Williams, accompanied by six other ships. Whether or not Drake welcomed the arrival of the Queen's current favourite is not clear but, in any case, his main focus of attention was now on the capture of Lisbon.

Sailing from the Berlengas, the English landed at the port of Peniche, a town situated on a peninsula with a perimeter of about 10 kilometres. About 100 kilometres to the north was Figueira da Foz, where 219 years later the Duke of Wellington would land a British army to fight and eventually defeat the French occupying forces.

The extensive beaches of Peniche, though much appreciated today by surfers and body boarders, did not hold the same attraction for the English sailors and soldiers in the flotilla of boats sent ashore to seize the town. One boat was overturned in the breakers and its twenty-five occupants drowned, though the remainder of the boats succeeded in making a landing. The local resistance was fierce but brief and the castle was soon taken. The full army was then landed under Norreys, Essex and Dom Antonio and, after taking the salute, Drake sailed down to the mouth of the Tagus to await events.

Cooped up in their boats, soldiers and sailors were falling to a fever that was ominously similar to the one that had swept the English fleet after the defeat of the Armada. Sir Thomas Fenner wrote to Walsingham that of his ship's company of 300 on the *Dreadnought*, fourteen had died and only eighteen were fit for work.

The expedition was also plagued with ill discipline. The Dutch shippers complained about the behaviour of the soldiers on board the flyboats, while Norreys' force marching from the north seemed somewhat unconvincing, without even a siege train and only a handful of cavalry. Their numbers were further depleted by disease and desertion. Although the Spanish forces withdrew, without the expected popular uprising to support the pretender, Norreys felt he had little choice but to withdraw.

The expedition was not without the occasional stroke of good luck. They captured eighty French and Hanseatic merchant ships en route from the Baltic with grain and naval stores, although fair fortune seemed mostly to be sailing elsewhere. The Dutch flyboat captains were not long in recognizing which way the wind was blowing and they set off for La Rochelle. The Queen still refused to supply a siege train and, to add injury to insult, twenty-five Spanish galleys sailed out from the mouth of the Tagus and succeeded in capturing three of the smaller English ships.

Although he called off a Channel raid on the Azores, despite all the setbacks, Drake was able to summon enough vigour to launch an attack on Vigo. Having occupied and burned the town, a violent storm put paid to any second thoughts about the Azores and, by the time she reached Plymouth Sound, *Revenge* was barely afloat.

If the attack on Lisbon was supposed to consolidate the victory over the Armada, it failed. Its objectives had not been achieved, English ships had been captured and thousands of English seamen had been lost either through conflict or disease – the casualty rate was over 40 per cent. When the soldiers were disbanded with five shillings apiece, though they were allowed to keep their arms, 500 made their way to London where the Lord Mayor had to call out the train bands to keep order.

Despite all this, the perception abroad was not entirely negative. The opinion of the Venetian ambassador was that the King of Spain's prestige had been damaged further by 'a woman, mistress of only half an island, with the help of a common soldier and a corsair'. The presence of the English fleet had repercussions, leading even to a mutiny in Parma's army when pay was withheld as a result of the delays to the Spanish treasure fleet.

The fact that Drake did not receive another command until the West Indies expedition of 1595, however, told its own story. During this period 236 English ships sailed out on various expeditions, taking over 300 prizes, while Drake did good works in his home town of Plymouth, strengthening the port, building mills and improving the water supply. He was not to sail in *Revenge* again, but that ship was soon to achieve immortality under a different master.

Chapter 3

At Flores, in the Azores
Sir Richard Grenville Lay

In the wake of the failed Lisbon expedition, Sir John Hawkins set about devising a new maritime strategy, based on the principle 'that first we have as little to do in foreign countries as may be (but of mere necessity), for that breedeth great charge and no profit at all'.[1] It proved to be one of the enduring themes of English foreign policy down the centuries.

The plan involved maintaining small squadrons of Queen's ships, with supporting vessels, between Spain and the Azores during the sailing season of the Spanish treasure-carrying *flotas*, coming from the Indies.

> Up to this point the English had shown very little strategic imagination ... But in 1590 a new approach can be glimpsed, which was to have a long and distinguished future in naval strategy. John Hawkins and Martin Frobisher were commissioned to cruise off the coast of Spain in order to intercept all ships passing to or from the Indies ... More important, they remained on station for seven months, being victualled at sea. They took virtually no prizes, but paralysed that aspect of Spanish commerce, an unsung exploit which testifies to the high level of discipline which could be maintained, and points to the whole fleet consisting of royal ships ... the strategy of blockade which it represented was still the dominant element in naval policy at the time of the Napoleonic wars.[2]

To be successful, the plan required a well-organized relay of relief vessels so as not to leave a gap for the Spaniards to slip through. It

50

also presupposed that the Spanish would be deterred by the English rather than just sweeping them out of the way.

The Spanish had not failed to learn some lessons from the Armada débâcle and were not only rebuilding their fleet but designing new super-ships that could more than match the English ships for strength and speed – these included twelve massive new galleons (the Twelve Apostles), designed on English lines, and a collection of *gallizabras*, a fast and deadly warship that could outsail anything it could not defeat.

Neither the 1589 nor the 1590 *flotas* were intercepted by the English but the Spaniards were indeed deterred by the presence of two English squadrons, one off the Azores under the command of Frobisher in the *Revenge*, and one off the coast of Spain under Hawkins.

Although some bullion was transported in 1591 between February and March, in frigates specially built in Havana, the main *flota* left much later in the year, the intention being to wait until the English ran out of supplies and also for Bazán to gather a strong enough fleet off the Azores to escort it home.

This time the English sent out twenty ships and pinnaces under the command of Lord Howard. Sir Walter Raleigh had originally planned to go but in the event was replaced by Sir Richard Grenville. Howard sailed in the *Defiance*, 600 tons, and Grenville in the *Revenge*; Richard Crosse commanded the *Bonaventure*, 600 tons; Sir Edward Denny commanded the *Nonpareil*, 600 tons; while other smaller ships included the *Charles* and the *Moon*, of 60 and 70 tons respectively, the *Bark Raleigh* and some pinnaces.

The Cornishman Sir Richard Grenville was something of a wild card in this line-up. He did not have the reputation to rank him among seamen such as Drake, Hawkins, Frobisher or even Lord Thomas Howard, and in fact, unlike the aforementioned, he had not even taken part in the defeat of the Armada. He had been responsible for organizing the defences of the west of England and had been employed more recently in Ireland.

Grenville was described by the Spanish ambassador as a 'notable pirate' and his exploits and behaviour did everything to support his fearsome reputation. A Spanish ship that dared to attack Grenville on his return from a voyage to Virginia in October 1585 was over-powered. Since Grenville lacked a boat with which to board her, he

51

put together a raft made of old chests and rowed across on that, the raft disintegrating as they boarded the vessel.

This pugnacious, somewhat unhinged, attitude to the enemy, and Spaniards in particular, valuable as it may have been when directed appropriately in the heat of battle, was to be the decisive factor in the fate of one of the Navy Royal's finest warships, the first *Revenge*.

Grenville was sometimes as unpopular among his own men as he was with the Spanish. He was arrogant, overbearing, hot-tempered and argumentative and, if this were not enough, he was also conceited about his knight-chivalric lineage which placed him a cut above the run-of-the-mill English admirals, by birth if nothing else.

According to Jan Huyghen van Linschoten, Grenville was 'a man of fierce temper, very unquiet in his mind and greatly affected to war. His own people hated him for his fierceness and spoke very hardly of him.'[3]

Ralph Lane, governor of the new Virginia colony, wrote to Walsingham about Grenville's 'intolerable pride, and insatiable ambition'.[4] Although Lane also had a reputation for being quarrelsome, in Grenville's case his complaint seems to have been justified.

It seems, however, that rays of sunlight sometimes penetrated this somewhat thundery picture. Philip Gawdy, a young gentleman volunteer, wrote to his brother in Norfolk in more flattering terms:

> The Queen hath commanded all speed to be made. Sir Richard and other captains will presently go to court with whom I will go. And so away as fast as the ships will fall down the Thames. I have already bought my arms and target, the very fellows to my Lord Thomas and Sir Richard. My apparel will be made tonight, what is necessary else I do provide besides the great kindness I find both at Sir Richard's hands and at Mr Langhorne's [captain of the soldiers aboard *Revenge*].[5]

Grenville returned the compliment by writing on the margin of another letter of Gawdy's to his brother that 'not sickness, no danger, no fear ... nor no extremities of weather, mutiny hard[ship] or other peril or grief could provoke'[6] him from his duty.

When Lord Thomas's squadron sailed in April it ran into what Captain Langhorne described as 'the extremest fury of the weather' which forced them all to take shelter in Falmouth, apart, of course, from Grenville, who continued in the teeth of the gale, riding it out between Scilly and Ushant. According to Gawdy: 'We spent both our masts, but by God's grace, they were espied in good time and strengthened with fishes, wolding and caulking, and now, thanks be to God, they be in very good plight.'[7]

Having weathered the storm, *Revenge* then sailed on to the rendezvous off Cape St Vincent, where Lord Howard's ships were to cruise, awaiting the arrival of the treasure fleets from Havana.

On about 18 April, *Revenge* captured a large Hanseatic hulk off the Berlengas, carrying about £10,000 worth of masts, timber and other stores, which were required for Philip's fleet. Having discovered that four of the treasure-frigates they had been awaiting had in fact already reached Spain, the English sent their prize home and headed for the Azores.

In England, there was a flurry of activity, as, fearing another Armada, Henry Palmer's squadron in the Channel was reinforced, a fleet of privateers was raised by Sir Walter Raleigh in the West Country and the Earl of Cumberland put to sea with his own squadron. Two Queen's ships, the *Lion*, George Fenner, and the *Foresight*, Thomas Vavasour, sailed to reinforce Lord Howard. Seven London merchantmen, the *Susan, Centurion, Cherubim, Mayflower, Margaret, John* and *Corselet* also left Plymouth Sound to join Howard.

Lord Howard's rendezvous was south-west of the island of Flores, where he planned to lie in wait for the treasure fleet until 30 August. According to Gawdy, he was 'almost famished for want of prey, or rather like a bear robber of her whelps'.[8] In the absence not only of the enemy but also of provisions and reinforcements, Howard had no choice but to abandon station and head for Flores, to take on water and give his crews some rest and medical attention. They also set about replacing the old soiled ballast in the ship, by now a repository for infection, cleaning the ship and replacing it with new ballast from the island.

Don Alonso de Bazán, meanwhile, had sailed from Spain and arrived at the island of Terceira, some miles to the east of Flores, on 15 August. They had been sighted by Captain Middleton in one of the Duke of Cumberland's pinnaces, who managed to warn Howard on 31 August. By then, however, it was almost too late. Howard's men were still ashore, embarking fresh water, ballast and provisions, when at about 5 o'clock in the evening the Spanish were seen rounding the island.

Howard had time to get his men ashore before weighing anchor, and some of his ships were forced to slip their cables, in their haste to get away. Howard managed to work his way to windward and was able to put himself out of immediate harm's way. *Revenge* was the last to weigh anchor.

There has been some speculation as to the delay. Raleigh's view was that Grenville simply took longer than the others to recover his men, of which ninety were diseased. There seems nothing remarkable in this. However, as his account goes on, Grenville's singular personality begins to impose itself. Urged by the master and others to cut his main sail, Grenville refused:

> to turne from the enemy, alleging that he would rather choose to die, than to dishonour himself, his country, and her Majesty's ship, persuading his company that he would pass through two squadrons, in despite of them: and enforce those of Seville to give him way. Which he performed upon diverse of the foremost, who as the mariners term it, sprung their luff, and fell under the lee of the *Revenge*. But the other course had been the better, and might well have been answered in so great an impossibility of prevailing. Nothwithstanding out of the greatness of his mind, he could not be persuaded.[9]

What Raleigh describes as 'greatness of mind' might otherwise be described as stubbornness or foolhardiness:

> deep down ... at the root of the man, there was, surely, an element of unbalance, of overstrain. It comes out in his impulsive temper, terrifying to his subordinates, which made him unloved where Drake was adored. It is not without significance that his very first appearance upon the public scene was an act of manslaughter.[10]

As the Spaniards came upon the single English ship, first the *San Phelipe* and then the *San Barnabé* under General Bertendona grappled the *Revenge*. According to the Spanish relation, the *San Phelipe* managed to put ten soldiers aboard the *Revenge*. According to Raleigh, despite the fact that there were no soldiers or marines

aboard the *Revenge*, the Spanish attempts at boarding were successfully repulsed by her crew. However, the Spaniards at one point
invaded *Revenge*'s poop deck, captured her ensign and had some
limited success before the *San Barnabé* had to sheer off due to the
damage she had received.

Two more Spanish galleons took her place and the men of
Revenge fired on them as best they could with muskets and grenades.
Not only that, but the *San Phelipe* also received a broadside of
crossbar shot from *Revenge* and as other galleons came up, *Revenge*
wreaked vengeance upon them; the *Ascensión* and Cuitino's flagship
were both sunk.

A brave little ship, the *Pilgrim*, under Jacob Whiddon, a Plymouth
man, hovered near the *Revenge* in the forlorn hope of rendering
assistance, 'but in the morning bearing with the *Revenge*, was hunted
like a hare amongst ravenous hounds but escaped'.[11]

The decks of the *Revenge* resembled a charnel house, with dead
and wounded bodies lying amidst a confusion of broken masts and
tangled rigging. Of the 100 men who had been fit to fight at the
beginning of the battle, forty had now been killed and most of
the remainder were wounded.

Grenville himself was among the more seriously wounded. He
had received a musket shot in the body during the night and was hit
again on the head while his surgeon was dressing his wound. The
surgeon himself was killed.

Although undefeated, Sir Richard Grenville recognized that the
situation was hopeless. Rather than surrender, however, he took a
similar decision to the German captain of the *Graf Spee* 348 years
later: he decided to scuttle the ship rather than hand her over to the
enemy, although this would mean drowning himself and his crew.

Although he found an ally for this plan in the master gunner, he
could not persuade the captain of the ship or the master, and their
resistance was vindicated when the Spanish General, Don Alfonso
Bazán, agreed to grant the crew safe passage to England, 'the better
sort to pay such reasonable ransom as their estate would bear, and
in the mean season to be free from gallery or imprisonment'.

Having failed to deny Her Majesty's Ship to the Spaniards, Sir
Richard was indifferent to his own safety and replied to Alonso
Bazán 'that he might do with his body what he list, for he esteemed
it not'. None the less, he was carried, swooning, out of the ship to be
received with considerable respect and admiration by the enemy.

Grenville survived two or three days but at last his wounds overcame him.

According to John Huyghen Van Linschoten, a resident of the island of Terceira, even at this point Grenville's indomitable spirit did not desert him. But, although he bequeathed his own memory in exalted terms, he was somewhat less complimentary about those who had fought with him:

> Here die I Richard Grenville with a joyful and quiet mind, for I have ended my life as a true soldier ought to do, that hath fought for his country, Queen, religion, and honour: whereby my soul most joyfully departeth out of this body; and shall leave behind it an everlasting fame of a valiant and true soldier that hath done his duty, as he was bound to do. But the others of my company have done as traitors and dogs, for which they shall be reproached all their lives and leave a shameful name for ever.[12]

There seem to be two readings of Sir Richard Grenville: on the one hand we see a man who, although unable to take part in the fight against the Armada himself, was imbued with such a spirit of love for his country that he would fling himself like a tiger at the enemy wherever he found him.

The Spaniards, indeed, continued to pose a dire threat to England, perhaps even more so now that they were equipped with the new super ships, the 'Twelve Apostles'. In the resolute opinion of Sir Richard Grenville, the enemy must not only be engaged more closely but at every possible opportunity. Such a reading might suggest that the final sentence of Grenville's dying soliloquy was aimed at Lord Howard and the rest of the English fleet that had allowed the winds of caution to fill their sails, and allowed discretion to overrule valour. In his view, they had failed their country.

On the other hand, the whole episode may be seen as typical of a man blinded by rage who put his ship and his crew at risk out of sheer foolhardiness, when he could well have slipped away from the immediate threat with the rest of the fleet in order to preserve a valuable ship and fight another day. Under this view, the final sentence reads not so much as patriotic dismay but as vindictive fury that his will had been thwarted. This crew, many of whom had fought to the death, taking a heavy toll among the Spanish galleons ranged against them, were not to be spared a lashing from their master's tongue for good measure.

Neither one of these readings appears to suffice on its own. Grenville's patriotism was bound up inextricably with his personality and neither the Spaniards nor his own crew were likely to be spared the effects of his whirling-dervish temper. If the Spaniards were present, they must be attacked; and if his crew disobeyed his orders they must be vilified, even if this vilification should have to be conveyed on his dying breath.

Sir Richard Grenville is the hero of the hawks and the enemy of the doves. Winston Churchill would have valued his mettle, if not his tactical nous. Grenville was a man of action and he saw his duty in straightforward terms. He was not a Protestant zealot, it just so happened that Spanish Catholics were the enemies of his Queen and were therefore his enemies. The Spaniards themselves described him as 'el Almirante de los mayors marineros y cosarios de Inglaterra gran hereje y perseguidor de catholicos'.

The last fight of the *Revenge* became an epic in the annals of English history as it epitomized, perhaps even more than the fight against the Armada, the spirit of resistance of a small nation faced with a larger foe. Tennyson is conscious of this value of the underdog in his epic poem – three times out of four that *Revenge* is directly named, she is prefaced with the adjective 'little'.

It was to be a peculiar and recurring theme of great moments in English history. Even when Great Britain was the greatest imperial power in the world, her survival in the summer of 1940 would depend on 'the few'. It is not surprising that William Shakespeare, with his genius for reading the signs of the times, should catch this spirit and insert it retrospectively into the account of Henry V's foray into France and that the lynchpin rallying call should be 'we few, we happy few'.

The 'little' *Revenge*, therefore, had found a master who most embodied the spirit of her name, more even than Sir Francis Drake, who used the ship in the height of national danger to skulk off in the night after rich pickings. And the ship itself embodied the spirit of a small nation that, although it was to become great, remained always spiritually attached to its relative size – a nation always proud to be a David among Goliaths.

The Cornishman A.L. Rowse was expansive about the significance of this particular incident and how it reflected so closely the mood of the Elizabethan age:

> It was the heroic age in our history, when the nation saw great opportunities of expansion and achievement opening before it. Young, fresh, vigorous, full of self-confidence and spirit, it knew how to take them ... It was the fact that the opportunities given were so triumphantly taken, our difficulties surmounted in spite of the odds against us, that made the Elizabethan age the heroic age in our history ...
>
> It was in the realm of action, at its most heightened and intense moments, that the pure quality of the heroic emerges: that sort of gesture by which a man goes down to posterity for something not only memorable in itself, but in which subsequent ages find significance, inspiration in its defiance, strength in its courage ...
>
> Of such was Grenville's last action in the *Revenge*. There was never any fight more famous in a nation's history; never any that was more purely heroic in quality – that mixture of dare-devilry, defiance of fate, supreme indifference to consequences, which men admire more than anything, because their own lives are at every point so circumscribed by circumstance, from which there is, save in such moments, no emancipation.[13]

Poets and prose writers have queued up to pay homage to the event, including Sir Francis Bacon:

> In the year 1591 was that memorable fight of an English ship called *Revenge*, under the command of Sir Richard Grenville, memorable (I say) even beyond credit and to the height of some heroical fable: and though it were a defeat, yet it exceeded a victory; being like the act of Samson, that killed more men at his death, than he had done in the time of all his life. This ship, for the space of fifteen hours, sate like a stag amongst hounds at bay, and was sieged and fought with, in turn, by fifteen great ships of Spain, part of a navy of fifty-five ships in all; the rest like abettors looking on afar off. And amongst the fifteen ships that fought, the great San Philippo was one; a ship of fifteen hundred ton, prince of the twelve Sea Apostle, which was right

glad when she was shifted off from the *Revenge*. This brave ship
the *Revenge*, being manned only with two hundred soldiers and
marines, whereof eighty lay sick, yet nevertheless after a fight
maintained (as was said) of fifteen hours, and two ships of the
enemy sunk by her side, besides many more torn and battered
and great slaughter of men, never came to be entered, but
was taken by composition; the enemies themselves having in
admiration the virtue of the commander and the whole tragedy
of that ship.[14]

The epitaph of Sir Richard Grenville may be echoed in the poetry
of Thomas Babington, Lord Macaulay, although intended for a
different hero in dire straits:

> *Then out spake brave Horatius,*
> *The Captain of the Gate:*
> *'To every man upon this earth*
> *Death cometh soon or late.*
> *And how can man die better*
> *Than facing fearful odd,*
> *For the ashes of his fathers,*
> *And the temples of his Gods?*
> *Now who will stand on either hand*
> *And keep the bridge with me?'*[15]

And what of the ship itself, her master having succumbed to his
wounds? Manned by foreign hands, the little ship was still to live up
to her name. The Spaniards could hardly believe their good fortune
in capturing the prize ship of the Navy Royal:

This Admiral-galleon was one of the best there were in
England; they called her the *Revenge*. She was the flagship that
carried Drake to Corunna ... she carried 42 pieces of artillery
of bronze without three which were given to another ship a few
days before, the 20 on her lower deck of 40 to 60 quintals, and
the remaining 22 of 20 to 30 quintals, all good.[16]

Their possession of this prize was not to last for long for, just as
at the time of the Armada, 'God blew and they were scattered', so
after the capture of the *Revenge* all the vengeance of God seemed to

rain down upon the Spanish fleet, manifested in the worst storm in living memory, which struck with the force of a cyclone – creation itself seemed to have been blotted out during this seven- to eight-day onslaught which wrought havoc among Bazán's naval craft and even worse among the *flotas*.

Revenge was among the many ships cast away in the storm:

> near to the Island of Tercera, where it brake in a hundred pieces and sunk to the ground, having in her 70 men gallegos, Biscayans and others, with some of the captive Englishmen, whereof but one was saved that got up upon the cliffs alive, and had his body and head all wounded, and he being on shore brought us the news, desiring to be shriven, and thereupon presently died.[17]

At a time when the hand of God was seen to be in everything, before the age of science or rational explanation, the demise of Grenville, the *Revenge* and the natural events that accompanied it were steeped in ominous significance:

> that the taking of the *Revenge* was justly revenged upon them, and not by the might or force of man, but by the power of God, as some of them openly said in the Isle of Tercera, that they believed verily God would consume them, and that he took part with Lutherans and heretics: saying further that so soon as they had thrown the dead body of the Vice admiral Sir Richard Grenville overboard, they verily thought that as he had a devilish faith and religion, and therefore the devils loved him, so he presently sunk into the bottom of the sea, and down into Hell, where he raised up all the devils to the Revenge of his death.[18]

The Grenvilles had grown up in Cornwall over the centuries, ancestors of Norman adventurers; and *Revenge* itself had grown up in ancient forests of England, its planks formed from the branches of vast forest titans with immeasurable girths. Solid, immovable, rooted in the soil of their country, both man and oaken ship were slow to succumb: Grenville, like an oak tree that takes many blows of the axe before its branches and trunk eventually fall with a crash into the undergrowth; and the *Revenge* itself, unsinkable except by an act of God Himself. Both, far from England, went to their watery graves at the bottom of the stormy sea.

Not only strong and solid, but fast and furious, the *Revenge*, with its greyhound lines, seemed to represent all the great potential of the Elizabethan era. Light and deadly, a ship for fast movement and adventure, she also proved at the last to be made of stern stuff.

The Revenge
Alfred, Lord Tennyson

I

At Flores, in the Azores Sir Richard Grenville lay,
And a pinnace, like a flutter'd bird, came flying from far away;
'Spanish ships of war at sea! we have sighted fifty-three!'
Then sware Lord Thomas Howard: ' 'Fore God I am no coward;
But I cannot meet them here, for my ships are out of gear,   5
And the half my men are sick. I must fly, but follow quick.
We are six ships of the line; can we fight with fifty-three?'

II

Then spake Sir Richard Grenville: 'I know you are no coward;
You fly them for a moment to fight with them again.
But I've ninety men and more that are lying sick ashore.   10
I should count myself the coward if I left them, my Lord Howard,
To these Inquisition dogs and the devildoms of Spain.'

III

So Lord Howard past away with five ships of war that day,
Till he melted like a cloud in the silent summer heaven;
But Sir Richard bore in hand all his sick men from the land   15
Very carefully and slow,
Men of Bideford in Devon,
And we laid them on the ballast down below:
For we brought them all aboard,
And they blest him in their pain, that they were not left to Spain,   20
To the thumb-screw and the stake, for the glory of the Lord.

IV

He had only a hundred seamen to work the ship and to fight,
And he sailed away from Flores till the Spaniard came in sight,
With his huge sea-castles heaving upon the weather bow.
'Shall we fight or shall we fly?   25
Good Sir Richard, tell us now,
For to fight is but to die!
There'll be little of us left by the time this sun be set.'
And Sir Richard said again: 'We be all good Englishmen.
Let us bang these dogs of Seville, the children of the devil,   30
For I never turn'd my back upon Don or devil yet.'

V

Sir Richard spoke and he laugh'd, and we roar'd a hurrah and so
The little Revenge ran on sheer into the heart of the foe,
With her hundred fighters on deck, and her ninety sick below;
For half of their fleet to the right and half to the left were seen,   35
And the little Revenge ran on thro' the long sea-lane between.

VI

Thousands of their soldiers look'd down from their decks and
laugh'd,
Thousands of their seamen made mock at the mad little craft
Running on and on, till delay'd
By their mountain-like San Philip that, of fifteen hundred tons,   40
And up-shadowing high above us with her yawning tiers of guns,
Took the breath from our sails, and we stay'd.

VII

And while now the great San Philip hung above us like a cloud
Whence the thunderbolt will fall
Long and loud,   45
Four galleons drew away
From the Spanish fleet that day.
And two upon the larboard and two upon the starboard lay,
And the battle-thunder broke from them all.

VIII

But anon the great San Philip, she bethought herself and went,   50
  Having that within her womb that had left her ill content;
And the rest they came aboard us, and they fought us hand to hand,
For a dozen times they came with their pikes and musqueteers,
And a dozen times we shook 'em off as a dog that shakes his ears
  When he leaps from the water to the land.   55

IX

And the sun went down, and the stars came out far over the summer sea,
But never a moment ceased the fight of the one and the fifty-three.
Ship after ship, the whole night long, their high-built galleons came,
Ship after ship, the whole night long, with her battle-thunder and flame;
Ship after ship, the whole night long, drew back with her dead and   60 *her shame.*
For some were sunk and many were shatter'd and so could fight us no more –
God of battles, was ever a battle like this in the world before?

X

  For he said, 'Fight on! fight on!'
  Tho' his vessel was all but a wreck;
And it chanced that, when half of the short summer night was   65 *gone,*
  With a grisly wound to be drest he had left the deck,
  But a bullet struck him that was dressing it suddenly dead,
And himself he was wounded again in the side and the head,
    And he said, 'Fight on! fight on!'

XI

And the night went down, and the sun smiled out far over the   70 *summer sea,*
And the Spanish fleet with broken sides lay round us all in a ring;
But they dared not touch us again, for they fear'd that we still could sting,

So they watch'd what the end would be.
And we had not fought them in vain,
But in perilous plight were we,   75
Seeing forty of our poor hundred were slain,
And half of the rest of us maim'd for life
In the crash of the cannonades and the desperate strife;
And the sick men down in the hold were most of them stark and
cold,
And the pikes were all broken or bent, and the powder was all of it   80
spent;
And the masts and the rigging were lying over the side;
But Sir Richard cried in his English pride:
'We have fought such a fight for a day and a night
As may never be fought again!
We have won great glory, my men!   85
And a day less or more
At sea or ashore,
We die – does it matter when?
Sink me the ship, Master Gunner – sink her, split her in twain!
Fall into the hands of God, not into the hands of Spain!'   90

XII

And the gunner said, 'Ay, ay,' but the seamen made reply:
'We have children, we have wives,
And the Lord hath spared our lives.
We will make the Spaniard promise, if we yield, to let us go;
We shall live to fight again and to strike another blow.'   95
And the lion there lay dying, and they yielded to the foe.

XIII

And the stately Spanish men to their flagship bore him then,
Where they laid him by the mast, old Sir Richard caught at last,
And they praised him to his face with their courtly foreign grace;
But he rose upon their decks, and he cried: 100
'I have fought for Queen and Faith like a valiant man and true;
I have only done my duty as a man is bound to do.
With a joyful spirit I Sir Richard Grenville die!'
And he fell upon their decks, and he died.

XIV

And they stared at the dead that had been so valiant and true,   105
  And had holden the power and glory of Spain so cheap
  That he dared her with one little ship and his English few;
  Was he devil or man? He was devil for aught they knew,
  But they sank his body with honor down into the deep.
And they mann'd the Revenge with a swarthier alien crew,   110
  And away she sail'd with her loss and long'd for her own;
When a wind from the lands they had ruin'd awoke from sleep,
  And the water began to heave and the weather to moan,
  And or ever that evening ended a great gale blew,
And a wave like the wave that is raised by an earthquake grew,   115
Till it smote on their hulls and their sails and their masts and their
    flags,
And the whole sea plunged and fell on the shot-shatter'd navy of
    Spain,
And the little Revenge herself went down by the island crags
  To be lost evermore in the main.[19]

Chapter 4

Prince Rupert

Like the stunned silence that follows the finale of a dramatic piece of music, or the last act of a great play, a pregnant pause hangs over the last act of the great *Revenge* tragedy and, as on those occasions when no one wants to be the first to break the silence, no order was given over the next fifty-nine years for a replacement to be constructed.

Perhaps what was also awaited was not only the time but the man, and the man who was to confer the famous name on another ship could overmatch Sir Richard Grenville in élan, dash and in lineage. He was, after all, the nephew of King Charles I.

Prince Rupert of the Rhine, son of Frederick V, elector of Palatine and King of Bohemia, and of Elizabeth Stuart, is probably best remembered for his inspirational leadership of Royalist cavalry during the English Civil War, his precipitous charge at the Battle of Edgehill becoming a trademark for brilliance bordering on recklessness, his gleeful pursuit of the enemy leaving the Royalist centre dangerously exposed. After defeats at both Marston Moor and Naseby, the favourite was dismissed by his patron, Charles I, and, after the Royalist surrender, banished from England. The erstwhile cavalry commander now took on a different variety of steed and, as Admiral and General-at-Sea, he took command of the Royalist fleet in 1648.

After occasional skirmishes with the Commonwealth fleet round the British Isles, Rupert set sail across the Bay of Biscay to Lisbon, where he was welcomed by the newly crowned King John IV, who, while maintaining cordial relations with the English Commonwealth, was predisposed to support the English Royalist cause.

Rupert and the Royalist fleet proceeded to play a game of cat and mouse with the Commonwealth fleet under Bacon, sent to blockade

Rupert. The Portuguese played a delicate game of attempting to aid Rupert without antagonizing the Commonwealth. After various brushes between the two fleets, and several unsuccessful attempts to get away, Rupert finally made his escape on 12 October 1650, much to the relief of the Portuguese.

After setting off into the Atlantic, Rupert sailed down the south coast of Spain, hunting English ships in ports such as Málaga and Motríl. Rupert in the *Constant Reformation* and his brother, Maurice, in the *Swallow* were not, however, to be found. At this point they were in pursuit of a merchantman, the *Marmaduke*, which was attempting to escape south towards the coast of Africa. This merchantman was, at 400 tons, well armed and full of fight. Rupert and Maurice caught up with her by nightfall and fierce hostilities flared in the morning. The battle raged until about mid-day when the *Marmaduke* finally surrendered due to the death of her captain.

The *Marmaduke*, now a prize, then accompanied Rupert and Maurice to Formentera. Not finding the other Royalist ships at the agreed rendezvous, the two princes and their prize sailed on towards Cagliari in Sardinia, whereupon the *Constant Reformation* became separated from the other ships in a storm. Maurice sailed to Toulon with the prize where he was eventually joined by Rupert, who had pulled in to Messina in Sicily to repair storm damage.

At Toulon, Rupert set about repairing and refitting the prize ship, which was renamed the *Revenge of Whitehall*. With this and four other ships, Rupert sailed on 7 May, deceiving the lurking Commonwealth fleet under the command of Penn by first sailing east and then doubling back close to the coast of Africa, before heading into the Atlantic.

Although there was some dispute among the captains as to their destination, they finally arrived at the Azores, an appropriate location for the second *Revenge*.

Rupert's squadron landed at São Miguel and he made this the base of his operations. Soon afterwards, however, one of his ships, the *St Michael the Archangel*, deserted and sailed off for England.

On 26 January, the squadron sailed for the Cape Verde islands, Prince Maurice having moved into the *Revenge*. After this, they sailed down to the Gambia where the Portuguese pilots managed to run both the *Swallow* and the *Revenge* aground. At this stage Marshall moved across to the *Revenge*.

At Mayo, in the Cape Verde islands, two English ships anchored near the *Revenge*, which promptly captured them and took their crews prisoner. This was to prove the undoing of the *Revenge*, for William Coxon, the mate of the *Supply*, one of the captured ships, organized the prisoners to take over the ship. Once this had been achieved, they sailed for England.

Thus ended the exploits of the second *Revenge* in the Azores, having revisited, like a ghost, the hunting ground of her illustrious namesake.

For Rupert, too, the time was approaching when he should return to northern waters. After a visit to the West Indies, Rupert's squadron approached the Azores, only to be fired upon by the Portuguese authorities who had decided in favour of the English Commonwealth.

Rupert's sally into the Mediterranean and the Atlantic was effectively a sideshow, with such little strategic interest as to be barely worth more than a few lines in a general history of the period. The interest it does have is mainly due to the sheer force of personality of Rupert and, for the purposes of this book, the passing presence of the ship named *Revenge*.

Rupert sailed to France and joined the court of the English King-in-waiting, Charles II. The captured *Revenge* was bought by the Admiralty in 1652 and renamed the *Marmaduke*. There would not be another *Revenge* until the *Newbury* was renamed in 1660.

While the Royalist fleet had been engaged on its somewhat fruitless diversions, significant developments were underway in the Commonwealth Navy, largely due to the skills and experience of two Generals-at-Sea, Robert Blake and George Monck.

Blake had led the hunt for Rupert in the Mediterranean and Rupert was fortunate to have escaped him, for Blake's exceptional talents were to turn the English Navy into an elite fighting force and in the forthcoming First Dutch War he won three out of four engagements with the distinguished Admiral Tromp, between May 1652 and June 1653. George Monck, who had fought for Charles I and who was to be a lead player in the Restoration of his son, although primarily an expert on land warfare, employed his organizational and tactical skills to develop a formula for naval engagements, to be known as the 'Fighting Instructions'.

A set of fighting instructions had been issued by Edward Cecil, Viscount Wimbledon (1572–1638) in 1625 for the expedition against Cadiz, and these contained one of the first references to fleet line ahead, though as has been noted above, a form of line ahead had been performed by Howard's ships in their attack on the *San Martín* of the Spanish Armada. The realization of this tactical idea was to come in the first Dutch War, not only under the influence of Blake and Monck but of William Penn (1621–1670), whose formulation of fighting instructions was to be the basis of James Duke of York's 'Instruction for the better Ordering His Majesties Fleet in Sayling of 1673'.

To begin with, however, despite the previous attempts to formulate fighting instructions, the first engagements with the Dutch at sea, concerning disputes over the honour to the flag (as stipulated in the Navigation Act of 1651) were haphazard.

In May 1652, Robert Blake met a fleet under the Dutch Admiral von Tromp and the Dutch lost two ships in the battle. In November of the same year, Von Tromp had his revenge by defeating Robert Blake's force at Dungeness. Before the English next went into action against the Dutch, at the Battle of Portland (18 February 1653), William Penn, Vice Admiral of the Fleet, had been issued with a set of fighting instructions, and, although these did not refer directly to 'line-ahead' tactics, the move suggests that the English were attempting to formulate tactics so as to maximize the effective use of the fleet. It may be significant that fighting instructions were issued at Portland and at the next two battles, since the Battle of Portland was won as well as the battles of the Gabbard (2 and 3 June) and of Sheveningen (31 July).

The 'Sailing Instructions' issued before the Battle of the Gabbard were clear and straightforward, uncluttered by less important administrative details, and their effect may have been to give the fleet a sense of unity and order that it had lacked in previous years. The captains of the English fleet were all reading from the same song sheet and, in a time of limited communication, they had at least an outline of what their Admiral was working from.

By the time of the Second Dutch War, the Restoration of the monarch had taken place and, along with his new monarch, Charles II, Prince Rupert returned to England. It seems highly appropriate that a new *Revenge* should be commissioned that year, the name being clearly associated with the Royalist camp during the Civil War and Commonwealth period.

Overall command of the fleet was given to James, Duke of York, at that time only twenty-seven years old and with no direct experience of maritime warfare. With his arrival came a new set of fighting instructions and the organisation of the fleet went a step further. There were specific instructions relating to the position of each ship in the line, all of which was to have been achieved before engaging with the enemy. Freelance pursuit of the enemy was discouraged. Gone were the days of Sir Francis Drake, when defence of the realm could be put on hold in the interests of private plunder. Ships were also organized into squadrons, within which they knew their exact position and were not expected to leave it for any other reason than *force majeure*.

The novelty of tactical instructions, which were supplemented on various occasions by the Duke of York, also produced a rigorous formalism which was disliked by some. The efforts to organize the fleet had produced a by-the-book attitude that stifled initiative and reduced the opportunities for attack that only spur-of-the-moment initiative could take advantage of. On the other hand, the fog of war would often break up the rigorous structure and produce opportunities for individual initiative by default.

The two schools of tactical thought were summarized as 'formalist' or 'mêlée':

> There was the 'formalist' view, upheld by seamen of the calibre of James, Duke of York, and Penn, who believed in the importance of rules and orderliness, even to the extent of stifling individual initiative; then there was the 'mêlée' point of view, with Prince Rupert and Monck as its protagonists. They believed in the orderly approach but in engaging the enemy immediately on arrival within close enough range, without relying on concerted tactical manoeuvres, accepting the inevitable shift of control from commander in chief to subordinate in the heat of battle and exploiting an unexpected advantage as soon as it presented itself.[1]

As suggested above, circumstances would largely dictate the actions on the day and much would depend on the commanders of individual squadrons. As it was, the 'formalist' school were to lose out to the 'mêlée' school by mere dint of the fact that James Duke of York and Lord Sandwich were removed from their command of the fleet, leaving Prince Rupert along with Monck in charge.

The Battle of Lowestoft, at which *Revenge* was present, had provided a salutary reminder as to how tactical theory and practice could diverge. Sandwich reported that, although ships attempted to get into line-ahead before the battle, many of them were three or four abreast. None the less, the English did manage to achieve a victory and there is little doubt that the fighting instructions would have helped in achieving a certain level of order.

The Dutch lost thirty-two ships at Lowestoft and sustained casualties of about 4,000 dead and 2,000 prisoners. The English only lost one ship, the *Charity*, 36 guns and 283 killed, including two flag officers, Vice Admiral Sir John Lawson, Rear Admiral Robert Sanson, and three captains, along with 440 wounded.

As a result of the presence of the English fleet in the Channel and North Sea, the Dutch East India Fleet had been forced to sail around Ireland and the north of Scotland, and had taken refuge in the Norwegian port of Bergen.

Conspiring with the King of Denmark and Norway, the British sent an expedition to Bergen to capture the Dutch ships. Led by Rear Admiral Sir Thomas Tydiman in the *Revenge*, along with thirteen other sail of the line, three fireships and four ketches, the English expedition entered Bergen harbour on the morning of 3 August 1665 and anchored. Unfortunately for the English, the governor of Bergen had decided to support the Dutch and the 300 guns of the castles and forts of Bergen provided a significant addition to Dutch firepower.

The English were badly mauled, losing about 400 killed or wounded, including six captains and two of *Revenge*'s officers. Tydiman was forced to slip the cables of *Revenge* and to scamper for the relative safety of the open sea, along with his squadron. To add insult to injury, Arthur Langhorn (Holmes's successor) was killed on *Revenge*'s quarterdeck in another engagement on 9 September.

There followed a period of relative quiet before the storm broke once again in the fateful year 1666. The two sides began the year fairly evenly balanced, with Prince Rupert and the Duke of Albermarle commanding eighty ships with 4,460 guns manned by 21,085 officers and men; while Admirals de Ruijter, Cornelius Evertsen and Cornelis Tromp had eighty-five ships, with 4,615 guns, manned by 21,909 officers and men. The declaration of war on England by France on 16 January 1666 was, however, to swing matters in favour of the Dutch, for the first action of the Four Days' Battle in June was fought on decidedly unequal terms.

Diverted by the French fleet, Rupert took twenty of the most powerful English ships on a strategically fruitless detour, leaving only fifty-four ships to fight a Dutch fleet of eighty-four. The action proved indecisive and on the second day Albermarle decided to husband his numerically weaker forces rather than snatch a favourable opportunity. On the third day he was continually shadowed by the Dutch, who, still smarting from the previous day's exchange, did not attempt to attack him. The orderly retreat into the Thames estuary was, however, marred when the *Royal Prince* ran aground on the galloper sands. The Dutch caught up like baying hounds on a wounded stag and attacked her with fireships. The *Royal Prince* lost about 150 men in the fight but eventually surrendered and was subsequently burned by the Dutch.

At this point a fleet of twenty sail was sighted to the westward, which the Dutch hoped was the French coming to their aid but which, fortunately for the English, proved to be Prince Rupert returning to the fray. Now the sides were more evenly matched for the fourth day, with the English able to deploy about sixty sail and the Dutch about seventy-eight.

On the fourth day, the wind was blowing fresh from the south-west as the two fleets ran past each other, with the Dutch to windward. Due to the superior weatherliness of the English ships, they were able to break the Dutch line in several places and on several occasions, and to get to windward. This reduced the consistency of naval gunfire but was an almost inevitable consequence of individual initiative and opportunism in the midst of battle. One such example was the duel fought between Albemarle and de Ruijter. While this was going on, Tromp and Admiral Jan Jassze van Nes came up to leeward of the Dutch centre with fourteen ships of the van, the English centre lying between them. De Ruijter then ordered the ships near him to break before the wind, which broke up the English centre, the Dutch passing through in irregular order. Although safely to windward, the battered English now found themselves in the teeth of a rising gale. Despite the fact that Albemarle shadowed the Dutch for a while, he was reluctant to commit his limping forces to another contest.

The Dutch had every reason to be content with their achievement. The English had lost seventeen ships, including two flagships, and nine captains. They had also lost about 5,000 casualties and between 2,000 and 3,000 taken prisoner. The Dutch had lost six ships and suffered about 2,000 casualties.

The *Revenge* herself had been in the thick of the action. Acting as second-in-command to *Victory*, she had followed in the wake of the flagship, repeating her signals and covering her every move. On the morning of the fourth day, Vice Admiral Sir Christopher Byngs was shot in the throat while standing on the quarterdeck of the *Victory*. He stayed on deck another half hour, pressing the wound closed to staunch the flow of blood, until a second shot struck him in the neck and killed him.

The result of the battle at first sight was in favour of the Dutch. The English fleet was more deeply scarred than their own and their casualties greater. But when the relative size of the forces is considered, and the length of time in which one side not only deterred the other but continued to inflict appreciable damage, the English appear to have had the moral victory. Their superior tactics, discipline and overall seamanship had made up for their lack of numbers and the authors of the various versions of 'Fighting Instructions' would appear to have been vindicated.

For all that it was battered, the English still had a fleet in being and the Dutch were to be astonished at the speed with which it was refitted and made ready for action. The ubiquitous press gang was the main source of new seamen and Monck and Prince Rupert made it their duty to write to port authorities either requesting or demanding seamen. On 14 June 1666 they wrote to the Bailiffs of Yarmouth to remind them that they had not provided the necessary number of seamen and to deliver the threat that, if they did not produce the men, 'we shall represent your neglect to the King's Council, which we shall be very unwilling to do.' On 16 June, they wrote on similar lines to the Governor of Falmouth, and on the 27th they wrote the following to the Bailiffs of Ipswich:

Whereas we are credibly informed, that there are many seamen fit to do his Majty Service lie concealed within your Town of

Ipswich, we therefore desire you forthwith, to cause strict and diligent search to be made for the said seamen, and that you would send them on board the degger, whereof Thomas Tyler is Mastr., belonging to his Majs. Ship the *Revenge* lying in Aldeborough Road or Haven in purpose to receive them. We will take care to see you repaid all such charges as you shall be at in pursuing of these are [sic] desires, and your diligence in the speedy performance hereof will be an acceptable service to his Majty.

There was no mystery surrounding the scarcity of willing volunteers for the Navy – conditions aboard were nothing less than appalling.

As a Third Rate of the 1660s, the *Revenge* had a complement of 300. She had a Captain in command, along with a Lieutenant as second-in-command, a warrant master, quartermaster, warrant boatswain, carpenter, master gunner and a surgeon, as well as their various mates. Many of these lived in tiny, damp, insanitary cabins that were more like chicken coops. In addition there was a complement of men called 'idlers' who worked only in the daylight hours on certain trades, as armourers, sail-makers, coopers, officers' servants, butchers, barbers, tailors and cooks.

Most of the ship's company slept in hammocks, every man normally near his place of duty: the quarterdeck men aft, the forecastle men forward. Personal space for sleeping in this place of de rigueur intimacy was 14 inches in which to sling a hammock. The only compensation was that the men were organized in two watches, so that the hammock belonging to the man in the other watch would normally be empty during sleeping hours. Seamen also slung their hammocks at different heights to give more space.

Food consisted of ship's biscuit, salt pork and beef, all cooked on a stove. Livestock such as hens, pigs, sheep and, in larger ships, cows, were kept in a special manger. Fresh water became foetid after a few days at sea, so the major liquid intake was beer, to which each man was entitled to a gallon each day.

Although there were the occasional mutinies in the Royal Navy, they were not normally about living conditions and the average sailor put up with these strictures for months and even years on end, with little complaint.

As a Third Rate in the 1660s, the *Revenge* had fifty-eight guns, including twenty-two 32-pounder demi-cannons on the lower gun tier, four 18-pounder culverins, twenty-four 9-pounder demi-culverins, distributed along the upper decks, and eight demi-culverin cutts. Cutts normally had shortened barrels, but there were a multitude of other differences between them and conventional cannons.

Shot was stored in such a way as to keep the ship's centre of gravity low, amidships, forward and in the hold. This also meant that rapid expenditure of shot would not alter the ship's trim. Powder was stored in a magazine situated in the forward hold, next to which was a filling room for making up cartridges. Entrance to the magazine was strictly controlled but there were few other safety precautions.

Like every other ship in the fleet, the *Revenge* sailed for the Four Days' Battle undermanned. Despite the efforts of the press gangs and protests by various commanders, the seventeenth-century Navy remained chronically short of men. Even popular captains, such as Elliott of the *Revenge*, had difficulty in meeting the recommended manning level of the ship. The sticking point was not bad living conditions, poor food or the near certainty of either disease or death in battle, but pay. Sailors were sometimes underpaid, but their pay was always in arrears. This contributed to discontent and desertion, mutinies and executions. The Four Days' Battle itself did little to increase enthusiasm for the Navy, but in this respect at least, the Navy was able to change public opinion.

Although the Dutch claimed to be the predominant force in the English seas, the Four Days' Battle had not proved enough of a victory to settle the argument. Another battle would be needed and it was not long in coming.

On 22 July, the majority of the English fleet assembled off the mouth of the Thames and anchored at the Gunfleet that evening. The Dutch fleet was at anchor about 18 miles to the north-east.

With joint command of the English fleet, Albemarle and Prince Rupert both flew their flags in the *Royal George*. The fleet consisted of eighty-nine ships and seventeen fireships, mounting 4,460 guns. It was divided into three squadrons –White, Blue and Red. As before, the *Revenge* was in the Red squadron. The Dutch fleet, commanded by Admiral de Ruijter, had eighty-five ships, twenty fireships and ten smaller vessels, mounting 4,700 guns altogether. The two fleets were thus fairly evenly balanced.

By 24 July, both fleets were manoeuvring to achieve the advantage of the weather gauge and by that night they were both in a wide stretch of the Thames Estuary, between Orfordness and the North Foreland, the English at anchor. Early on 25 July, St James's Day, the English weighed, and both fleets slowly approached each other. The battle began at about 10 a.m.

Aided no doubt by the discipline of the 'Fighting Instructions', the English managed to maintain a better line than the Dutch, who were arranged in an irregular half-moon. Led by Admiral Sir Thomas Allin, the White Squadron engaged the Dutch van, which was led by Evertson. Sailing parallel, the squadrons exchanged fire and then broke away to become involved in close-range duels. The English centre carried out a similar manoeuvre against the Dutch centre, led by de Ruijter. Meanwhile, the English rear, the Blue Squadron, led by Admiral Sir Jeremy Smyth, encountered the Dutch van led by Tromp, who once again acted independently and broke through in the face of the English van, becoming detached from the main Dutch fleet.

Tromp's inspired act of tactical opportunism might have placed the Dutch at a distinct advantage, especially in view of the fact that he was ranged against the weakest English squadron under Admiral Sir Jeremy Smyth, but unfortunately for the Dutch, de Ruijter was not on the same wavelength and did not sail to support his fellow admiral. The two squadrons, therefore, detached themselves from the main battle, fighting a furious micro battle as they went.

[Captain] Taylor wrote to [Captain] Williamson:

> This dispute continued till night even as long as they could see to fire, during which time 4 of the enemy's ships were seen on fire, and we lost the Resolution by a fireship of the enemy's (she being much disabled before). This day about 6 or 7 in the morning they began again, and the guns were heard here till 10 and ceased that we could hear no more, and what the issue of this day's engagement may be we do not yet hear, yet hope well because the Dutch in our judgment seemed to draw our fleet further from our coast by the loss of the report of the guns.[2]

Taylor was right to some extent, though the Dutch were not so much drawing the English away from the English coast as being chased by Smyth. Eventually, with no support on offer from either Albemarle or Rupert, who were both too far to leeward, Smyth called off the chase.

The actions of the Blue squadron were later criticized by Rupert in the House of Commons on 31 October 1667: 'I must not forebear to tell you my judgment that the Blue squadron was in that action guilty of a great miscarriage, otherwise, in probability, the whole Zeeland squadron had fallen into our hands.'[3] Rupert also took the opportunity to gripe again about both the lack of provisions and manning:

> This want of provisions did manifestly tend to the extraordinary prejudice of his Majesty's service in that whole summer ... The want of seamen was also too great to be forgotten, which I believe was occasioned partly by the hopes they had to go into merchant ships and colliers, where their pay was greater, and the hazard less, and partly by the ill-management of those who were intrusted to impress them.[4]

The outcome of the battle was that the Dutch lost twenty ships, with 4,000 men killed, including four flag officers and numerous captains, and 3,000 wounded. The English lost five captains, two or three fireships and about 300 men. The *Revenge* suffered structural damage to her upper deck and several wounded among her gun crews in what proved to be her last battle. This *Revenge* did not take part in the Third Dutch War, but she had contributed to a decisive victory. By midnight on 26 July 1666, the English van and centre were at anchor off the Dutch coast and the English had regained control of the Narrow Seas.

This strategic advantage was, however, short-lived. Once peace negotiations began in 1667, to save money Charles II's government thought themselves into a false sense of security and laid up the main fleet in reserve, with all stores taken ashore and their crews reduced to a handful. Once the Dutch got wind of this, they decided not only to cock a snook at the English, but to thoroughly tweak the King's nose.

In June 1667, de Ruijter sailed up the Thames and into the Medway, broke a chain boom at Gillingham, landed armed parties at Upnor, captured or burned ten ships and, as the final insult, towed away the *Royal Charles*, with the Royal Standard still flying at the main mast. As if this were not enough, de Ruijter continued to blockade the Thames and London for a month. The Treaty of Breda of July 1667 ended the Second Dutch War, with the Dutch again commanding the Narrow Seas.

Having needlessly squandered the English advantage, and having his face rubbed in it, Charles proceeded to pursue policies that were almost guaranteed to bring the Dutch back to war. Despite a triple alliance between England, Holland and Sweden designed to offset the success of King Louis XIV's campaign in the Spanish Netherlands, Charles began to negotiate with Louis for an Anglo-French alliance against the Dutch. So dazzled was Charles by the Sun King that he even agreed to become a Catholic in return for money to fit out the English fleet.

On 28 May 1672, a large English and French fleet of seventy line-of-battle ships and even more fireships, transports and smaller vessels, under James, Duke of York, flying his flag in the *Royal Prince* (120 guns), lay at anchor off Solebay, on the Suffolk coast, preparing for an invasion of the Netherlands. The Earl of Sandwich flew his standard in the flagship *Royal James* (100 guns) and the French Admiral d'Estrées, flew his in the *St Philippe* (78 guns).

The Dutch, however, decided to get their retaliation in early and launched a pre-emptive strike on 28 May. Due to a failure in communications, the French turned away to the south-east and took no part in the main action, which centred round a fierce duel between Van Ghent and Sandwich in which Van Ghent was killed. The *Royal James* was burned to the waterline and Sandwich was drowned when a boat crowded with survivors was capsized.

The Duke of York was also under fire and had to shift his flag twice during the day. In the evening, the English disengaged and allowed the Dutch to withdraw, the English fleet having suffered severe losses, with 2,500 men dead. The Dutch lost two ships but de Ruijter's skilful handling of his fleet that day disabled the English fleet for a month, gave the Dutch command of the Channel once more and, most important, thwarted the Anglo-French invasion of the Netherlands.

Chapter 5

The Navy of Pepys

The *Revenge* that took part in the Battle of Schooneveld was not the veteran of the Four Days' Battle and St James's Day but a new and larger ship: a 1,065-ton Third Rate of 70 guns, 150 feet in length and 40 feet in width, built at Deptford in 1699. *1669*

In 1671, as part of a squadron of six ships under Vice Admiral Sir Edward Spragge (known as 'Old Trekky') despatched to the Mediterranean to suppress piracy, *Revenge* took part in an attack on Bugia Bay (Port de Bougie), in which seven warships and three Algerine Corsairs were burned, and the town and castle were bombarded, killing about 400 people. Old Trekky was wounded in the action.

In 1673, James Duke of York, who was a Catholic, resigned from his post of Lord High Admiral as a result of the Test Act. Rupert took over command and made two attempts to destroy the Dutch fleet off the Schooneveld in May and June 1673, but de Ruijter managed to foil both attempts through brilliant handling of his ships and also succeeded in opening Dutch ports once again to incoming convoys.

The final battle of the war took place off the Texel on 11 August 1673. The Dutch managed to separate the French van from the main body so that it took no part in the battle in the rear between Sir Edward Spragge and Tromp, in which Spragge was killed. The battle was a stalemate, but de Ruijter had succeeded in preventing an invasion and Charles had little choice but to end an unpopular war at the Treaty of Westminster in February 1674.

So ended an extraordinary episode in naval warfare, which was full of implications for the future of the Royal Navy. The *Revenge* and the Navy in which she sailed was at the centre of myriad influences, personalities and events, each of which could have had a decisive influence on the course of subsequent history.

The tenure of James, Duke of York, as overall commander of the Royal Navy was a fruitful one, as the issue of the fighting instructions bears witness, but it was limited in duration by matters that had little to do with naval tactics. The Catholic Duke of York was also married to a Catholic, Mary d'Este. His wife's Chaplain was Claude de la Colombière, a highly gifted French Jesuit who had previously been spiritual director to Margaret Mary Alacoque, a Visitandine nun and visionary of the Sacred Heart, at the convent in Paray-le-Monial.

So great was Claude de la Colombière's influence that Protestants began to convert back to the Old Faith. This inevitably caused jealousy and both Titus Oates and Israel Tonge went to great lengths to discredit the Jesuits as plotters on the life of the King. Claude de la Colombière was imprisoned as a result of the scandal and his life was only saved through the direct intervention of Louis XIV.

The devotion to the Sacred Heart is said to have had far-reaching implications for the Roi Soleil. After a holy revelation in 1689, Margaret Mary Alacoque wrote to her Superior to tell her that the French King should arrange for public reverence to the Sacred Heart and that its symbol should appear on the Royal coat of arms.

According to the Cavalier Parliament, by helping to bring the Dutch to their knees, the Duke of York's navy was participating in a global Catholic plot in league with the Jesuits and the French King. The Test Act of 1673, which barred Catholics from high office, put an end to this alleged scheme.

Revenge, which at the Armada had been the scourge of Catholic Spain, had now become the agent of the Catholic Church in a navy commanded by a Catholic Duke under a King with distinctly Catholic sympathies allied to a French monarch who, by all accounts, had been designated by Jesus Christ Himself as the Catholic nemesis, empowered, should he obey the requests of the Sacred Heart, to avenge himself upon his Protestant foes. But it was not to be. Louis XIV was too distracted by his court and mistresses to comply with the request of an eccentric mystic. The Protestant nations remained bloodied but unbowed and the English Parliament took steps to ensure that a Catholic future should be the last thing that would await them. The sun began to set on the Roi Soleil.

These were not the only troubled waters on which *Revenge* had to sail. The seventeenth century was a period of important developments for the Navy: it saw the development of the tactical arts in the 'Fighting Instructions'; the crystallization of the administration of the Navy in the Navy Board and the Admiralty; and the emergence of some startling personalities, such as Blake, Monck, Prince Rupert, the Duke of York and, of course, Samuel Pepys.

Born in London on 23 February 1633, Pepys came into a comparatively humble family that had left behind greater things when the family had lived in the countryside. After St Paul's School and Magdalene College, Cambridge, he found his way into the service of Edward Montagu, later to become a General-at-Sea. When Montagu sided with Monck at the Restoration, Pepys found himself elevated beyond his wildest dreams, first as Admiral's Secretary and Treasurer to the Fleet, and later Clerk of the Acts to the Navy Board. In 1673 he was to join the Admiralty, after the departure of the Duke of York, as Secretary to the Commission. In 1679 he was made Secretary for Admiralty Affairs.

Initially Samuel Pepys's dealings were with the Navy Board, otherwise styled 'the Principal Officers and Commissioners of the Navy'. The board had a wide remit that included: the production and supply of naval requirements in both peace and war; the building and repair of ships; the procurement of all equipment and stores; and the management of the dockyards.[1]

As Clerk of the Acts, Samuel Pepys was the Navy Board's chief administrative officer and was immersed in every detail pertaining to ships such as *Revenge*, from the commissioning of the ship itself to the detail of how blocks were purchased.

Being at Deptford today, among other things, to inform myself in the business of blocks, of which [we] are now to buy great quantity to send to Portsmouth for the ships now going forth – I inquired of Mr [Sh] how they were measured, for we buy them at so much for all above that diameter. He told me that he measures them always the breadth way. By and by, when Edgehill the blockmaster comes and I asked him the like, he told me that we measure them and take them from him always the length-ways and never otherwise anywhere.[2]

This attention to detail extended to almost every other item, including ship's lanterns: 'Measuring of lanterns ill regarded ... Fletcher [timber measurer] ... tells me plainly, that he never measured one in his life – nor knows how they are to be measured.'[3]

It was clear that, under the supervision of Samuel Pepys, no stone was to be left unturned and that every kind of irregularity, anachronism and oversight would be levelled off and planed down until the system was as smooth as a well-turned mast. In doing so, he was carrying out to the letter the injunction to principal officers: 'Take care that no provision of any considerable quantity or price be served into His Majesty's store without contract made for the same at a public meeting, where both the provisions in quantity and goodness, dimensions and price may be maturely scanned and accordingly specified in the contract.'[4]

Pepys's large capacity for work, allied to his eagle-eyed attention to detail, was applied to essentials such as masts, hemp, tar and pitch, as well as the supply of anchors. Reliable in small things, he was also responsible for large ones, and as member for Castle Rising he was instrumental in gaining approval for a major shipbuilding programme in 1677, for which £600,000 was voted for the building of thirty ships, including one First Rate, nine Second Rates and twenty Third Rates.

The fourth *Revenge* would have been commissioned according to a contract similar to that made for another famous Royal Navy ship, HMS *Warspite*, also a Third Rate, in 1665: 'one good and substantial new ship or frigate of good well seasoned timber and plank of English oak and elm ... [at £7.00 per ton] as measured and calculated according to the accustomed rule of Shipwrights Hall.'[5]

This apparently innocuous order concealed a larger problem that Pepys wrestled with for a large part of his career – the shortage of English oak to build the ships. While supply was generally equal to demand up to the time of the First Dutch War, the switch to specially commissioned ships for the Royal Navy, as opposed to the extensive reliance on converted merchantmen, of which the second *Revenge* is an example, heightened demand not only for English oak, which was regarded as superior to other varieties, but also oak of the correct shape.

Due to the difficulties in shaping timber to meet the norms of naval architecture – as Fred T. Jane said, 'The limitations of the tree proved the limitations of the ship' – a great deal of care and time was expended in finding trees of the correct size and shape. This special timber, known as 'curved' or 'compass' timber was usually sourced from trees that stood apart from the main forest growth, as these isolated trees were likely to grow their branches in the required shape.[6]

The unique properties of oak allowed it to resist enemies that were more likely to put a ship out of service or send it to the bottom than enemy cannon balls: the *teredo navalis*, or sea worm, which attacked the ship's timbers from the outside, and dry rot, which attacked them from the inside. Oak was rich in tannic or gallic acid that deterred the sea worm, adding to the demand for this particular wood, when shortages might otherwise have easily been resolved by the use of alternative trees.

Nevertheless, if not properly attended to and not sufficiently aired, dry rot would eventually penetrate the wood with macabre white fibres, weakening the supporting frame timbers in the area of the waterline and causing the ship to collapse under its own weight and founder. The problem was exacerbated by insufficient seasoning which in turn was caused by limited supply and urgent demand, especially in time of diplomatic tension or war.

The scale of the problem faced by Pepys and the Navy Board can easily be gathered from a report on the state of ships in 1666, the year of the Four Days' Battle. The defects of the third *Revenge* are described as follows:

Hull	Masts
The scarf of the stern, 3 beams, cathead, lower tier of ports, clamps, cut cross pillar, the rudder loose, several knees in hold between decks unserviceable. Bitt prime, several timbers shot	Main mast, main partner

Many of her sister ships were described as 'very leaky' (*Henrietta, Portsmouth, Newcastle, Old James, Delft*) or, in the case of the *Antelope*, 'Extremely leaky underwater'.

Many of the ships in the list also had defective main masts, foremasts or mizzen masts. Since there were fifty-three ships listed, all of them requiring substantial attention to hulls and/or masts, not to mention sails and cordage, it is not difficult to imagine the pressure the Navy Board must have been under to provide not only sufficient quantities of replacement materials, but at the right price and at the right time.

Oak, elm, beech and fir were the main timber woods used in the King's ships up to 1804 and, although many of these could be obtained from abroad, foreign timber tended to be more susceptible to dry rot by the time it reached its destination and was ready for use by the Royal Navy. This was due to the simple fact that the process of rot infestation was likely to have already begun in the manky and poorly ventilated holds of the ships that were transporting them. But, these factors apart, 'To an English shipwright there was not wood in the world superior to English oak ... The solution of the timber problem was now strongly affected by the stupid and conservative partiality for certain woods, and an equally unjustifiable discrimination against others. This tended to exhaust the supply of the favoured timbers when the drain could have been relieved by using the others.'[7] This preference was not due to sentimental patriotism, however. There something about English oak that made it a genuinely better raw material.

Quercus robur, otherwise known as pedunculate or English oak, grows to a height of between 30 and 40 metres, and can reach an age of 1,000 years or more. Its ideal habitat is in fertile soils with a pH of between 4.5 and 7.5. The oak has an immensely strong close-grained heartwood that is ideal for shipbuilding or house building, and also has numerous other uses including the manufacture of oak casks. Although commonly associated with England, the tree grows widely across Europe, from Scandinavia down as far as Sicily and across to the Urals. Supply of this material should therefore in theory have been relatively straightforward. The soil and climate, however, affected the quality of the timber and, in the opinion of English shipwrights, the native soil and climate produced the best quality of wood. Trees from Sussex were a particular favourite.

This choosiness in itself limited the supply, but there were other factors at play. Whereas England had once been superabundant in this muscular tree, the incursions of agriculture, the profit-seeking of new landowners and the competing demands from such areas as the housebuilding trade combined to make the problem of limited supply more acute.

An appropriately sized English oak was not an easily renewable resource – it was not an option to put the country's political and naval ambitions on hold for the 100 years that it took for an oak to mature. Sensibly managed plantations would, however, relieve the headaches of future generations.

A plan to bring the Royal Forests into the equation met with little success and private individuals were encouraged to do their bit by replanting and maintaining the trees that would be used to protect the nation and their own interests.

The Navy Board worked out a scheme to cover timber districts, including Berkshire, Essex, two parts of Suffolk, Sussex, Salisbury, Winchester environs, Chichester and neighbourhood, Norfolk, Nottingham, Yorkshire and Staffordshire. A typical purchase was from Sir William Warren of 4,000 loads of oak timber and fifty loads of knees. The price of timber varied between £3 2s 6d and £2 13s per load, depending on the quality and whether it was straight timber or the more highly prized and rare 'compass' or curved timber. Knees were normally purchased at between £4 10s per load and £3 10s. Home supply was not enough: 'The Navy Board had early on contracted for substantial quantities of timber from Scandinavia and the Baltic. The first purchases were made on 23 May 1677 and were for 1,000 loads of oak timber and plank, 300 loads of drawn timber and 10,000 deals.'[8]

Due to likely interruption of supply, especially when England was at war, the Navy Board switched supply of masts from the 'East Country' to North America, though in due course this would also prove to be a problem due to the American Revolution, though this was still some time hence. On 10 September 1663, Pepys had the satisfaction of closing a deal with Sir William Warren for the supply of masts from Gottenburg, Norway and New England.

In 1691 a new Massachusetts Charter was signed whereby all pine trees suitable for masts of a diameter of 24 inches and more from 12 inches above the ground would be reserved for the English Crown.

The abundance of nature often leads to careless overuse by man. It is also not always in the nature of men to plan for succeeding generations when faced with immediate problems in the present. The timber shortage experienced by Pepys, the Navy Board and the English Navy in the seventeenth century was, sadly, not to be resolved. It is a testament to the strength of *Quercus robur*, the English oak, that it would one day rule the seas, despite desperate shortages in supply for the building of new ships and for repairs.

Pepys's frustration with the inadequate supply not only of oak but a whole range of other essentials is evident from his correspondence:

> By this means in general, I may observe, it is very true that our many demands at this day made from every yard for the dispatch of twelve ships now going forth with all imaginable dispatch in expectation of a Dutch war, there is not sufficient stores of all sorts in any one of his Majesty's yard to set forth one ship – without borrowing of some other ship that possibly may be in the River or of the rigging that lies by belonging to another ship, and these are but few too, God knows.[9]

Hemp was one of these necessities, a product that was a prerequisite for a fully functioning ship, and which had to be obtained far and wide, including Italy and Russia, the best-quality hemp coming from the Baltic. In order to obviate the complications of importing supplies, efforts were made to develop the domestic industry.

Canvas for sails was another necessity and, again, the best-quality materials came from abroad, this time from Brittany. Good canvas could also be found in the Netherlands, known as Holland Duck canvas, but with England at war with the Netherlands supply was obviously curtailed from that quarter. Although English canvas could be sourced from areas as diverse as Suffolk and the West Country, it was not considered strong enough for heavy sails.

Tar was also required and had to be imported – as it was used for caulking it was therefore an essential. International tensions could easily limit the supply from the 'East Country', namely Russia and the Baltic, and so Pepys and the Navy Board endeavoured to ensure enough reserves were built up to provide in time of war and to avoid the commercial blackmail that could take place when a few contractors had a monopoly on the supply of essential materials:

> Tar ... had to be imported ... it was desirable, if funds were available, to buy forward and stockpile against a possible emergency. This trade again was largely in the hands of a group of City merchants. Pepys hoped he had broken one of these rings (Bowyer, Hill and Stacy) by doing a private deal with Stacy's office, but when it came to the point Stacy would not implement the agreement.[10]

Deptford, where *Revenge* was built, was frequented by Samuel Pepys and the fourth *Revenge* was a result of the considerable surge in shipbuilding that took place in the first decade of the eighteenth century.

A Third Rate was a two-decker ship, and one of the most common ships in the Navy. The most famous of these was the 74-gun Third Rate. Not a great deal had changed since the days of Elizabeth I, though the fourth *Revenge* had a less racy design than her successor. The fourth *Revenge* was effectively a frigate, comparatively light on the water, though heavier, due to the greater weight of guns, and not as manoeuvrable as her more famous ancestor. The guns were comparatively unchanged, including the short-barrelled, medium-range culverin.

With the arrival of William of Orange in England in 1688, Pepys's star began to wane, having collaborated with George Legge, Lord Dartmouth's unsuccessful attempt to intercept William's fleet. Pepys, whose work for the Navy had contributed to the creation of a national naval force that would one day dominate the oceans of the world, allowed himself to be mixed up in a disastrous muddle that resulted in a change in the monarchy.

William's accession meant a radical change in foreign policy and whereas the third *Revenge* appeared to be the agent of a Catholic revival, the fourth *Revenge* was once again the servant of Protestantism ranged against the French. War was declared on France on 5 May 1689 and negotiations for co-operation with the Dutch fleet were wrapped up, turning the naval arrangements of the previous few years completely on their head.

The fourth *Revenge* sailed almost immediately into the cauldron that was the War of the Spanish Succession. Carlos II having died heirless, the succession went to Philippe of Anjou which in turn precipitated French military advances in the Spanish Netherlands and Italy.

With the death of William, the war against France proceeded under Queen Anne and the major historical emphasis switched to the exploits of John Churchill, Duke of Marlborough, who proceeded to unravel French ambitions with the help of Prince Eugene of Savoy.

Sir George Rooke had unsuccessfully attacked Cadiz in order to repeat Drake's singeing of the King of Spain's beard, but the attempt was badly organized and failed to achieve the intended result.

Sir George Rooke (1650–1709) was born near Canterbury and entered the Navy as a volunteer. He commanded a squadron at the siege of London in 1689 and became a Rear Admiral in 1690, when he participated at the Battle of Beachy Head. He made his mark at the Battle of La Hogue, when he contrived to burn six enemy ships and was rewarded for his action with a knighthood. He served in various posts in the Channel and in the Mediterranean until 1702, when he led the expedition against Cadiz, followed by the conspicuously successful raid on the Spanish and French fleet at Vigo. He was accompanied by Sir Cloudesley Shovell on the attack on Gibraltar on 21 July 1704, which received popular acclaim and which proved to be a milestone in British maritime history. On 13 August he commanded the fleet in an attack on the French off Malaga. The battle was inconclusive, with neither side losing a ship, and Rooke was subject to criticism for the poor preparation of the English fleet at the battle – the ships' hulls had not been careened and the guns were short of ammunition after the extensive barrage at Gibraltar. On this negative note, he retired from the Navy in 1705 and died in 1709.

After the failure at Cadiz, Rooke's face was saved when he got wind of some Spanish treasure ships in Vigo Bay. At a council of war held on the *Royal Sovereign* on 17 October 1702 it was decided to sail to Vigo and 'insult them immediately with our whole line, in case these be enough'.[11]

On arrival at Vigo on 18 October, Rooke sent in two boats to scout which reported back that there were about twenty-two Spanish galleons and eighteen French men-of-war. The ships had unloaded some of their treasure and were secured in an inlet above Vigo, near Redondella, protected by a boom made up, according to Captain Nathaniel Uring, thus:

> They having unrigged their ships, laid their Masts and Yards abreast each other, and lashed them securely together which spread the whole breadth of the Channel, with their cables stretched out a length upon them and well fasten'd; and their Top and other chains were stapled down to the Mast, to prevent them being out by our Men. They moored it without Side and within, with several anchors and cables; it was 8 or 10 foot broad, which altogether made it so strong, that they thought it impossible to be forced.[12]

The Allied fleet anchored near the boom and another council of war was held in which it was decided that it was too risky to attempt to enter the enemy's lair in full strength, due to the lack of sea space, and it was decided instead to send in a detachment of fifteen English and ten Dutch ships along with fireships, backed up by frigates and bomb vessels, with the major ships watching for any opportunities at the back.

The population of Vigo, having been visited upon years before by the legendary Drake, were understandably alarmed, as a French historian recounts:

L'inquietude puis la panique gagnerent toute la region; le vieux racontaient de terrible histoires du temps de leurs grands-parents; c'etait l'attaque de la ville en 1589 par Francis Drake qui brula les maisons, profana les eglises et laissa le pays ruine pour trent ans, c'etait la mise a sac de Cangas en 1617 par les pirates barbariques qui ne laisserent pierre sur pierre, qui massaeraient enfants et viellards et mutilaient les prisonniers a grand coups de cimeterre, qui couperent les seins de femmes don plusieurs nonnes.[13]

On Monday, 22 October, having landed troops in a bay 'about a league above Vigo' [Rooke], Vice Admiral Topsonn in the *Torbay* was ordered to make an attempt on the boom, which he succeeded in making. The *Swiftsure* accompanied the *Berwick* and the *Essex* under Rear Admiral Fairborne. Meanwhile the Marines attacked and took the forts, putting them out of action while the Allied ships passed beneath them.

What ensued was effectively a turkey shoot, with every French and Spanish ship being either burnt (16), sunk (8) or captured (12). On the Allied side, the *Torbay* came off worst, having been attacked by a fireship which then blew up.

Carlos di Risio has little doubt about the reasons for the crushing victory: the English gunners were better trained and could fire faster than either the French or Spaniards, and these two fleets were in any case a shadow of their former selves. Just over a hundred years later, at Trafalgar, the English would once again defeat a Franco-Spanish fleet, with once again a bold strategy and superior gunnery.

Following this victory, England made an alliance with Portugal and some Portuguese soldiers were present in the attack that took place on Gibraltar on 24 July 1704. Joined by Sir Cloudesley Shovell, Rooke held a council of war on 16 June in which the best possible targets were debated, the onus being on them to make good use of the considerable naval resources at their disposal, including the *Swiftsure*, a 70-gun ship built in 1673 which would be renamed *Revenge* in 1716. At a second meeting, on 17 June, Gibraltar was finally settled upon as the best option, though it is unlikely that the strategic impact of that decision for the next two centuries would have crossed the minds of those in attendance. It seemed to them to be a useful place to hold for the purposes of the war and it was also relatively lightly defended in comparison with ports such as Cadiz, on which Rooke had already burnt his fingers.

On 21 July, the Anglo-Dutch fleet arrived in Gibraltar Bay and 1,800 English and Dutch marines landed under the command of the Prince of Hesse, cutting the town off from the mainland. They received a barrage of cannon fire the next day, after the governor refused to surrender, but the marines took the fortifications and the governor of the town eventually surrendered on the 24th.

Leaving the Prince of Hesse in charge, the fleet then withdrew and some days later, on 9 August, spotted a French fleet and gave chase. By the 14th, the French had formed for action off Málaga and consisted of fifty-two ships and twenty-four galleys. The Anglo-Dutch fleet was fifty-two ships. The ensuing action was sporadic, with the enemy disinclined to stand and fight, eventually disappearing into the mist.

The *Swiftsure* was part of a division commanded by Sir Cloudesley Shovell, which also included the *Barfleur*, *Eagle*, *Orford*, *Assurance*, *Warspite*, *Nottingham*, *Tilbury* and *Lenox*. The English lost 691 men, the Dutch 400 killed and wounded and the French 3,048 men, along with one rear admiral, five captains, six lieutenants and five ensigns. The French, however, contrived to portray the battle as a victory – an early example of propaganda.

The *Swiftsure* remained under her original name for another decade, during which the Duke of Marlborough and Eugene fought a series of victorious campaigns over the French, prefaced by the Battle of Blenheim in 1704, with Ramillies and Oudenarde following in 1706 and 1708 respectively. When the war eventually drew to a close, the Treaty of Utrecht was signed in 1713, which set the seal on Rooke's capture of Gibraltar in perpetuity. This great lump of igneous rock was henceforth to be a lynchpin of British naval strategy in the Mediterranean and a stone in the shoe for Spain. Flying the Union Jack, it was emblematic of the rise in fortune of the British colonial empire and the relative decline of Spain and France.

Chapter 6

Guarding the Channel

In 1704, *Revenge* was involved in the vital duty of protecting trade in the Channel, particularly the Soundings, that area of sea roughly south of the Lizard in England and north of Forne Head in Britanny. *Revenge* was under the command of Commodore the Honourable William Kerr (1622–1722) who had the unenviable task of protecting British trade coming in from the Americas or Portugal from the depredations of French squadrons based at Brest and Dunkirk.

The Brest squadron was led by a privateer called Duguay-Trouin whose skill in hunting down straggling traders had been applauded and officially recognized by the French Government. His opposite number at Dunkirk was Saint-Pol-Hecourt.

Réné Duguay-Truin (1673–1736) led a career that was radically different to the one his family had intended for him. Having trained in a Jesuit College for Holy Orders, after which he entered the University of Caen, he decided to answer instead the call of the sea and became a corsair. Various successful actions led to his appointment as captain of a frigate in 1692, when he was eighteen, and later a larger ship.

Taking a leaf out of the book of the successful English Elizabethan privateers, the French Government decided to equip French corsairs with navy ships, thus granting a semi-official status to the swashbuckling escapades of the privateers and taking advantage of their natural talent and bravado for the benefit of the nation. One of the tactics practised by Duguay-Trouin and other corsairs was to fly the enemy flag before launching a surprise attack on an often unsuspecting enemy. At one point the British managed to capture Duguay-Trouin but their efforts to charge him with ungentlemanly deceit fell flat when he managed to escape from imprisonment.

His continued success led to an official invitation to join the French Navy, which he was delighted to accept, and by the age of twenty-four he had been appointed to the rank of captain. Realizing that his new formal status was constricting his debonair talent, it was decided on the outbreak of the War of the Spanish Succession that Duguay-Trouin should leave the Navy and return to privateering.

After his exploits in the Channel in 1704, often against the *Revenge*, he was honoured by the French Crown and, in 1704, when HMS *Revenge* was no longer cruising in that station, he captured twelve British merchantmen off the Lizard.

To begin with, the French had to contend with a larger British force under the command of Sir Cloudesley Shovell, who had been appointed to deal with a bustle of activity round the French ports of Rochefort, Brest and Port Louis. If the French fleet were to set sail for the straits, then Shovell had orders to detach part of his force, up to twenty-two ships, to reinforce Admiral Rooke.

Shovell's plan was to take his squadron from a rendezvous at Plymouth to the location of the cruisers on the Soundings, to ascertain at that point whether the French fleet, under the command of the Comte de Toulouse, had left Brest. If there was no sign of Toulouse, Shovell would gather the combined fleet, which included merchantmen bound for the West Indies, and bring them into the Soundings. If there were still no sign of the French, he would take his ships to a point 140–150 leagues west or west-south-west of the Scilly Isles. Again, if there were no sign of enemy, the ships for the West Indies would be allowed to set off, while store ships would be despatched to replenish Sir George Rooke's fleet at Lisbon.[1]

On 15 May, Shovell's fleet was positioned between the Lizard and Forne Head, with *Revenge* in the squadron commanded by Rear Admiral of the Red George Byng. Having come to the conclusion that Toulouse was probably at sea, the fleet then moved into the Soundings.

By 28 May, when there was still no sign of the French fleet, Shovell detached the major part of the fleet and set sail for Lisbon. This left the Westward end of the Channel under the command of Sir Stafford Fairborne, based at Portsmouth. At least two thirds of the Channel fleet, consisting of thirty-five English ships of the line and eleven Dutch, were based in the North Sea, leaving Fairborne and Kerr with the difficult task of defending a considerable area with limited resources. It was all the more difficult, in this game, to be on the defensive rather than on the offensive.

The French, for their part, could call on two large ships and two or three smaller ones under the command of Duguay-Trouin, and three large ships and three or four smaller ones under Saint-Pol.

The English cruisers in the Soundings focused on the safe passage of the merchant ships returning across the Atlantic, from Portugal and the West Indies.

In early July, Duguay-Trouin sailed from Brest with two large ships, *Le Jason* (54 guns), *L'Auguste* (54) and the corvette *La Mouche*. He was later joined by *La Valeur* (28) and some St Malo privateers.[2]

When Kerr spotted the French on 15 July, he was cruising alone in the *Revenge* some 50 miles west of Scilly. *Revenge* first of all engaged *Le Jason*, over which the *Revenge*, with its 70 guns, should have had the advantage. After a battle of nearly two hours, Kerr noticed *L'Auguste* and three other ships approaching, and decided to break off the action and return to Plymouth. Fortunately for Kerr, although heavier than the French ships, the *Revenge* proved to be faster and managed to get away without further incident.

Having had the opportunity to lick his wounds, Kerr came out of Portsmouth on 20 July accompanied by the *Falmouth* (54), Captain Thomas Kenny. Three days later he captured the corvette *La Mouche* and the following day chased and fired at *La Valeur*.

After this display of bravado, when Kerr sighted Duguay-Trouin 150 miles west of the Lizard on 27 July, he once again appears to have become more circumspect. According to Kerr, the French detachment appeared to consist of 'six tall ships' and his reason for declining the opportunity of a fight was that he felt it would distract him from his primary duty, which was to protect the Virginia fleet and incoming trade.

This raises an interesting point with regard to the tactics of the cruising squadrons. Should they, considering their small numbers, have engaged the enemy more closely, whatever the cost, or should they have continued to maintain themselves as a deterrent force, only taking their opportunities when the odds were obviously in their favour? After his somewhat inconclusive wrangle with *Le Jason* on 15 July, Kerr was clearly of the opinion that it was best not to throw caution to the winds. His case was not helped by the fact that the French force turned out to consist of only two armed ships, *Le Jason* and *L'Auguste*, as well as some prizes.

The French, for their part, were also probably aware of the limitations of their force and did not appear to want to commit to a battle either, so the two sides tracked each other warily over the next two days until the French broke away on the 29th. The wisdom of Kerr's tactic may be seen by the fact that he was able to sail to the west to meet a fleet arriving from Virginia.

At eight o'clock on 2 August, Kerr sighted some ships about whose identity he was unsure. In squally weather, he set a cautious course to the north until one of the ships hoisted English colours. The ship turned out to be the *Salisbury*, but Kerr was not fooled. The *Salisbury*, now renamed *Le Salisbury*, had been captured and was now part of the Dunkirk squadron.

Two more 'tall ships' now appeared to windward,[3] which turned out to be the *Moderate* and the *Gloucester*. By this time the enemy were upon the *Falmouth* and, despite Kerr's efforts to come to her aid in the *Revenge*, she was soon taken by a boarding party from a fifty-gun ship. *Revenge* engaged *Le Salisbury* and *Le Jersey*. According to the French account, it was *L'Amphitrite* that attacked the *Falmouth*, aided by *L'Heroine*. Captain Kenny of the *Falmouth* was mortally wounded.

Despite being supported by Kerr on the *Revenge*, the *Moderate* and the *Gloucester* did not make an appearance at this engagement, Captains Lumley and Meads having had several discussions on 4 August as to what to make of the ships they had sighted, sometimes disguised by fog. On 5 August, the *Moderate* and *Gloucester* engaged *L'Auguste* and *Le Jason* respectively, the battle continuing until midday, when the French broke away. Both the English ships then headed for Portsmouth where they joined the *Revenge* and the *Mouche*.

The French had turned the tables on the English and had beaten them at their own game. Faced with the challenge of patrolling a wide area of sea, the English had broken their ships up into small detachments, and indeed *Revenge* was sometimes on her own. This did not give them sufficient firepower when it came to engaging with the enemy and driving them off, and it also resulted in some rather tentative behaviour by the English commanders. If Captains Kerr and Kenny had been able to work together with Meads and Lumley, they could have formed a much more potent force that would have been likely to see the French off with somewhat less risk to themselves.

Although to some extent slamming the door after the horse had bolted, the Admiralty did order Fairborne to gather reinforcements from Portsmouth, Chatham and the North Sea. Kerr, whose original orders were to wait for the reinforcements at Plymouth, was later despatched to escort ninety incoming merchantmen from Oporto and Vianna in Portugal. The traders put in at Plymouth on the 11th and sailed again on the 13th for the Thames, accompanied by the *Revenge*, *Medway*, *Exeter* and *Mary*. The *Medway* captured two French privateer frigates off the Lizard.

Having fulfilled their duties to the Portuguese traders and escorted their prize home, the English squadron did not see action again until 4 September, when Kerr in the *Revenge* sighted seven sail, probably under Saint-Pol, and gave chase. As there was a gale blowing from the west, the *Medway* sprung her mainmast while the *Mary*'s fore-yard was carried away. Having lost his quarry, Kerr returned to Plymouth on 6 September.

When Kerr sailed again on 21 September, it was with Fairborne in the *Exeter*, along with the *Rochester* and *Deptford*. Fairborne sent a disgruntled note to the Secretary of State informing them that his ships were foul. The fleet was forced to put into Torbay due to a gale.

On 28 September, the squadron was at sea again under Fairborne and on 30 September they met a convoy of ships returning from the East Indies, which were escorted up the Channel by 7 October. Fairborne had eight major warships cruising off the Lizard and he spread six of them, including the *Revenge*, in a long line south-wards between 11 and 22 October. Fairborne eventually returned to Plymouth on 28 October and went on leave.

The efforts to protect the valuable trade returning from England, and the important part played in this by the *Revenge*, showed how the times had changed. In this game, it was the daring French privateers, Duguay Trouin and Saint-Pol, who took on the parts once played to such effect by Francis Drake, Raleigh and Frobisher. It was the French who had the initiative, lying in wait for the rich pickings of heavily laden transports shepherded by scanty escorts, and were able to choose their moment to run in and take their prey by surprise while the English Channel cruisers might be miles away, patrolling in the wrong spot, by guesstimate or intuition.

In February 1942, the British home fleet and coastal defences, with all the benefits of radar and aircraft reconnaissance, were to be caught napping by the German Kriegsmarine, which slipped the pocket battleships *Gneisenau* and *Scharnhorst* up the Channel to their ports at Wilhelmshaven and Brunsbuttel. It is not difficult to imagine, therefore, the level of difficulty required in the eighteenth century to intercept raiders without such aids, who even when in sight were difficult to identify or who might be flying the wrong colours.

When the enemy was intercepted and correctly identified, there then arose the issue of whether the defending cruisers had the strength to engage them effectively, and all too often this proved to be seriously in doubt. The English tactics and organization proved to be at fault, for even when there were enough ships in the area to see the enemy off, complications in the chain of command and poor communications meant that the forces remained separated and weakened, as evinced by the fiasco on 2 August 1704.

In the context of this book, however, the conclusion is more heartening: *Revenge* was almost invariably on the scene, acting as a deterrent if not actually engaging the enemy. Like her first forebear, *Revenge* defended the English coast against all comers, not as part of a large fleet, but alone or in the company of two or three other ships. If the tactics were at fault, then at least there was some measure of success: most of the incoming trade reached home safely and the French were thwarted in their attempt to challenge the emerging maritime power of England.

As if to emphasize the point, on 21 September, Fairborne's squadron had passed Sir George Rooke's Grand Fleet which was returning from the successful action against Gibraltar. While *Revenge* had been defending home waters against the odds, a foundation stone had been laid for the extension of English naval power and maritime trade into the Mediterranean and beyond.

Chapter 7

Keeping the French at Bay

Following the major fleet action off Málaga in August 1704, which proved to be inconclusive and which tarnished George Rooke's reputation, the English Navy focused on the protection of trade or land operations, such as the protection of Gibraltar from a French attack in 1705, an unsuccessful assault on Toulon harbour in 1707 and the strategically important capture of Port Mahon on Menorca in 1708.

The Duke of Marlborough had notched up a host of victories, including the Battle of Ramillies in 1706 and Oudenarde in July 1708. But, despite capturing Ghent and Bruges in January 1709, the war still carried on. Determined to obtain an unconditional surrender from the French, Marlborough pushed into France, capturing Tournai, before fighting his last major battle at Malplaquet in September 1709.

By the time the Treaty of Utrecht was signed in 1713, the new naval bases at Gibraltar and Port Mahon glinted propitiously in the English crown. England's status as a world naval power had been underwritten and the new bases helped her to extend her reach in the Mediterranean, particularly against the recalcitrant Spaniards, whose monarch, Philip V, had been obliged to drop his pretensions to the throne of France. The following year the Spanish Netherlands and Spain's possessions in Italy were given to Austria. Spain's empire was no longer the Habsburg imperial one of the last two centuries, but a collection of colonies in the Americas. This was no longer the confident Spain that had come so close to bringing England to its knees in 1588, but instead an unwieldy country that was barely able to manage its internal affairs, let alone those of an empire.

With the demise of the Spanish Habsburg Empire, and with the failure of France to seize the opportunity that lay before it, the bright morning star now seemed to stand over England. Nevertheless, the French naval base at Toulon was a thorn in the side for the Allies operating in the Mediterranean and, in order to counter its effect, the English generals then campaigning in Spain urged the Government in London to assign a squadron to remain on station in the straits.[1]

The Navy considered that locating the fleet at Spezia, in the north of Italy and within easy reach of Toulon, posed too many administrative and logistical difficulties, and so the Duke of Marlborough wrote to the British Commander-in-Chief in Catalonia, General Stanhope: 'I am so entirely convinced that nothing can be done effectually without the fleet that I conjure you if possible to take Port Mahon and to let me have your reasons for any other port that I may continue to press them in England.'[2]

The Duke of Sunderland also wrote to Stanhope:

Everyone is ready to agree that nothing could be of greater use [referring to a squadron wintering in the straits] but the great question is: how shall such a squadron be secure in any port of Italy from insults of the French by a superior force from Toulon? ... I conclude open this head, unless we can take Toulon from the French or Port Mahon, this thing is in no way practicable with safety ... It remains that you should dispose yourselves to be masters of Port Mahon.[3]

Marlborough then reported back to the authorities in London:

We must submit to the judgement of the admirals and sea officer on the safety of the port and other accommodation for ships of the line. It is certain they are the best judges, and Sir John Leake has order for it; but I must tell you plainly that, so far as I can learn, these gentlemen do not believe any port safe and fit except that of Mahon. I have written to Mr Stanhope to do his utmost to make himself master of it, after which there will be no difficulty.[4]

Marlborough's confidence in the judgement of the Navy, in their competence and in that of General Stanhope, is evident.

The naval operation against Port Mahon was entrusted to Sir John Leake, who had participated in the attack on Gibraltar and who had seen off the French forces under the Comte de Toulouse that were besieging Barcelona in 1706. Leake arrived at Port Mahon on 25 August 1708 and Stanhope on 3 September.

Leake placed at Stanhope's disposal a strong squadron under Sir Edward Whitaker, who had led the attack of the marines on Gibraltar. The troops were landed 2 miles away from Port Mahon, at a point that had been secured by the Navy, and Whitaker also seized Port Fornells on the north of the island to provide refuge for transports. Whitaker's squadron consisted of eighteen ships of the line and frigates, one fireship, two bomb vessels, two hospital ships and three Dutch ships.

Leake was keen to emphasize the importance of the naval role in this operation, which he considered may have been overshadowed by General Stanhope's and the army's success.

Once the port was taken, Sir George Byng was instructed to take a squadron to winter in the Mediterranean. Despite the success in capturing Minorca to complement England's strategic prize of Gibraltar, Toulon continued to simmer with intent and the threat to England's new acquisition remained very real.

In 1744, Admiral Matthews, sailing with Vice Admiral Lestock and Rear Admiral Rowley, failed to seize their opportunity when faced with a Franco-Spanish fleet off Toulon under Admiral de Court and Cabaret and the Spanish under Don Juan Joseppo Navarro, the English Admiral Lestock somehow contriving not to engage the enemy who seized their opportunity and escaped.

This failure led to a spate of internal administrative wrangling and courts marshal, and the dismissal of Matthews. Part of the problem, as Matthews pointed out in his own defence, was the evident superiority of the French and Spanish ships, not only in speed and agility but in firepower:

> There was no really effective line of battleships in the British fleet. The First and Second Rates were too large and it was difficult to obtain crews for them; between 1739 and 1745 it was rare to find more than half of them in service at any given time. They had originated as great prestige ships in the Dutch

Wars but the more advanced navies of the 1740s, like the French and the Spanish, had little use for them. Below them, the smaller ships were equally far from perfect. The 80s were unstable, the 70s too small to stand up to the great French 74s, and the 60s and 70s were even worse.[5]

The problem had been highlighted four years before Matthews' fiasco at Toulon by an incident involving a Spanish 70-gun ship called the *Princessa*. She was chased by three British 70-gun ships and eventually run to ground due to the fact that she had lost a topmast in a previous accident. Once overhauled, however, she proceeded to fight off her opponents in a manner not dissimilar to the first *Revenge* in 1591. It took six hours for the British to finally make the most of their three-to-one advantage and even so the Spanish ship survived to sail another day.

The reason for the *Princessa*'s impressive performance, apart from the bravery of her crew, lay in her build: at 165 feet, she was considerably longer than the British ships and, at 50 feet, also wider. These dimensions enabled her to perform as a stable gun platform and to take considerable punishment.

After the Battle of Toulon had rubbed the point home, the Admiralty put in hand measures to increase the size of English ships across the board and to improve their design. Unfortunately, the disadvantages of design by committee, with shipwrights from Deptford, Woolwich, Chatham, Sheerness and Portsmouth all putting in their pennyworth, resulted in a camel rather than a thoroughbred. The new 80-gun ship, as opposed to the recommended 74, was still smaller than its French and Spanish counterparts.

The Admiralty, however, preferred the 74 and gradually the 80s died out. The new 74s were something of a breakthrough, although when ordered the fiction was maintained in the early stages that they were 70s:

In fact the new ships were not 70s at all, but 74s and the original draught clearly shows provision for 74 gunports: the upper and lower decks were designed for 28 guns each, as in the latest 70s; the quarterdeck was fitted for 14 guns instead of 12, and the forecastle could carry four guns instead of two. The actual difference in gun power was small – the addition of four extra 9-pounders, raising the weight of metal from 1526 to

1562 pounds would not greatly increase the fighting power of the ships; but it did have great symbolic importance. Perhaps this is why the Admiralty was so secretive about it.[6]

The inspiration for the new 74s was taken not only from Spanish ships such as the *Princessa* but from French ships such as the *Invincible*, which had been captured in 1747 and much admired. The change, as has been seen above, was not welcome in all quarters:

> The 74 stood for everything the old surveyors had been against: it was of foreign ancestry; it was a large two-decker, whereas they had put their faith in small three-deckers; above all building 74s meant not just breaking the 1745 establishment, but destroying the whole system by which ships had been designed for the last half-century. With a major war just around the corner, the Admiralty had to move quickly, but also carefully. Construction of the new ships was well advanced before their full significance became clear, and traditionalists were faced with a fait accompli.[7]

The effectiveness of the new class of ship would be underlined by the Royal Navy in due course, but first it would have to pass through a period of agonizing that was to follow the loss of the island of Menorca to the French and the performance of a certain Admiral Byng.

As Britain's imperial ambitions and responsibilities grew, the Navy was forced to consider a variety of pressing needs and to prioritize accordingly. As has been seen, the Port of Toulon was a more or less endless source of potential menace of one sort or another and much time was given to trying to predict where the menace would next be directed – if not in the Mediterranean itself, then perhaps at Canada, or even an invasion of England, with a sideshow in Minorca for the purposes of distraction. There was also the question of trade and the powerful lobby of merchants demanding protection in and out of the Channel. As it was, the last of these options won the day and, while the fleet was largely taken up with sentinel duty in the Channel or escorting convoys, a French army embarked at Hières on 12 April 1756 and set sail for Minorca.

An analysis of Admiral Byng's instructions at this time[8] indicate that the Admiralty itself was unclear as to what direction his mission might take him, but that he should proceed to Gibraltar to ascertain whether the Toulon squadron had sailed that way.

When Byng arrived at Gibraltar, he heard that the French had already landed at Minorca. The French landing on the island did not, of course, mean that they had taken the citadel or that they could not be thrown off again, but Byng appears to have taken a decidedly negative approach to the whole prospect. As he said at his court martial:

> If I had been so happy to have arrived at Mahon before the French had landed, I flatter myself I should have been able to have prevented their getting a footing on the island: but as it has so unfortunately turned out, I am firmly of opinion from the great force they have landed, and the quantity of provisions, stores and ammunition of all kind they brought with them, that the throwing men into the castle will only enable it to hold out but a little time longer, and add to the numbers that must fall into the enemy's hands, for the garrison in time will be forced to surrender, unless a sufficient number of men could be landed to dislodge the French or raise the siege.[9]

As it was, the garrison held out valiantly, only succumbing when the French discovered an Achilles heel in one of the outer works. The French, surprised by the strength of the fortifications and the determination of the defenders, were in little doubt themselves that their efforts could have been thwarted if the English had managed to reinforce the garrison.

> On n'aurait jamais entrepris le siege de cette fortresse si l'on eut connu jusqu'a quel point les Anglais l'avaient rendue redoubtable.[10]

Unfortunately 'redoutable' was not an adjective that could be applied to the English authorities on Gibraltar. They worried that if they sent a detachment from Gibraltar it would not be able to land, and furthermore they managed to conjure up an awful scenario whereby Byng's squadron might be overcome by the Toulon squadron, leaving Gibraltar more susceptible to attack with a reduced garrison. Assuming, therefore, that the garrison on Minorca would succumb almost without a fight, assuming also that the French force was so powerful it was liable to defeat the English Navy, and assuming that the French supermen they had conjured up for themselves had time on their hands not only to take Minorca but Gibraltar as well, the Council on Gibraltar let Byng sail away without military reinforcements.

Armchair warriors will swear that they would have been more decisive and more courageous, but the evidence seems to show that Byng and the authorities at Gibraltar did have some cause to doubt the effectiveness of the resources at their disposal, and cause for worrying over the problems consequent on their late arrival on the scene.

Captain Richmond comments:

> Throughout January and February a considerable force of ships of the line was kept in home waters for the protection of the kingdom and the defence and attack of trade, and no attention was paid to the advices from the Mediterranean. What strikes me in this matter is the large number of ships of the line employed cruising on purely trade protection or attack, when an important strategic position was reported, from most trust-worthy sources, to be threatened ...
>
> Not only could ships have been sent earlier without the least danger to the United Kingdom, but a stronger force could have been sent.[11]

It was Byng's fatal error to have wavered in the way he did, thus giving a government eager for a scapegoat the opportunity it needed. It seems, however, that his indecision was just part of a train of unfortunate events and, in hindsight, it can be seen that, rather than shoot Byng, 'pour encourager les autres', as Voltaire put it, the authorities might have done better to reprimand him and put their own house in order. For instance, a letter from General Blakeney on Minorca dated 10 February makes it clear that there was ample warning that something was afoot:

> I can't be too early in acquainting you, Sir, that by different informations sent me from France and Spain there is equal reason to believe the French intend very shortly to make an

attack on this island; 'tis publicly talked of at Marseilles and Barcelona, and founded on 25,000 men being immediately ordered to march to the sea coast of Provence, officers of all their Militia being ordered to join their corps in order to replace the regular troops drawn from the inland garrisons. Several large boats have been just built at Toulon to contain 60 men each, and a 24-pounder; twelve sail of the line are absolutely to be ready to put to sea in this month, and five frigates that were lying in the road ready victualled are said to have received their orders.[12]

Once he had tracked down the enemy, Byng took a decidedly more aggressive stance, but unfortunately it did not have the desired effect.

When he arrived off Minorca on 20 May, Byng's squadron consisted of *Ramillies*, *Buckingham*, *Culloden*, *Trident*, *Captain*, *Revenge*, *Lancaster*, *Kingston* and *Defiance*.

Blakeney announced he had called a Council of War who 'were unanimously of opinion that, considering who these informations came from, and the reports everywhere about which seemed to tally with them, that this island, with the greatest speed, be put in the best state of defence it can.'[13] He noted later: 'A great quantity of timber for buildings of ships is arrived at Toulon, especially from Holland, and the number of hands in the yard for building and equipping ships are doubled.'

Commodore Edgcumbe wrote on 22 March:

The advices I have received, of the 24th ultimo, say that at Toulon everything is getting ready with the greatest speed; 14 large ships are taken up at Marseilles and more will be soon, they say, as far as 15,000 ton, to serve as transports. Those already taken are to be at Toulon the 15th of this month, against which time 22 battalions of foot will be in the neighbourhood, besides a battalion of the Royal Artillery, with some companies of miners and other workmen used in sieges, and a strong train of artillery with bombs are preparing.

Most people continue to think these preparations are against Minorca.[14]

Consul Dick wrote from Leghorn: 'The Toulon fleet is fitting for the sea with the utmost expedition ... It is said the force is intended against Minorca and is to be commanded by the Count de Maillebois.'[15]

He said in his letter of 13 March:

I have received the enclosed accounts and all the letters that are lately come hither from Provence, Languedoc, and Lyons mention an attempt on Minorca as intended and resolved upon by the Court of France, and to be executed as soon as the battalions now in full march towards the coast of Provence are arrived, and the squadron together with the transports can be got in readiness, which probably will require some weeks longer.[16]

For all that Byng showed some trepidation in his forecast of the usefulness of his intervention, he did eventually engage the enemy aggressively, but the able French Admiral de la Gallissenière continued to deprive him of the close battle and victory that Byng so desperately needed. Firstly, his trepidation was shared by others, such as the authorities on Gibraltar; second, his cautious manner of anticipating events was probably a natural effect of his personality; and third, the larger error was not his but lay in the strategy adopted by the authorities in England.

Quiberon Bay

The French were fast discovering that their ambition to create a colonial empire was seriously compromised by their inferior status at sea. British strategy in this respect was relatively straightforward: keep the French bottled up in port, thus depriving them of the option of reinforcing their colonial armies, carrying out trade or attempting to invade England. The British maintained their own trade while denying this privilege to their enemies. In May 1747, Vice Admiral George Anson attacked a French convoy off Cape Finisterre bound for India and Canada, and in October of the same year Admiral Hawke intercepted a French convoy bound for the West Indies. Under this kind of stranglehold, France had little choice but to acquiesce to the peace of Aix-la-Chapelle in 1748.

The French, however, would not easily lie down and, despite British successes in North America, crowned by the capture of

Quebec by General George Wolfe, the French actively planned to invade England itself. With most of their forces concentrated at Brest under Admiral Conflans, the French options were severely limited by the constant presence of a British blockading squadron. Their only window of opportunity was created by the weather, which forced the British to take refuge in a home port.

On one such occasion, in November 1759, Conflans took his chance and put twenty-one ships of the line out to sea. His orders were to rendezvous at Morbihan with transport boats before setting course for Scotland. Hawke, however, had not left the door entirely open, having detached some frigates to Douarnenez Bay, and the French fleet was sighted by two British transport ships. Conflans next sailed to Quiberon Bay, where he planned to embark an army of invasion, but here his nemesis in the shape of Hawke's fleet finally overtook him.

Having attempted to chase away two English frigates that were keeping an eye on him, Conflans suddenly noticed the main English force approaching. In view of the weather conditions and the perils of rocks and shoals in the vicinity of the Bay, Conflans was confident that he could find refuge in the Bay until, once again, the English were forced by nature to retire. Against a more cautious opponent such faith might have been rewarded but Hawke had a hunter's instinct and the moment he saw his prey he sounded his horn for a general chase. His captains duly spurred their steeds and it was every man for himself.

Once the reins were loosed, *Revenge* was one of the quickest off the mark. Along with *Magnanime, Torbay, Dorsetshire, Resolution* and *Warspite*, she was soon involved in a mêlée with the French. Punished severely by English guns and battered by squalls, French ships began to run aground on the treacherous shoals. The French flagship itself ran aground, while trying to escape the guns of Hawke's *Royal George*. The ship was then burned by her crew.

Although a couple of English ships also ran aground, there was no doubt where the victory lay. Seven French ships had been lost while the remainder scampered off to a safe haven. The tactics may have been messy but the strategic impact was immense: France would no longer attempt to face down the English at sea.

Chapter 8

Interlude

The next *Revenge* to be commissioned was a Sixth Rate, built at the Port of Bombay in 1755, headquarters of the East India Company. As a Sixth Rate, the new *Revenge* was typical of the growth in the cruiser force which had risen to 30 per cent of total British warship tonnage in 1760.[1] Ships of this size were useful for fast patrolling and for keeping a check on interlopers.

In 1750, Bombay acquired a dry-dock and the ships were built by naval shipwrights. *Revenge* would have been used to patrol the Indian Ocean.

Bombay had originally been a Portuguese possession, a relic of the discovery route to India via Cape of Good Hope by the early Portuguese navigators, notably Vasco da Gama. The Portuguese had named it Bom Bahia (literally Good Bay), in recognition of its ample proportions. In 1661, as part of the dowry of Catherine of Braganza on her marriage to Charles II of England, Bombay was ceded to England and later leased by the East India Company in 1668.

Bombay provided a deep-water port and the East India Company made sure that they took full advantage of the natural features of building up their own facilities, including causeways, forts and a castle. By 1687, the Company had turned Bombay into its Indian headquarters. Later it would even develop its own navy, the Bombay Marine, which would form the basis of the future Indian Navy. The Bombay Marine played an important role in fighting off marauding ships from rival European nations, namely Portugal, France and Holland, but also a range of pirates and other unwelcome guests. This *Revenge* foundered in 1782. A brig was named Revenge in 1778 and was captured by Americans in 1779.

The next *Revenge* was a Third Rate of 74 guns, laid down at Chatham in 1800 and launched on 13 April 1805. The order for the

Revenge, among seven other ships, was in response to the growing threat to Britain, not only from France, but from Holland and Spain as well.

Although built in 1805 and thus a brand-new ship when she sailed at Trafalgar that same year, *Revenge* did not represent a significant change in design from ships that had been launched half a century earlier – 'The methods of construction used in 1805 did not permit any great expansion of the two-decker.'[2] The materials used, largely comprising oak and other timbers, had numerous advantages, but also limitations, and no radical design had been developed that would change the shape, capacity or handling of ships of a particular weight designed to carry a particular number of guns. This is not to say there had been no innovations in the preceding period – far from it. There was a constant urge to refine methods of ship design and a consequent pressure on relevant departments to adapt so as to enable new systems to function more efficiently. Shipwrights became more and more specialized and the fulcrum of other sub-trades. The Surveyors' Office took on a new prominence in the last years of the eighteenth century, although it was too early for science to make a significant contribution to the design of a ship's hull or her superstructure. In both cases, experience and wisdom handed down over centuries was the most important factor, notwithstanding the frequent recourse to French designs, which were considered superior. The ship's displacement had to be balanced against its potential speed through the water. As far as the superstructure was concerned, space had to be found for stores, men and guns, and there was the knotty problem of how to deploy guns effectively through open gun ports when the ship was heeling in a high wind. Guns that were placed too high above the waterline, on the other hand, were likely to seriously destabilize the ship.

Chatham

By the time *Revenge* was laid down, Chatham had diminished in its importance as a naval base, its heyday having been the period of the Dutch Wars, for which for obvious geographical reasons it was strategically well placed. After this golden age, the emphasis at Chatham was on its less glamorous but still strategically vital role of building, repairing and maintaining the fleet.

The increasingly rare oak having been ordered and the ship's design received at the yard, the wood would be cut to shape to form the various parts of the ship, the first and most fundamental being the keel. Other parts included the floor timbers and various shapes and sizes of 'futtock' that were cut over templates to produce the shape of the ship. At either end there was a sternpost and stempost. The ship was then framed, leaving spaces for the gun ports.

Once the main structure of the hull had been completed, the ship was left to stand for a period of several months or even years to allow the wood to season, a process which would be complete when the sap had drained from the wood. Once the seasoning was complete, the planking would be added to the frame. Deck beams were then added which provided essential structural strength and bracing, as well as providing support for men, guns and stores. Depending on the size of the ship, there might be an orlop deck, a gun deck, a middle deck and an upper deck. Added to these were the forecastle, quarterdeck and poop deck. The decks were supported by 'knees' – L-shaped pieces of timber which were sometimes difficult to obtain due to the relative scarcity of trees of the right type and shape from which they could be cut. Once all these processes were complete, *Revenge* would have been ready to be launched into the Medway prior to fitting out.

The next essential for the new *Revenge* was her masts. These would probably have been sourced from either the Baltic or New England, and finished by shipwrights in England. There were three masts in a 74 – the main mast, the foremast and the mizzen mast. The other masts were positioned in such a way as to minimize their interference of and from the sails of the main mast. In addition to the vertical masts, there was the angled bowsprit in the bows of the ship which had a number of uses, including part of the bracing of the main mast and an anchor for the forestays. Although the bowsprit had traditionally carried sails, known as spritsails or later staysails, the *Revenge* of 1805 broke new ground and carried neither. Instead, the gaff mizzen, which hung diagonally off the back of the mizzen mast, was extended on *Revenge* in comparison with earlier designs.

In order to carry the weight of sails, which typically would include a lower sail, topsail, topgallant and loyal, the masts were constructed from several sections. By virtue of the huge natural forces to which they would be exposed, the masts, particularly the main and foremasts, ran through all of the decks of the ship and were secured at their base in the keelson. On each deck, the masts were also secured to deck beams. Where the lower mast met the upper mast, constructions known as trestletrees and tops were built. These allowed shrouds to support the topmast and provided a platform to be used for tactical shooting and so on.

Rigging was an art in itself and rope was often made in the Navy's own yards. The rigging both supported the masts themselves, with an emphasis being placed on holding the mast from the rear against the forward pull of the sail, and it was also used for pulling sails into position and keeping them trimmed. The rigging that went forward from the mast was known as the forestays, whereas the shrouds were angled to the rear.

Shrouds were designated according to the mast they served, namely 'the main, fore and mizzen shrouds, the main top-mast, fore-top-mast, or mizzen top-mast shrouds, and the main top-gallant, fore top-gallant or mizzen top-gallant shrouds.'[3] The shrouds would stretch under the force of the sails and would need to be tensioned. This was achieved through a system of lanyards and blocks, one attached to the shroud and the other to the deck.

Running rigging can be broken down into braces, sheets, haliards, clue-lines, brails and so on. The sheet, for example, was a rope fastened to the corner of a sail in order to keep it in a particular position. The yard was a piece of horizontal timber which supported the sail. This was designed to be turned according to the direction of the wind. It could also be lowered and raised. The brace was a rope that was used to pull the yards into the required position and they were attached for this purpose to the ends of the yards.

The sail was so called due to a derivation of the Dutch word 'seyhel' or 'seyl'. It was made up of several pieces of cloth stitched together, the individual pieces being known as cloths. The sails of a 74 would consist of 'courses, or lower sails, the top-sails, which are next in order above the courses; and the top-gallant sails, which are expanded above the top-sails. The courses are the main-sail, fore-sail, and mizzen, main-stay-sail, forestay and mizzen-stay-sail; but more particularly the three first.'[4]

The sails were hauled up to the yards by means of lines. When the sail was furled it was attached to the yard by ropes known as gaskets. These could only be tied by men who had gone aloft and worked their way along the foot ropes suspended under the yard. The brave men who did this work in all weathers were known as topmen.

The forces that would be exerted on the sails would be counter-balanced by the weight of the ship, including the ballast in the hold, weight of provisions and armament, and other stores on top of that. The ballast for a 74 normally consisted of a mixture of iron and shingle, on which provisions such as barrels of water, beer and rum would lie. Proper ballasting was a skilled job as it would have a direct effect on the ship's trim and speed through the water, and also on her stability in rough seas and strong winds. It was the responsibility of the master of the ship to find the right balance, so that the ballast was neither too high nor too low, too far forward or aft. In calculating the trim, the master would be aware of the gravitational forces pulling downwards and the contrary flotation forces pushing in the opposite direction. A correct trim would mean that the centre of gravity was neither too high so as to cause the ship to capsize, nor too low so as to cause her to be unwieldy in the water, or for her masts to break due to the over-weight of the ship.

British designers tended to build heavier ships than the French, whose ships were comparatively lighter, more buoyant and with guns set higher.

Seamen

Once built and fitted out with masts and rigging, and with ballast and preliminary stores on board, the *Revenge* would start to receive her crew.

The skills of the seamen of large sailing ships are still celebrated today in mast drills at tournaments. The seaman was a highly skilled individual who had to demonstrate considerable courage and physical prowess to be able to scramble up the rigging, often in rough and stormy weather, and work his way along the yardarms at great heights, his feet only supported by a rope and his arms over the yard itself, leaving hands free to haul in unpredictable, wind-lashed sail cloth. A wrong move meant certain death.

In addition to his physical aptitude, the seaman had to learn how to tie a host of knots and to recognize myriad styles of rigging and ropes, with associated blocks and tackle. Not surprisingly, such men were both prized and relatively scarce. It was not enough to send an ordinary landlubber aloft in the hope that he would learn the trade through experience. The seaman, and particularly the topman, had to be carefully trained as the efficiency of the ship and his own life depended on it.

Seamen for ships such as *Revenge* were largely impressed men and there was always a danger of desertion. Leave was therefore limited to reduce the likelihood of seamen opting for an easier life ashore.

The official ship's complement for HMS *Revenge* was 640, though the actual number aboard was probably typically around 630.

Stores

The stores that were taken on included 478 casks of water, 32 casks of beer, 4 tons of wine and 16 tons of spirits. Food included 13 tons worth of beef, about the same weight of pork and a list of additional supplies including oatmeal, bread and cheese.

The armament of seventy-four guns included: twenty-eight 32lb guns for the lower deck; thirty 24lb guns on the main deck; and sixteen 9lb guns and carronades on the upper deck and poop. The guns were supplied by the Ordnance Board and, once taken aboard, they were supervised by the master gunner, who was responsible for their maintenance, for their correct fitting with tackles and for their supply with a variety of shot and powder. Under the master gunner there was a crew consisting of mates and a quarter gunner who would be attached to a group of four guns.

A typical 32lb gun was a smoothbore of just over 9 feet in length. It was tapered towards the muzzle and was moulded with trunnions on each side to fit into a gun carriage, and a mounting at the rear for attaching the breeching tackle. When the gun was loaded, a cartridge of gunpowder would first be rammed down the barrel via the muzzle. The ball would then be inserted, followed by a wad. The wad was required due to the disparity between the size of the ball and the bore of the cannon, known as windage. This was due to the inaccuracies in boring cannon which meant that extra room for error had to be built in. The end result was loss of efficiency when firing as a significant proportion of the expelling force of the explosion would be lost round the sides of the ball.

The gun carriage was a simple construction with four wheels which was typically fitted with tackle on each side fed through two blocks, attached to the side of the gun carriage and to the side of the gun port. The tackle was designed to facilitate the rolling out of the gun but, even so, it required at least thirteen men to roll out a 32lb gun. The extent of recoil of the gun was defined by the breeching rope which was fed round the back of the gun via the cascabel and attached with ring bolts to the hull. Another piece of tackle, known as the train tackle, was designed to stop the cannon rolling forward when it was being loaded.

The projectile was normally a round cannon ball but could also include chain shot (two balls joined by a chain), which was designed to destroy rigging, or a thin-cased grapeshot canister which could be fired at enemy personnel, or the less commonly used bar shot.

Gunpowder was stored in barrels in the magazine. In view of the obvious dangers of a spark igniting such a large concentration of gunpowder, which could blow the ship apart, the barrels were rested on leather skins to prevent sparks caused by friction, especially in bad weather or when the barrels were being moved. The magazine was lined with copper so as to prevent rats getting in and trailing gunpowder around the ship. Lighting for the magazine was kept in a separate room, the light penetrating through thick glass. Gun charges or cartridges were made ready in the filling room and laid on racks prior to use.

The traditional method of firing a cannon had been to put a lighted match on a touch hole. This had disadvantages due to the delay that sometimes ensued before the charge ignited. British cannon were increasingly fitted with a flintlock mechanism which made firing more efficient and accurate – it was one of the contributory factors to the greater efficiency of British gun management at Trafalgar and elsewhere. The other factor was training. The gun deck of a British man-of-war, once cleared for action, was an efficient space in which every man was highly trained in his role. The rate of fire of British ships was greater than that of their enemies and their aim was generally more accurate.

The first captain of the new *Revenge* was Robert Moorsom, born at Whitby, Yorkshire in 1760 to a family of seafarers. He joined the Royal Navy in 1777 and, after seeing action at the Siege of Gibraltar and Cape Spartel, as well as against a French convoy, he was made a lieutenant in 1784. As war loomed, he was made up to post captain in 1790. Moorsom's association with *Revenge* was to prove the highlight of a career which might otherwise have gone unremarked.

Moorsom's new command – like her 'race-built' ancestor of Armada fame – was significantly sleeker and faster than many other ships of the line, qualities that would contribute to her significant role in what was to be the most important battle ever fought by the Royal Navy.

Revenge's first station was with the Channel fleet and here, as William Robinson narrates in his personal account of his experiences on board *Revenge*, the ship was worked up into full fighting order and the watches were set up – starboard and larboard.[5] The starboard watch went on duty at eight o'clock at night, and the larboard watch at twelve o'clock. The half hours on board were marked by bells which were sounded as the hour glass was turned. The period of channel watch would have allowed some of the less experienced men to become accustomed to the rigours of naval life and for the crew to learn to work together as a team, which was essential for the efficient running of the ship. Soon HMS *Revenge* was ordered to sail for the Bay of Biscay and down the Spanish coast towards Cadiz.

Chapter 9

Trafalgar

In May 1803, Britain had declared war on France and in May 1804, Napoleon Bonaparte had proclaimed himself Emperor of the French. An army was assembled at Boulogne which *Revenge*, on its first duty in the Channel, was deployed to oppose. Boulogne and other French embarkation ports received a great deal of investment to make it capable of holding up to 1,000 landing craft, but the realities of crossing the Channel in unwieldy rowed landing craft when the British Admiral Lord Leith had 218 ships at his disposal to intercept them made the invasion of England a pipe dream.

British tactics largely involved keeping the French blockaded in port. Nelson had kept a watch on Toulon in the south and there were at least sixteen ships deployed to watch Brest. Spain needed to be handled diplomatically and an eye was kept on El Ferrol where *Revenge* would drop in on her journey south. An ill-judged attack by British naval forces on a Spanish treasure fleet returning from the Americas, however, hastened what was almost inevitable. Spain declared war on Britain in December 1804 which gave Napoleon a strong hand of naval cards. The Spanish fleet was not only substantial, it was also well commanded and trained.

Emboldened, Napoleon hatched new plans which would help him achieve his ultimate goal: the invasion of England. His direct involvement in creating these plans was not welcomed by the French Navy who found themselves in receipt of orders and counter-orders. Although the French naval commander at Toulon, Admiral Villeneuve, protested, he did not have sufficient character to influence events. Eventually Villeneuve managed to slip out of Toulon and evade British watches at Gibraltar and Cadiz and, accompanied by the Spanish Cadiz squadron under Admiral Gravina, sailed for the

West Indies. The plan was that they should join with the French forces at Martinique and return across the Atlantic to surprise the British and cover the invasion of England.

Hindered by limited communications, Nelson got wind of French movements late and set off in pursuit about a month later. As Nelson raced west across the Atlantic, the Admiralty ordered fourteen ships under Collingwood to set sail for Cadiz. *Revenge* was among them.

When Villeneuve heard that Nelson had arrived in the West Indies there was only one thought in his mind: to head back towards Europe. Having been a month behind, Nelson was now catching up. He was now only two days behind Villeneuve as he set off in pursuit of the French. When he became aware that Villeneuve and Gravina were heading for El Ferrol, Nelson sent a brig with a message to that effect for the Admiralty in London and steered course for Gibraltar.

Although the French had succeeded in drawing Nelson away, they had not managed to weaken British defences in the Channel. Some of the credit for seeing through French intentions seems to be owed to Admiral Collingwood. Collingwood had noticed intelligence reports that showed Villeneuve's force included a cavalry unit. He realized that such a unit could not be intended for use in the West Indies. He wrote to Alexander Carlyle:

> I think it is not improbable that I shall have those fellows coming from the West Indies again, before the Hurricane months, unless they sail from thence directly for Ireland, which I have always had an idea was their plan, for this Bonaparte has as many tricks as a monkey. I believe their object in the West Indies to be less conquest, than to draw our force from home.[1]

As they approached their destination, Villeneuve and Gravina ran into a squadron of fifteen British ships under Admiral Calder. There was an indeterminate scrap in bad weather and the next day Calder failed to renew the attack, leaving the allies to find refuge in Vigo. Some took the view that Calder would have done better to throw caution to the winds and launch a kamikaze action against the superior allied forces – anything to prevent their escape.

So what was the argument between Britain and France and why was Trafalgar so significant? Was it merely a question of trade and the spoils of empire?

It is certainly true that England and France were arch rivals but HMS *Revenge* had also fought with the Spanish and the Dutch. What was so special about this battle?

The Spanish Armada had threatened England and, if it had succeeded, would have imposed the Catholic faith on a defeated England. This, however, would have been no profound change, for England was a Christian country and had been Catholic for far longer than it had been Protestant. The arguments with the Dutch were largely mercantile and did not pose a major threat to the English body politic. The French Revolution had, however, brought about a political change that was at odds with the entire constitution and way of life of the English. For those who were interested in revolution in England, this was not such an issue but for all those who subscribed to the idea that English liberties were passed on from one generation to the next and presupposed a maintenance of liberties that had been won by previous generations, France and the French Revolution as embodied by Napoleon Bonaparte posed a fundamental threat.

English suspicion of the French Revolution was voiced most lucidly by Edmund Burke, for whom it was little less than a nightmare:

> Out of the tomb of the murdered monarchy in France has arisen a vast, tremendous, unformed spectre, in a far more terrific guise than any which ever yet have overpowered the imagination, and subdued the fortitude of man. Going straight forward to its end, unappalled by peril, unchecked by remorse, despising all common maxims and all common means, that hideous phantom overpowered those who could not believe it was possible she could at all exist, except on the principles, which habit rather than nature had persuaded them were necessary to their own particular welfare, and to their own ordinary modes of action.[2]

The elements of this revolution that appalled Burke could be itemised as: 'The spirit of total, radical innovation; the overthrow of all prescriptive rights; the confiscation of property; destruction of the Church, the nobility, the family, tradition, veneration, the ancestors, the nation – this is the catalogue of all that Burke dreaded in his darkest moments, and every item in it he would have discovered in Marxism.'[3]

Burke, however, was not a believer in monarchies growing fat while the poor crawled in the gutter. His instinct was to preserve the 'revolution' without an 'r', that had been the British way of achieving change and progress over the centuries. Only by evolution could they preserve the good that had been inherited from the past while contributing a measure of useful change to posterity. The ideas of the French Revolution incorporated the thinking of those such as Rousseau who stated that individuals should 'be forced to be free'. As Napoleon gathered an army at Boulogne and waited impatiently for his navy to wipe out the English fleet, this was precisely his intention. The English would become free, their history erased in order to make a clean start under the forced freedom of the general will.

Despite the English Reformation and despite a civil war and other ups and downs, the English and the British had consistently maintained the principle of freedom of the individual, which Edmund Burke described as 'an entailed inheritance derived to us from our forefathers, and to be transmitted to our posterity'.[4] If there was any question as to where this concept of individual freedom derived from, it was from Christian principles which had formed the bedrock of the English law and constitution: 'Christendom for long synonymous with Europe – with its recognition of the unique and spiritual nature of the individual, on that idea, we still base our belief in personal liberty and other human rights.'[5]

Despite the unpropitious movements of his fleet, Napoleon still awaited the moment when Villeneuve and his Spanish allies would arrive in the Channel to sweep away the British blockade of Brest and unleash a storm upon England.

Although his recent engagement with the British had proved inconclusive, Villeneuve was by now sufficiently nervous to choose to sail not northwards, where his Emperor eagerly awaited him in person at Boulogne, but south. In doing so, he narrowly avoided an even greater shock, for Nelson was still on his scent and sailing north to meet him. Weather conditions intervened, however, to keep the fleets apart, and the allies slipped into Cadiz where Collingwood and *Revenge* kept an eye on them.

By this time even Napoleon had to acknowledge that if the English were to be rescued from their perfidious ways and illusory liberties, it was not now. Habeas corpus, Magna Carta, the Common Law and the monarch in Parliament would all remain standing. The British had missed their opportunity to be forced to be free.

As German forces would do 135 years later, Napoleon turned his attention to the east, where there was an ominous tramp of marching feet heading in his direction, leaving the sceptred isle to shimmer tantalizingly in the setting sun. The battle at Trafalgar, therefore, would not be about saving England from the immediate threat of invasion so much as underlining British naval mastery for the next century or so and all that was consequent upon that mastery.

The naval focus was once again on Cadiz, though the French had received unwelcome orders from the supreme commander, this time relating to a campaign in Sicily. Nelson now joined Collingwood at Cadiz, and the French and Spanish watched for their opportunity to escape without having to do battle with the British. The arrival of English reinforcements, including the *Revenge*, made their chances appear increasingly slim.

Due to the long periods on station, some of Nelson's ships were detached to Gibraltar to restock with essential provisions, including water. Villeneuve saw his chance and on 20 October the allies sailed out of Cadiz, hoping to reach the straits of Gibraltar before the English could catch up with them.

In order to tempt the enemy to make a move, Nelson had deliberately kept his main force at a distance, using frigates as his eyes and ears. Once he had news of the enemy movement, he set course to cut them off. In view of the relatively light winds, Villeneuve realized he would not reach the straits of Gibraltar by nightfall and made plans to return to Cadiz, but by now destiny had caught up with him.

Captain Lucas of the *Redoutable* described the complications in forming the line in the Combined Fleet as battle approached:

On the 28th Vendemiaire

An XIV (20th October, 1805) 1 the Combined Fleet got under sail to leave Cadiz Bay. The wind was southerly; light at first, afterwards fresh. The fleet comprised thirty-three sail of the Line, of which eighteen were French, fifteen Spanish; with five frigates and two brigs, French. We were hardly outside when the wind shifted to the south-west and came on to blow strong. The admiral then ordered the fleet to reef sail, which was done, though some of the Spanish ships were so slow over it that they fell considerably to leeward. Some time was lost by that, but at length all worked back again, and then the fleet stood on, in no regular formation, heading to the west-north-west. The Redoutable was next astern to the Bucentaure, and a short distance off, when, towards noon, the flagship suddenly signalled 'Man overboard!' I brought to at once, lowered a boat, picked the man up, and regained my station. West, and the fleet went about all together. As soon as that was done, the Bucentaure signalled for the battle-squadron to form in three columns on the starboard tack, flagships in the centre of their divisions. In this order of sailing the Redoutable, as leader (chef de file) of the first division, should have been at the head of her column, and I manoeuvred the ship to take that post. All the afternoon, however, was spent without the fleet being able to get into the formation designated, although the admiral kept signalling repeatedly to ships to take station.

Towards seven in the evening the wind went down a little; but the sea was still rough, with a swell setting in from the south-west. The fleet was now steering to the south-south-west. I signalled at this time to the admiral that I could make out a fleet or squadron of the enemy to windward. They did not, to me, seem very far off. The ships of this squadron, as the evening went on, made a great many signals, showing for their purpose quite a remarkable display of coloured fires.

About nine o'clock at night the flagship made the general signal to the fleet to form in the order of battle at once, without regard to the stations of individual ships. To carry out this evolution those ships most to leeward ought to have shown a light at each masthead, so as to mark their positions. Whether this was done I do not know: at any rate I was unable to see such lights. At that moment, indeed, we were all widely scattered. The ships of the battle squadron and those of the squadron of observation were all mixed up. Another cause of confusion was this. Nearly all the ships had answered the admiral's signals with flares, which made it impossible to tell which was the flagship. All I could do was to follow the motions of other ships near me which were closing on some to leeward.

Towards eleven I discovered myself close to Admiral Gravina, who, with four or five ships, was beginning to form his own line of battle. I was challenged and our name demanded, whereupon the Spanish admiral ordered me to take post in his line. I asked leave to lead it and he assented, whereupon I stood into station. The wind was in direction and force as before, and we were all still on the starboard tack.

The whole fleet was at this time cleared for action, in accordance with orders signalled from the Bucentaure earlier in the night. In the Redoutable we had, however, cleared for action immediately after leaving Cadiz, and everything had been kept since in readiness to go to quarters instantly. With the certainty of a battle next day, I retained but few men on deck during the night. I sent the greater number of the officers and crew to lie down, so that they might be as fresh as possible for the approaching fight.[6]

Admiral Gravina himself was a skilled commander and seaman. He gave his own account of the preparations for battle aboard the *Príncipe de Asturias*:

On the morning of the 19th some of the French and Spanish set sail in obedience to the signal made by Admiral Villeneuve. In consequence, however, of the wind shifting to the S.E., we could not all succeed in doing so until the 20th, when the wind got round again to the E.S.E. Scarcely was the Combined Fleet clear of the harbour mouth, when the wind came to S.S.E., blowing so strongly, and with such a threatening appearance, that one of the first signals made by the Bucentaure, the flagship of Admiral Villeneuve, was to set double-reefed topsails. This change of wind also necessarily caused a considerable dispersal of the fleet, until two o'clock in the afternoon. Then, fortunately, the wind veered to the S.E., and the horizon becoming clear and unobscured, signal was made to form five columns, and afterwards for all to close. An advanced frigate signalled eighteen sail of the enemy in sight, in consequence of which news we cleared for Action, and sailed in fighting order. At three we all tacked and stood for the Straits, still preserving the same disposition of five Columns in which we had been before the last evolution. After having so done, we descried four of the

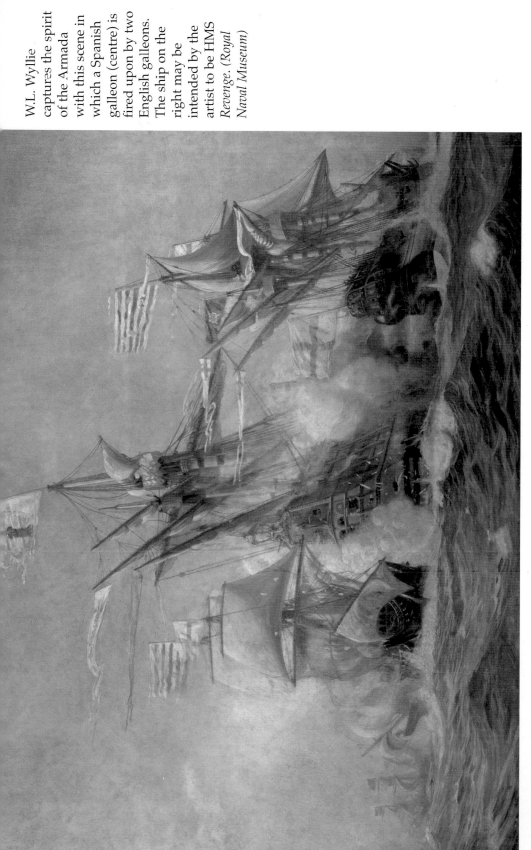

W.L. Wyllie captures the spirit of the Armada with this scene in which a Spanish galleon (centre) is fired upon by two English galleons. The ship on the right may be intended by the artist to be HMS Revenge. (Royal Naval Museum)

Sir Francis Drake (1540-96) was the captain of HMS *Revenge* at the time of the Armada. Probably the most famous English sea captain alongside Nelson, his name reverberates down the ages the sound of Drake's drum. *(Royal Naval Museum)*

Infante Dom Henrique, Duke of Viseu (1394-1460). Popularly known as Prince Henry the Navigator, he was the son of King John I of Portugal and the English princess Philippa of Lancaster, daughter of John of Gaunt. Henry had huge influence on the early European voyages of discovery by fostering the development of maps and navigational aids such as the astrolabe and developing more seaworthy ships such as the caravel. All these initiatives would influence the explorations of the English navigators, including Drake, while the design of the caravel influenced the design of the first *Revenge. (Royal Naval Museum)*

PRINCE HENRY OF PORTUGALL

os locked in battle at
Falgar in a painting by
mas Luny. After the
nada, this was perhaps
most critical naval battle
British history, though by
time it was fought the
nediate threat of invasion
Napoleon had passed.
yal Naval Museum)

niral Lord Nelson by
drich Heinrich Fuger.
son embodied the spirit
ndividual initiative which
its roots in the derring-
of the Elizabethan Navy
al, and which meant that
pre-eminence of the
al Navy in the nineteenth
ury and beyond was not
rely based on size.
val Naval Museum)

HMS *Revenge* as a 91-gun, screw-powered, second-rate two-decker, launched in 1859. S
served in the Channel Squadron and made various expeditions to the Mediterranean a
to American waters before becoming flagship of the Port Admiral at Queenstown. *(Ro*
Naval Museum)

The Royal Sovereign class battleship HMS *Revenge* launched on 3 November 1892. The
understated power of the Royal Sovereign class battleships was emblematic of the
British Empire in its heyday. Designed by Sir William White, these were the most
powerful ships afloat prior to the creation of HMS *Dreadnought*. *(Royal Naval Museum)*

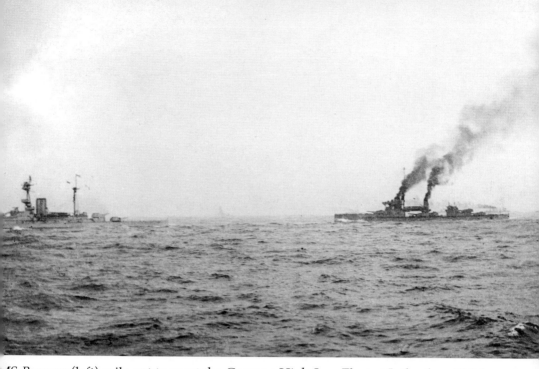

HMS *Revenge* (left) sails out to meet the German High Seas Fleet at Jutland on 31 May 16. Although she was barely run in, HMS *Revenge* was once again present at a critical ttle in British history, in this case the largest naval battle ever to be fought. *perial War Museum SP604)*

HMS *Revenge* as a Revenge class battleship in all her pristine glory. At Jutland and ring the inter-war years she could influence policy both at sea and ashore. By the cond World War, however, although she remained a formidable presence, she could rely keep pace with newer and faster battleships. *(Royal Naval Museum)*

A range-finder team watch the fall of shot in the crow's nest of HMS *Revenge*. *(Imperia War Museum A1513)*

The breach of a 15in MKI naval gun as fitted to HMS *Revenge* in 1913. The gun could a 1,920lb (871kg) shell at a range of 32,500 yards (29,720m). *(Royal Naval Museum)*

HMS *Revenge* leaving Portsmouth harbour, accompanied by a destroyer, by Richard Ernst Eurich. The painting underlines the sterling work of HMS *Revenge* in bolstering home defences. Despite being comparatively old by the Second World War, HMS *Revenge* retained a strong image in the national consciousness. (© *National Maritime Museum, Greenwich, London*)

Two planesmen guide the nuclear submarine HMS *Revenge* somewhere deep in the oceans. They have no visual references other than the instruments all round them. *(Imperial War Museum TR42813)*

Enemy's Frigates, to which, by order of Admiral Villeneuve, we gave chase. Signal was made, at the same time, from our ship, for the Achille, Algeciras, and San Juan, attached to the 'Squadron of Observation', to reinforce the ships sent in chase. They had orders to rejoin the main body of the Fleet before nightfall. At half-past six o'clock a French ship informed us that they had made out eighteen of the enemy, all in line of battle; and shortly afterwards we ourselves began to observe, at no great distance, gleams of light. They could only be from the enemy's frigates, which were stationed midway between the two fleets. At nine o'clock the English squadron made signals by firing guns, and, from the interval which elapsed between the flash and report, they must have been about two miles from us. We informed the French Admiral by signal-lanterns that it was expedient to lose no time in forming line of battle on the leeward ships, on which an order to that effect was immediately given by the Commander-in-Chief. In this situation we beheld the dawn of the 21st, with the Enemy in sight, consisting of twenty-eight Ships, eight of which were three-deckers all to windward of us, and in Line of Battle on the opposite tack.[7]

Nelson had made his main plan beforehand and he also had some fall-back plans in reserve. The tactic of attacking the enemy line at right angles in parallel columns was not new, but this time it had a devastating additional ingredient – the Nelson touch. The English sailors were not so interested in the viability of the tactics on paper, or the quality of their ships, as the fact that their beloved Nelson was leading them. His presence inspired every man with an indomitable spirit and there was no doubt whatsoever that they would do their duty.

Admiral Collingwood had transferred his flag from *Dreadnought* to the newly copper-sheathed *Royal Sovereign*. It was fitting for the style of this battle that both Admirals would lead from the front. *Revenge* was ninth in line in Collingwood's column, which would be the first to bisect the enemy line. The reason for this was that Collingwood had been allocated most of the sleek and fast 74s, among which *Revenge* was one of the swiftest. All ships were under full sail and all had their full colours flying. Bands played patriotic tunes. England, recently threatened with invasion, had come to wreak her revenge.

The British Fleet

Victory – Admiral Lord Nelson; Captain Thomas Masterman Hardy

Temeraire – Captain Eliab Harvey

Neptune – Thomas Francis Fremantle

Leviathan – Henry William Bayntun

Conqueror – Israel Pellew

Britannia – Rear Admiral Rt Hon. Earl of Northesk; Captain Charles Bullen

Ajax – Lieutenant John Pilford

Agamemnon – Captain Sir Edward Berry

Orion – Captain Edward Codrington

Prince – Captain Richard Grindall

Minotaur – Captain Charles Moore Stanfield

Spartiate – Captain Sir Francis Laforey

Royal Sovereign – Admiral Collingwood; Captain Edward Rotheram

Belleisle – Captain William Hargood

Mars – Captain George Duff; Lieutenant William Hennah

Tonnant – Captain Charles Tyler

Bellerophon – Captain John Cooke; Lieutenant William Pryce Cumby

Colossus – Captain James Nicoll Morris

Achilles – Captain Richard King

Revenge – Captain Robert Moorsom

Defiance – Captain Philip Charles Durham

Dreadnought – Captain John Conn

Swiftsure – Captain William Gordon Rutherford

Polyphemus – Captain Robert Redmill

Thunderer – Lieutenant John Stockham

Defence – Captain George Hope

Africa – Captain Henry Digby

Euryalus – Captain Hon. Henry Blackwood

The Combined Fleet

Scipion – Captain Charles Bellanger

Intrépide – Captain Louis-Antoine-Cyprien Infernet

Formidable – Rear Admiral Pierre-Etienne René-Marie Dumanoir le Pelley; Captain Jean-Marie Letellier

Mont-Blanc – Captain Guillaume Jean-Noel Lavillegris
Duguay-Trouin – Captain Claude Toufflet
Heros – Captain Jean-Baptiste-Joseph-René Poulain
Bucentaure – Captain Jean-Jacques Magendie
Redoutable – Captain Jean Jacques Etienne Lucas
Neptune – Commodore Espirit Tranquille Maistral
Indomptable – Captain Jean Joseph Hubert
Fougueux – Captain Louis Alexis Baoudoin
Pluton – Commodore Julien-Marie Cosmao-Kerjulien
Algésiras – Rear Admiral Charles-René Magon de Medine; Captain
   Laurant Le Tourneur
L'Aigle – Captain Pierre-Paul Gourege
Swiftsure – Captain C.E. L'Hopitalier-Villemadrin
Argonaute – Captain Jacques Epron
Achille – Captain Louis Gabriel Denieport
Berwick – Captain Jean-Gilles Filhol-Carnas
Neptuno – Captain Don H. Cayetano Valdés y Flores
Rayo – Captain Don Enrique MacDonnell
San Francisco de Asís – Captain Don Luís de Flores
San Agustín – Captain Done Felipe Jado Cagigal
Nuestra Señora de la Santíssima Trinidad – Rear Admiral Baltasar
   Hidalgo de Cisneros; Captain Francisco Javier de Uriarte y Borja
San Justo – Captain Don Francisco Javier Garstón
San Leandro – Captain Don José Quevedo
Santa Ana – Vice Admiral Ignacio Maria de Álava y Navarrete;
   Captain Don José de Gardoquí
Bahama – Commodore Dionisio Alcalá Galiano
Montañés – Captain Francisco Alcedo y Bustamente
Argonauta – Captain Don Antonio Parejo
San Ildefonso – Captain Don José Ramón de Vargas y Varaéz
Príncipe de Asturias – Admiral Don Federico Carlos Gravina; Rear
   Admiral Don Antonio de Escaño; Commodore Rafael de Hore
San Juan Nepomuceno – Commodore Don Cosmé Damian
   Churruca y Elorza
Monarcha – Captain Don Teodoro de Argumosa

Captain Lucas of the *Redoutable* recalled:

By nine o'clock the enemy had formed up in two columns. They
were under all sail they even had studding sails out and heading

directly for our fleet, before a light breeze from the west-south-west. Admiral Villeneuve, being of the opinion, apparently, that they were intending to make an attack on our rear, tacked the fleet all together. In this new order the Redoutable's place was third ship astern of the flagship Bucentaure. I at once made every effort to take station in the wake of the flagship, leaving between her and myself the space necessary for my two immediate leaders. One of them was not very far out of its station, but the other showed no signs of trying to take post. That ship was at some distance to leeward of the line, which was now beginning to form ahead of the admiral.

Towards eleven o'clock the two columns of the enemy were drawing near us. One was led by a three-decker, the Royal Sovereign, and headed towards our present rear squadron. The other, led by the Victory and the Temeraire, was manoeuvring as if to attack our centre, the Corps de bataille.[8]

So fast was the *Royal Sovereign* that it pulled ahead of the rest of the line and Collingwood ordered his men to lie down as the first enemy shot began to fly over. Moorsom ordered the gunners on *Revenge* to hold their fire until they were more closely engaged and would give the signal himself by firing a carronade from the quarter deck. New and fast, *Revenge* began to pull ahead of some of the older ships in the column and in no time she was in the thick of it. At first she became entangled in the bows of a French ship of equivalent size, the 74-gun *L'Aigle*, but she managed to fire two broadsides into the French ship before breaking free. The next engagement was not such an equal one. This time her opponent was a ship much larger than herself – the Spanish flagship *Príncipe de Asturias* (112 guns), which ran her bowsprit over the poop deck of *Revenge* with the intention of boarding her. This dire threat was defeated by skilful use of the carronades on the poop deck which were loaded with grapeshot and also by the skill at arms of the *Revenge*'s Royal Marines detachment. After this devastating response, the Spaniards thought better of it and sheered off to find easier prey, as William Robinson relates:

A Spanish three-decker ran her bowsprit over our poop, with a number of her crew on it and in her fore rigging. Two or three hundred men were ready to follow; but they caught a Tartar, for their design was discovered and our marines with their small arms, and the carronades on the poop, loaded with canister-shot, swept them off so fast that they were glad to sheer off.[9]

Revenge was then engaged by four more French ships but was unable to make any headway due to damage to mast and sails. As William Robinson wrote: 'In this condition we lay by the side of the enemy, firing away, and now and then we received a good raking from them, passing under our stern. This was a busy time for us, for we had not only to endeavour to repair the damage, but to keep to our duty.'[10]

One cannot help at this point remembering the action of the first *Revenge* at the Azores against the Spanish 'Twelve Apostles'. Here she was again, the indomitable *Revenge*, surrounded by no less than four enemy ships, not knowing the meaning of the word surrender. If there was a fight to be had, *Revenge* would fight it, whatever the damage she had sustained.

This same spirit was evident throughout the British fleet. Although British ships, and especially the first ones in each column, sustained considerable damage, they meted out two or three times what they received and the enemy were often sent reeling. The rate of fire was such that, as Robinson tells us: 'as to hearing, the noise of the guns had so completely made us deaf, that we were obliged to look only to the motions that were made.'[11]

The superb gunnery on the British ships inexorably wore down the enemy. Well-trained gun crews aided by advanced flintlock mechanisms fired at a greater rate than their opponents, and kept firing, no matter how seriously damaged the ship was. Captain Jean-Jacques Magendie of the *Bucentaure* noted afterwards:

From the nature of the attack that the enemy delivered there could not help resulting a pele-mele battle, and the series of ship-to-ship actions that ensued were fought out with the most noble devotion. The enemy had the advantage of us, owing to his powerful ships, seven of which were three-deckers, the smallest mounting 114 guns (sic), in weight of metal of his heavy guns and carronades; and in the smartness with which his ships were handled, due to three years' experience at sea a form of training which, of course, had been impossible for the Combined Fleet.[12]

It was significant that the two most heavily damaged ships in the British fleet were the ones sailed by the two British admirals, Nelson and Collingwood. *Royal Sovereign* and *Victory* led their respective lines and both received the brunt of the initial enemy response. *Victory* was the most heavily damaged and sustained the most casualties, with fifty-seven dead, including Nelson himself, and 102 wounded. Collingwood's *Royal Sovereign* was close behind with forty-seven dead and 100 wounded, including Collingwood himself, who received a gash in his leg.

This was the British way of battle, where officers led from the front and set an example that others might follow. A Spanish admiral later expressed his admiration for the habit of initiative displayed by the British, which contrasted with the somewhat hidebound attitude of the French and Spanish:

An Englishman enters a naval action with a firm conviction that his duty is to hurt his enemies, and help his friends and allies, without looking out for directions in the midst of the fight; and while he thus clears his mind of all subsidiary distractions, he rests in confidence on the certainty that his comrades, actuated by the same principles as himself, will be bound by the sacred and priceless law of mutual support. Accordingly, both he and all his fellows fix their minds on acting with zeal and judgment upon the spur of the moment, and with the certainty that they will not be deserted. Experience shows, on the contrary, that a Frenchman or a Spaniard, working under a system which leans to formality and strict order being maintained in battle, has no feeling for mutual support, and goes into action with hesitation, preoccupied with the anxiety of seeing or hearing the commander-in-chief's signals for such and such manoeuvres ... Thus they can never make up their minds to seize any favourable opportunity that may present itself. They are fettered by the strict rule to keep station, which is enforced upon them in both navies; and the usual result is that in one place ten of their ships may be firing upon four, while in another four of their comrades may be receiving the fire of ten of the enemy. Worst of all, they are denied the confidence inspired by mutual support, which is as surely maintained by the English as it is neglected by us.[13]

The criticism was a general truth but it did not apply to all French and Spanish officers. Some in particular were excellent, including Captain Lucas of the *Redoutable*, whose effective training regime for his men led to the death of Nelson.

The truth of the Spanish admiral's opinion is probably best evidenced in Nelson's own words: 'That his Admirals and captains, knowing his precise object to be that of a close and decisive action, would supply any deficiency of signals, and act accordingly. In case signals cannot be seen or clearly understood, no captain can do wrong if he places his ship alongside that of an enemy.'[14]

Back on *Revenge*, they fought off their enemies with the aid of *Dreadnought* and *Thunderer* which had come to their assistance and set about repairing the significant damage sustained by the ship. Enough was done in the short term to allow her to tow a Spanish prize.

> We were now enabled to get at some of the shot-holes between wind and water, and plug them up; this is a duty performed by the carpenter and his crew. We were now unable to work the ship, our yards, sails, and masts being disabled, and the braces completely shot away. In this condition we lay by the side of the enemy, firing away, and now and then we received a good raking from them, passing under our stern. This was a busy time with us, for we had not only to endeavour to repair our damage, but to keep to our duty. Often during the battle we could not see for the smoke, whether we were firing at foe or friend, and as to hearing, the noise of the guns had so completely made us deaf, that we were obliged to look only to the motions that were made. In this manner we continued the battle till nearly five o'clock, when it ceased.[15]

Following Admiral Collingwood's orders, as many survivors, both friend and foe, were rescued as possible before they made their way to Gibraltar. One of these was a Frenchwoman, who caused something of a stir, as related by a lieutenant of the *Revenge*:

> Towards the conclusion of the battle the French 80-gun ship Achille, after surrendering, caught fire on the booms. The poor fellows belonging to her, as the only chance of saving their lives,

leaped overboard, having first stripped off their clothes, that they might be the better able to swim to any pieces of floating wreck or to the boats of the ships sent by those nearest at hand to their rescue. As the boats filled, they proceeded to the Pickle schooner, and, after discharging their freight into that vessel, returned for more. The schooner was soon crowded to excess, and, therefore, transferred the poor shivering wretches to any of the large ships near her. The Revenge, to which ship I belonged, received nearly a hundred of the number, some of whom had been picked up by our own boats. Many of them were badly wounded, and all naked. No time was lost for providing for the latter want, as the purser was ordered immediately to issue to each man a complete suit of clothes.

On the morning after the action I had charge of the deck, the other officers and crew being at breakfast, when another boat load of these poor prisoners of war came alongside, all of whom, with one exception, were in the costume of Adam. The exception I refer to was apparently a youth, but clothed in an old jacket and trousers, with a dingy handkerchief tied round the head, and exhibiting a face begrimed with smoke and dirt, without shoes, stockings, or shirt, and looking the picture of misery and despair. The appearance of this young person at once attracted my attention, and on asking some questions on the subject, I was answered that the prisoner was a woman. It was sufficient to know this, and I lost no time in introducing her to my messmates, as a female requiring their compassionate attention. The poor creature was almost famishing with hunger, having tasted nothing for four-and-twenty hours, consequently she required no persuasion to partake of the breakfast upon the table. I then gave her up my cabin, for by this time the bulk-head had been replaced, and made a collection of all the articles which could be procured to enable her to complete a more suitable wardrobe ... altogether, our guest, which we unanimously voted her, appeared a very interesting young woman.

'Jeannette', which was the only name by which I ever knew her, thus related to me the circumstances. She said she was stationed during the action in the passage of the fore-magazine, to assist in handing up the powder, which employment lasted till the surrender of the ship. When the firing ceased, she ascended to the lower deck, and endeavoured to get up to the main deck, to search for her husband, but the ladders having been all removed, or shot away, she found this impracticable; and just at this time an alarm of fire spread through the ship, so that she could get no assistance. The fire originated upon the upper deck, and gradually burnt downwards. Her feelings upon this occasion cannot be described: but death from all quarters stared her in the face. The fire, which soon burnt fiercely, precluded the possibility of her escaping by moving from where she was, and no friendly counsellor was by with whom to advise. She remained wandering to and fro upon the lower deck, among the mangled corpses of the dying and the slain, until the guns from the main deck actually fell through the burnt planks. Her only refuge, then, was the sea, and the poor creature scrambled out of the gun-room port, and, by the help of the rudder chains, reached the back of the rudder, where she remained for some time, praying that the ship might blow up, and thus put a period to her misery. At length the lead which lined the rudder-trunk began to melt, and to fall upon her, and her only means of avoiding this was to leap overboard. Having, therefore, divested herself of her clothes, she soon found herself struggling with the waves, and providentially finding a piece of cork, she was enabled to escape from the burning mass. A man, shortly afterwards, swam near her, and, observing her distress, brought her a piece of plank, about six feet in length, which, being placed under her arms, supported her until a boat approached to her rescue ...

Although placed in a position of unlooked-for comfort, Jeannette was scarcely less miserable; the fate of her husband was unknown to her ... It was on about the fourth day of her sojourn that she came to me in the greatest possible ecstacy and told me that she had found her husband, who was on board among the prisoners, and unhurt. She soon afterwards brought him to me, and in the most grateful terms and manner returned her thanks for the attentions she had received ... On leaving the ship, most, if not all of us, gave her a dollar, and she expressed her thanks as well as she was able, and assured us that the name of our ship would always be remembered by her with the warmest gratitude.[16]

William Robinson relates that on *Revenge* a popular member of the crew was saved from an untimely death while an unpopular midshipman met an untimely end. The first was the ship's cobbler who, concussed in battle, was taken for dead and would have been thrown overboard if he had not started kicking at the last moment. He joked later that it was his dancing steps that saved him. The other was a tyrannical midshipman who enjoyed beating the men manning the guns and who was literally splattered against the sides by enemy grape shot.[17]

As *Revenge* towed its Spanish prize towards Gibraltar, it became clear that she was too badly damaged to make the voyage. English seamen went aboard to rescue as many of the Spanish crew as they could but some had to be left to their fate.

Having arrived at Gibraltar, *Revenge* received urgent repairs to make her seaworthy for the long voyage back to England and the men also had the opportunity to go on shore to celebrate the success and compare notes with crews of other ships. She then set sail for England, arriving at Spithead where crowds were waiting to cheer her in. The news of the battle had by now spread nationwide.

Chapter 10

Basque Roads

The following year, Robert Moorsom was succeeded as captain by Charles Elphinstone Fleming, who had not fought at Trafalgar and who immediately made himself unpopular with his new crew by ordering the ship to be repainted. *Revenge* had been painted in a yellow and black chequered livery ordered by Nelson to distinguish his ships in battle. This was now regarded by the crew as something equivalent to a battle honour and to have to paint it over was adding insult to injury, as Fleming was a tryrannical disciplinarian. Unlike Moorsom, he had never fought in battle. The story has a happy ending, however, as before she was redeployed, Fleming was in turn replaced by another captain who immediately returned *Revenge* to its original Trafalgar colour scheme.

Revenge was then deployed to blockade Bordeaux and Rochefort. William Robinson describes a night when twenty men set off in a pinnace with muffled oars to enter Bordeaux harbour and attempt to cut out one of the merchantmen there. However, the enemy were alerted and opened fire. A lieutenant and one of the sailors were killed in *Revenge*'s pinnace and the boat eventually sank, the survivors becoming prisoners of the French. Boats from other British ships succeeded in capturing one French gun brig but otherwise the operation had to be abandoned.

On another occasion five French frigates came out of Rochefort after dark, headed for the West Indies. *Revenge* and the rest of the squadron gave chase and soon caught up with the French ships, four of which were captured.

After being caught in a fierce storm in which she was almost lost, *Revenge* returned to England. Having refitted, *Revenge* sailed back for blockade duties off Cadiz where the situation was somewhat confused. The governor of the town was in league with the French but was lynched by a local mob. The French ships in the port then came under fire from the Spanish shore batteries. *Revenge* was ordered to take Spanish representatives back to England and set sail again. They also carried with them a Spanish friar who had escaped from the monasteries desecrated by the French. As a result of the representations of these Spaniards to the British Government, an army was sent out to Spain under Sir John Moore. Eventually another British army would land in Portugal under Arthur Wellesley.

After a spell of rest and recreation, which included boat loads of women being brought on board to entertain the sailors, the new captain joined the ship and it was back on station with the Channel fleet blockading the French port of Brest.

In February 1808, Robinson relates that, while sailing alone, *Revenge* came upon eight French ships of the line apparently making for the West Indies, filled with provisions. *Revenge* was also laden with provisions for the relief of the blockading squadron. The French squadron had seized the opportunity to put to sea on 21 February when westerly gales drove Admiral Gambier's squadron away from its watching position at Ushant. The French might have got away unseen had not *Revenge*, then commanded by Captain Charles Paget, been away on other duties. Having warned the other British ships, *Revenge* continued to shadow the French squadron until about 12.30, when she temporarily lost the scent, picking it up again at about 3 o'clock in the afternoon.

The orders of the French Admiral Willaumez were that on his journey south he should attempt to chase away the British ships guarding the port of Lorient, allowing the Lorient squadron to join him as he headed south for Rochefort. Once he had reached his destination, Willaumez would take with him whatever vessels were available at the port and cross the Atlantic to Martinique which was thought to be in danger of imminent attack by the British.

Now part of Beresford's squadron, *Revenge*, along with *Theseus*, *Triumph* and *Valiant*, headed towards Willaumez in a westerly direction. The squadrons lost sight of each other for a while and the French arrived off the Île Groix, opposite the port of Lorient, at about 6 p.m.

The next morning Willaumez sent word to the French ships in Lorient before continuing his journey south, with the British in sight and giving chase. The French sailed past Saint-Nazaire and towards the Île d'Yeu. Here they were spotted by the *Amethyst* and by the 24th they had entered Basque roads, adjacent to the mouth of the Charente River.

Further north, three French 40-gun frigates left Lorient and were chased by the frigate *Amelia* and the brig-sloop *Dotterel*. To the south was the squadron commanded by Admiral Stopford. The French frigates took refuge under the batteries of Sable d'Olonne whereupon Stopford's squadron attacked them. Two of the French frigates cut their cables and were washed onto the shore, soon followed by the third one. All three French frigates subsequently became wrecks.

After this action, Admiral Stopford's squadron sailed south to join the blockade of the Basque roads where the Brest squadron was anchored roughly south of the Île d'Aix. When Stopford's squadron of eight ships was joined by Gambier's five, the British had a total force of thirteen against the enemy's nine, although two British ships then departed.

Meanwhile, the Admiralty in London had called on the dashing Lord Cochrane whom they considered well qualified to deal with the trapped French squadron. When interviewed by the Admiralty, which considered that a fireship attack might be the best option in the circumstances, Cochrane pointed out that fireships on their own would not be enough to defeat the French squadron, especially as a reasonably alert enemy would have boats out, ready to tow away any fireships. Cochrane was confident, however, that a fireship attack accompanied by force of rocket ships and bomb vessels would have a high chance of success, especially as the French gun batteries on the Île d'Aix were relatively ineffective.

Impressed by Cochrane, the Admiralty ordered him to join Gambier and made it plain that they wanted him to be at the forefront of the attack. Cochrane was cautious about this, however. He must have sensed that the politics of his position could be tricky and in this he proved to be correct. But the Admiralty, and Lord Musgrove in particular, would not take no for an answer and Cochrane duly sailed south in the frigate *Imperieuse* to take part in a battle that was to prove at best controversial.

Cochrane arrived at Rochefort on the morning of 3 April 1809 and went straight across to meet Admiral Lord Gambier on his flagship *Caledonia*. Gambier was regarded in the fleet as overly pompous and pious and, although he had proved himself a competent naval officer at the battles of the Glorious First of June and Copenhagen, he was not made of the same stuff as the firebrand Cochrane.

Under orders from the Admiralty itself and with both the experience and confidence to undertake the mission, Cochrane was now to run into an admiral becalmed both by doubts and by faulty intelligence. Whereas the Admiralty and Cochrane realized that fireships might prove to be a useful tactical option, Gambier was apprehensive; whereas Cochrane's assessment of enemy batteries on the Île d'Aix was that they did not pose a major threat, they loomed large in Gambier's mind, along with a host of other reservations, including shoals.

Gambier had written a letter to the Admiralty which reveals something of his nervous state of mind:

> The enemy's ships are anchored in two straight lines, very near each other, in a direction due south from the Île d'Aix, and the ships in each line not further apart than their own length; by which it appears as I imagined, that the space for their anchorage is so confined by the shoaliness of the water, as not to admit of ships to run in and anchor clear of each other. The most distant ships of their line are within point-blank shot of the works on the Île d'Aix; such ships, therefore, as might attack the enemy would be exposed to be raked by red-hot shot, etc, from the island, and should the ships be disabled in their masts, they must remain within range of the enemy's fire until they are destroyed – there not being sufficient depth of water to allow them to move to the southward out of distance.[1]

Cochrane handed Gambier a letter from the Admiralty in which their Lordships made it abundantly clear that they wished Cochrane to command the fireship attack, although at that stage some of the fireships, along with rocket and bomb vessels, were still assembling at the Downs.

Although the letter did not create any immediate friction with Gambier himself, the superimposition of the young 'upstart' Cochrane over the heads of other senior officers in the squadron caused, as

Cochrane had predicted, ructions among some of those officers, notably Admiral Harvey. Harvey lost his temper with Gambier and made it plain that he would not brook having a junior officer taking command of a major attack over his head. Harvey then stormed out to vent his opinion as to Gambier's failings as a commander to Cochrane, and to anyone else within earshot. As a result, Harvey was sent back to England to be court-martialled.

Despite the fact that his predictions as to the politics of his unexpected promotion over the heads of superior officers had proved true, Cochrane was not deterred by the noises off and continued with the planning for the attack. At first light he set out to discover for himself the state of the enemy dispositions and the lie of the land. As Cochrane had already surmised, the gun batteries in the Île d'Aix were not a real threat. Although some were operational, many were out of action. Those that could fire would barely be able to find the range to pose a real threat. Cochrane took the precaution of firing at the French ships to gauge their reaction and, again, the result was encouraging. The English would, he reckoned, have substantial room to manoeuvre while remaining out of range of enemy fire.

Having been given his orders by the highest naval authority, and having assured himself that the way was comparatively clear, Cochrane lost no time. Rather than wait for the fireships to arrive, he began preparing transport ships from the fleet for the task. Cochrane also personally supervised the fitting of the bomb vessels. These vessels were filled with barrels of gunpowder with fuses that were long enough to allow those sailing them to get out of harm's way. By the time reinforcements from England had arrived on 10 April, Cochrane had twenty fireships at his disposal.

The French ships were moored in a staggered line, facing northwards and near them, across the channel from Basque to Aix roads, there was a boom formed of cables hung from buoys secured to the seabed by anchors, which were, at 5¼ tons, heavier than the heaviest anchor in the Royal Navy.[2] The French batteries numbered about thirty guns, most of which were 36-pounders.[3] There were shoals on both the northern and southern ends of the Île d'Aix.

At about 8.30 p.m. on 11 April, the fireships were set loose, accompanied by two bomb vessels, one of which was commanded by Cochrane himself. Each of these vessels was loaded with about 1,500 barrels of gunpowder, as well as about 400 shells and as many more grenades.

As the fireships approached the French squadron, some were ignited too early, but the *Mediator* successfully crossed the French boom, clearing a path for others. The bomb vessels, however, were slowed by the boom, which diminished the effect of their explosions. Like a massive firework display, however, the visual effects outweighed the actual damage. A particularly inky dark night exploded with rockets, tongues of fire and looming ships ablaze. The effect on the French was devastating.

The French frigates cut their cables and scrambled to the rear of the line of French battleships. As the fireships descended among them, the other French ships also cut their cables and desperately tried to manhandle the fireships away. As a result of cutting their cables, almost the entire French squadron ran aground. The crews took frantic remedies to try to refloat their vessels, including throwing all the guns overboard, but some could not be saved.

Despite the fact that it was apparent as dawn came that the French squadron was mostly stranded and helpless, a series of signals from Admiral Gambier caused the British ships to pull away into deeper water, and by midday no action had been taken by the British against what were in effect sitting ducks. At length Gambier ordered Captain Bligh to take *Revenge*, *Bellona* and *Valiant*, along with some frigates and sloops, to support the bomb vessel *Aetna* and the gun-brigs *Insolent*, *Conflict* and *Growler*, which were to attempt to finish off the stranded French ships.

The tide by now was coming in and the French ships, having made all necessary efforts to refloat themselves, began to get under way. They headed for refuge further up the Charente River, though some grounded on the shoals at the entrance. Lord Cochrane, seeing the enemy getting away, moved closer in the *Imperieuse* to intercept those that were still grounded and opened fire on the *Calcutta*, *Aquilon* and *Varsovie*. As *Imperieuse* was clearly outnumbered, Gambier ordered *Revenge*, *Valiant* and the frigate *Indefatigable* to go to her aid. Once these ships arrived, a heavy fire was unleashed on the French. The French ship *Calcutta* had already surrendered and the other two soon followed. The British did, however, sustain casualties, the *Revenge* losing one seaman and two marines, with others mortally or seriously wounded. *Revenge* also suffered a considerable amount of structural damage, including to rigging, sails and hull. The damage was sustained not only by fire from the two French ships but also from the batteries on the Île d'Aix. *Revenge* had come close to the French battleship *Ocean* but the water was too shallow for her to position herself for an effective broadside.

When *Revenge* and the other ships had moved to deeper water by 8 p.m., some transports were prepared for conversion to fireships in an attempt to finish off the remaining French ships. At 5 a.m. *Valiant*, *Theseus* and *Revenge* set sail towards the Charente and at 8 a.m. Lord Cochrane sent the bomb vessel and brigs against the remaining grounded French ships. The *Beagle* came close to *Ocean* and fired upon her for five hours.

Four of the French ships managed to refloat and head further up the Charente, while the French battleships *Ocean* and *Tourville* remained grounded close to the mouth of the river. By 3.50 a.m. on the 16th, *Ocean* had also managed to free herself and get to safety. By the 17th, both the *Foudroyant* and *Tourville* had escaped up-river. By the 29th, the last stranded French ship, the *Regulus*, had also got herself afloat and up-river to safety.

Back in England, Admiral Gambier appeared before a court-martial to answer the charge that he 'did, for a considerable time, neglect or delay taking effectual measures for destroying' the enemy's ships. Despite being 'honourably acquitted' of this charge, some were inclined to the view, with hindsight, that more could have been done earlier and that if this had happened most of the French squadron would have been destroyed.

The action at Rochefort was far from glorious, though the intervention of *Revenge* patched up what was becoming a shambles. The British had failed to tackle their enemy head on and the French had been in a state of near panic. Not much was lost on the British side, however, and French morale took another hammering. Although the British had been tested by the escape of the French fleet from Brest – another fleet had escaped almost simultaneously from Toulon – the action at Rochefort underscored British naval dominance.

Chapter 11

From Portugal to the Adriatic

Once she had refitted and repaired the damage done to her by the French batteries, *Revenge* was allocated to support a secret military expedition against Walcheren on 30 July. *Revenge* took troops on board and sailed with another forty ships of the line in addition to a variety of other ships and craft of all sizes. The military element consisted of about 40,000 soldiers and 15,000 horses, along with field artillery and two siege trains.

One member of this expedition was a young Captain of the 95th Rifles (2nd Battalion of the Rifle Brigade) by the name of John Kincaid. In his celebrated book, *Adventures in the Rifle Brigade*, Kincaid tells us how he arrived at Deal with a 'donkey-load of pistols in my belt',[1] possibly an indication of his apprehension. Kincaid was embarked first upon the frigate *Hussar* and then the 74, *Namur*, which took them to the island of South Beveland. Kincaid was among many who were victims of what Robinson calls an 'ague', which became known as 'Walcheren fever', but which was in fact malaria. Although Kincaid survived, at least 4,000 British troops died, only 106 of whom lost their lives in combat.

The task of the Navy was to destroy the French fleet which was thought to have been at Flushing. Although the British captured Flushing, poor co-ordination between the Navy and the Army allowed the French to escape upstream to Antwerp.

Captain John Kincaid returned to Scotland after this disaster in order to recover from his illness. He was then posted to join Wellington in Portugal where he would write one of the most celebrated personal accounts of the Peninsular War. Like many of the soldiers who had been through the Walcheren experience, the malarial disease continued to dog him for years to come:

I cannot shake off that celebrated Walcheren fever without mentioning what may or may not be a peculiarity in it – that a brother-officer and I experienced a return of it within a day of each other, after a lapse of five years, and again, within a week, after the lapse of the following three years.[2]

William Robinson recounts that, after *Revenge* returned from the Walcheren expedition at Christmas 1809 there was little sense of satisfaction among the crew. This had not been a noble feat of arms and indeed Dutch civilians had taunted them for doing little more than destroying the houses of local citizens.

Revenge was soon back on station in the Channel, this time watching the port of Cherbourg. At one point she went in pursuit of a French frigate near the batteries of La Hogue and as a result received a severe raking of fire.

In Spain and Portugal, the comparatively small British army was making its presence felt, though it was still not powerful enough to deal a decisive blow. Arthur Wellesley had advanced into Spain and defeated the French at Talavera (27–28 July 1810) but he was not able to push through to Madrid. The British army then retreated to Portugal, followed by Marshal Massena, though they dealt a stinging temporary defeat on the French on the ridge of Bussaco (27 September 1810) before continuing the retreat to Lisbon. As they went, they laid waste to the countryside and villages around them in a deliberate scorched-earth policy and evacuated the local population of about 200,000. This, however, was not a sign of desperation and this was not an army in headlong flight. Wellington, as he now was, had predicted this eventuality over a year before and had ordered Colonel Richard Fletcher of the Royal Engineers to construct a line of about 152 fortresses and redoubts, making best use of the natural features of a series of high rounded hills extending from the small town of Torres Vedras near the west coast, across to the Tagus River to the east. The sea and flanks were protected by Royal Navy vessels. The 'lines', as they came to be called, were largely manned by Portuguese militia and British marines and artillerymen, while first-line troops were ready to intervene where required.

The lines of Torres Vedras were an extraordinary engineering achievement and one can only imagine the reaction of Marshal

Massena as he first came upon them. French map-making was not of a high standard at that time and Massena may have been unfamiliar with the local geography. He was to discover that there were enemy forces perched on almost every hill in carefully constructed redoubts and with accurately enfiladed artillery. All the tree and scrub cover had been cleared and every valley was either filled with obstacles or had been flooded, in addition to being covered by deadly firepower. The Portuguese *Ordenança*, or 'militia', were roaming around the countryside, waiting to pick off any Frenchmen who strayed in small enough groups. The countryside had been methodically cleared of anything that might pass for a square meal.

As Wellington had predicted, Massena could neither attack without losing a large part of his force nor stay for long without his men starving or morale plummeting. By 14 November, Massena had had enough and began his retreat. The tide had turned.

Despite his tactical success, Wellington was always short of resources and *Revenge* was despatched in 1811 to disembark fresh troops at Lisbon. Among these was a Private William Wheeler of the 51st Foot, who, like Kincaid, would record his experiences in a memoir. Wheeler comments on the high standards he found aboard *Revenge* and on the concern that Captain Nash showed for his crew. This was in marked contrast to the behaviour of some of the captains William Robinson had served under. However Admiral Strachan, who commanded the Channel fleet, for all that he was terse by nature, was also well liked as the men knew that beneath the tough exterior he had their best interests at heart.[3] Admiral Collingwood was also well meaning and took the view that if the men were happily occupied, albeit the work was hard, they would be less inclined to what Saint Benedict has described as 'murmuring'.

The fact that seamen such as William Robinson and privates such as William Wheeler could write so vividly about their experiences was a sign in itself that the world was changing. Education was making even the humblest aware of their circumstances and able to write about them. They had also demonstrated their ability to influence events by uniting in mutiny when maltreatment went too far.

The tradition of flogging was a vicious one and William Robinson takes care to describe it in grisly detail. A man could be almost literally flayed alive by the vicious cat-o'-nine-tails and some died of their wounds. Some floggings included twenty-five lashes on each ship present by way of example to the others. Instilling fear by degrading a particular offender was seen to be an effective way of maintaining discipline.

By October 1813, Wellington's army had pursued the French as far as Bayonne and the Royal Navy continued to harry the French Navy wherever it could find it. The French brig-corvette *Flibustier*, for example, anchored near Bayonne, did not have much choice but to put to sea, filled with armaments and provisions for the French garrison at Santana. She was almost immediately spotted, however, by the British schooner *Telegraph* (Lieutenant Timothy Scriven), the 18-gun brig sloop *Challenger* (Captain Frederick Vernon) and the 12-gun brig *Constant* (Lieutenant John Stokes). Although the *Flibustier* sought protection from some shore batteries, the *Telegraph* came within close enough range to fire a broadside which persuaded the French crew to abandon their ship and to set fire to it.

This continual watch on the Spanish and French coasts meant that the French forces could barely move by sea without being spotted and marines being landed to destroy enemy batteries and other fortifications.

On 2 May 1813, the *Repulse* landed a force of 100 marines, to combine with marine detachments from *Volontaire* and *Undaunted*, to destroy new enemy fortifications near Marignon. The marines attacked and held back local enemy forces while boats were sent out to capture enemy vessels. The guns in the enemy batteries were destroyed.[4]

The 38-gun frigate *Bachante* – commanded by Captain William Hoste, who hailed, like Nelson, from Norfolk – and its marine detachment under Lieutenant Hood, made their presence felt, capturing gunboats near Cape Otranto and forcing the enemy battery at Karlbego to surrender. Off the coast of Gela-Nova, marines despatched from *Bachante* under Lieutenant Hood took on seven large gunboats, three smaller gun vessels and fourteen armed merchant vessels, which were backed up by enemy forces on land. The marines pressed home the attack, captured the enemy shipping and forced the enemy troops on the nearby beach to surrender. Two British seamen and one marine were killed.

Under the command of Rear Admiral Thomas Fremantle, *Bachante* and other ships attacked the town of Fiume, forcing the garrison of about 350 to retreat and capturing about ninety vessels.

The *Revenge* was also involved in this inshore naval warfare in the Adriatic, which bears so much resemblance to the exploits of what would later be called the Commandos in the Second World War. On 8 November 1813, *Revenge*, by now commanded by Captain Sir John Gore, sent boats under Lieutenant William Richards and Captain of Marines John Spurin into the harbour of Palamos to attempt the capture of a French felucca privateer. They set out under cover of darkness at about 8.30 p.m. and reached the felucca at 11 p.m. Having boarded the enemy vessel, they brought her back to *Revenge*, which they reached at about 1 a.m.

Revenge continued with her duties and after the end of the Napoleonic Wars and the defeat of Napoleon the Royal Navy continued its work of endless patrols, and both major and minor actions. There was a substantial naval presence in the Mediterranean and the Navy took the responsibility of dealing with pirates whenever it could find them. The pirate base of Algiers was attacked by the Royal Navy in 1815 and, temporarily at least, brought to heel. The Battle of Navarino in 1827 resulted in the defeat of Turkish and Egyptian navies by the Royal Navy, which bore the brunt of the battle, though French and Russian ships assisted the British later in the day.

When Mehemet Ali Pasha of Egypt seized Syria from Turkey, the British came to the aid of Turkey and provided arms for rebels against Egyptian rule in Lebanon. The next target was Acre, where Admiral Stopford began a bombardment on 3 November 1840. *Revenge*, along with *Rodney*, *Cambridge*, *Carysfort*, *Medea* and *Vanguard*, had previously been detached to blockade Alexandria to prevent Egyptian vessels from sailing to relieve Acre. Then, with the support of *Revenge*, the British squadron destroyed the batteries at Acre, the success of the operation being partly due to a fortunate misalignment of the enemy's guns.

This demonstration by the British of accurate gunnery against shore targets underlined the range and effectiveness of the Navy and its deterrent influence.

The new *Revenge*, launched on 16 April 1859 at Pembroke Dockyard, was a Second Rate two-decker with a wooden hull. She had a displacement of 5,260 tons, was 245 feet in length and carried 91 guns. What distinguished her from her predecessors was that she had the option of screw propulsion. The new *Revenge* represented a navy in a state of fundamental transformation. The days of sail were almost over and the shape and means of propulsion of new ships demonstrated the advances achieved by the Industrial Revolution.

The new *Revenge* was built at Pembroke in Wales by the firm of Maudslay, Sons, and Field. Henry Maudslay (1771–1831) had been employed by Marc Isambard Brunel (1769–1849) to build machines to manufacture ships' blocks. Maudslay later took an interest in the development of marine steam engines, but his greatest contribution was to be in the design of precision machines that could be used to create other machines, such as steam engines. His attention to detail and insistence on high-quality materials demonstrated that British industrial strength was built on virtues of attention to detail and quality that later were to become associated with German manufacturing. The engineers who were apprenticed under Maudslay maintained his standards. Henry Maudslay's son, Joseph (1801–1861) followed his father's example and was responsible for manufacturing the first steam engine used by the Royal Navy.

The Admiralty had used a number of paddle steamers which proved popular for inshore actions and by 1836 a successful design for a screw was being developed. The *Ratler* was fitted both with a screw and a Maudslay steam engine, and trials demonstrated to the Admiralty that the screw had several advantages, one being that the paddles of a paddle steamer were far more vulnerable to damage from enemy attack.

Pembroke Dockyard superseded Milford Haven as a shipbuilding establishment from about 1815. Apart from building *Revenge*, it would be famous for building such historic ships as the *Dreadnought* and *Empress of India*. Pembroke remained a viable shipyard by adapting to the rapid changes that were taking place at the time as hulls changed from wood to iron, and later from iron to steel, as propulsion changed from paddles to screws and from sail power to steam-engine power. Although the building of the *Dreadnought* was an epic achievement for the yard, it also proved its limitations and it only survived into the early 1920s by building a smattering of smaller vessels. Although Milford Haven was used as a flying-boat base for the RAF during the Second World War, the great days of shipbuilding were over in the region.

In the same year that *Revenge* was launched, Isaac Watts, naval architect and chief constructor, designed the *Warrior*, the British response to the French armoured warship *Gloire*. Having gained naval mastery by defeating the French at Trafalgar in 1805, the British were not going to sit back and concede technical mastery at the noon of empire. The *Warrior* effectively knocked *Gloire* into a cocked hat. It was an all-iron ship, about a third larger than *Gloire*, with about double the horsepower and a significant advantage in speed. It carried more and bigger guns. The *Warrior* carried technically advanced armour which resolved the problem of vital bolts failing under impact.

Watts had been involved with the development of the screw battleship and had taken wooden battleships to almost unimaginable lengths. Having reached the limit of wood construction, it was appropriate that Watts should design the ground-breaking, all-iron *Warrior*.

The Crimean War (1854–1856) now over, the new *Revenge* sailed into a period of relative peace. After she was commissioned at Plymouth in 1861, she became the flagship of Rear Admiral Robert Smart in the Channel Squadron, carrying out duties familiar to her ancestors. Later she was to serve in the Mediterranean and otherwise saw duty as far afield as the Mediterranean and Queenstown, County Cork, Ireland.

Chapter 12

Dawn of a New Age

The next *Revenge* was built at Jarrow in 1892. She was part of a new design concept for battleships known as the Royal Sovereign class which came about in the context of concern about Britain's ability to maintain its maritime supremacy in certain areas. The Prime Minister, Lord Salisbury, taking into account the possibility of powers such as France and Russia combining their fleets against England, adopted the two-power standard whereby the Royal Navy should be equal to the next two powers combined. The Naval Defence Act of 1889 allocated £21 million to a massive overhaul of Royal Naval assets, which included the building of ten new battleships, forty-two cruisers and eighteen other vessels. The Act would underline British supremacy but, just over a decade before the beginning of the twentieth century, it also demonstrated the lengths to which Britain had to go to maintain that supremacy.

The main architect of the new Royal Sovereign class of battleships was Sir William Henry White (1845–1913). White had been apprenticed as a shipwright in Devonport, where he had been born, and moved from there to the new Royal School of Naval Architecture and Marine Engineering in South Kensington. He was appointed to the Admiralty at a time when the transformation was taking place from wooden to iron hulls, which gave White the opportunity to study in detail the issues surrounding the introduction of new materials.

After leaving the Admiralty to join Armstrong & Co. in 1883, White returned in 1885 when he was appointed Director of Naval Construction. In 1888, the characteristics of the new Royal Sovereign class were decided. They were ships with a relatively high freeboard and with guns mounted on barbettes. They were equipped with 18in armour and, despite the weight of both armament and armour, they proved to be highly seaworthy.

The guns were manned by thirty-one men, including eight men to man the gun itself, eight in each of the two magazines and seven in the shell room. The guns in the barbettes demonstrated in themselves the extent of engineering mastery required for modern naval warfare. Each gun took over eighteen months to manufacture at Woolwich Arsenal and cost approximately £13,500.

Although the guns were not as highly visible on these ships as on the subsequent Dreadnought-class battleships, and although the superstructure and paint scheme gave them the look of a cruise ship, these were the most powerful battleships afloat in their time. They were also extremely fast.

In 1896, *Revenge* was commissioned at Portsmouth as the flagship of Rear Admiral A.T. Dale who commanded the Special Flying Squadron. This unit was created in response to raised tension following the Jameson Raid (29 December 1895 to 2 January 1896) in which Leander Starr Jameson had led a force of Rhodesian and Bechuanaland policemen on a raid into the Boer Transvaal republic led by Paul Kruger. Tension between the British and Dutch Boer community had been simmering ever since the British had taken control of the Cape during the Napoleonic Wars, and from 1828 when the British authorities passed legislation that stated that everyone, regardless of race, was equal under the law.

Following the Jameson Raid, the German Emperor, Wilhelm II, sent a telegram of support to Paul Kruger which immediately raised tension in Europe, precipitating talk of war. It was perhaps the first cloud on the horizon that would warn of the impending Great War eighteen years later.

A sister ship of HMS *Revenge* in the Special Flying Squadron was HMS *Royal Oak*, also launched in 1892 and commissioned in 1896.

In 1897, *Revenge* was deployed to Crete with an International Squadron to intervene in a rebellion which was part of the Greco-Turkish war. *Revenge* helped to impose a blockade on supplies from the mainland and also landed a detachment of Royal Marines on the island.

The Special Flying Squadron, which was briefly attached to the Mediterranean fleet, was stood down in November 1896. It had demonstrated the continuing deterrent power of the Royal Navy and the formidable power of the Royal Sovereign class of pre-Dreadnought battleships. While Britain was to become heavily involved in the Boer War, however, where she would learn painful lessons of a military nature, the threat of the industrial power of Germany continued to grow. In 1898, Germany made explicit her intention to considerably increase the size of her fleet, which meant that Britain was faced with maintaining a larger home fleet than she had previously envisaged.

Although the Royal Sovereign-class *Revenge* was to be overtaken by a revolutionary new warship design, she went out with a growl rather than a whimper. In October 1914, she was recalled from retirement in order to bombard troops in Flanders, her guns having been relined for the purpose. She returned to bombard the coast in December 1914 and in September 1915 to considerable effect.

Despite the success of her design, *Revenge* and the other ships of her class were soon to be rendered effectively obsolete by a revolutionary new warship, HMS *Dreadnought*, which was laid down in October 1905 and launched in 1906.

The development of the *Dreadnought* owed much to the influence of Admiral of the Fleet John Arbuthnot Fisher (1841–1920). Fisher saw the need for a flexible approach to the Navy's challenges, encompassing not only big-gun battleships but also submarines and fast super-cruisers. Ironically, although Fisher thought that the age of the big battleship was over, at least for close-quarter engagements in home waters, he was to preside over the development of a battleship that would prove to be the standard for all those preceding it, by putting them in the shade, and for all those to come, by setting the benchmark from which they could be developed. Fisher set up a Committee of Designs which came up with the revolutionary Dreadnought concept.

The main difference between the *Dreadnought* and the Royal Sovereign class, of which the current *Revenge* was part, was that the *Dreadnought* was designed as an all big-gun ship, whereas *Revenge*'s armoury was distributed between her big barbettes and secondary armament consisting of a range of 6in, 6pdr and 3pdr guns. One advantage of a uniform big-gun design, although it did not provide as many options at short ranges, was that it made the system of fire control much easier to handle, as calculations could be made more speedily and accurately for guns of a similar type. In addition, the restricted options due to lack of secondary armament were to a large extent cancelled out by improvements in the speed of firing of more technologically advanced guns. The first *Dreadnought* could fire fifteen rounds per minute of 850lb (385.6kg) shells at any enemy, whether near or far. Despite these advances in firepower, however, a predictive gunnery control system as originally devised by Arthur Pollen was not developed to its full potential, which led to unfortunate failings in British gunnery at the Battle of Jutland in 1916.

The Royal Navy was now on a new battleship development journey that would take it through a variety of post-Dreadnought and then super-Dreadnought designs, before arriving at what was to be the last battleship named *Revenge*. In order for the last *Revenge* to be built, the Royal Sovereign Class *Revenge* would first have her name changed to *Redoubtable*.

The first class of battleships designed to improve on HMS *Dreadnought* was HMS *Bellerophon*, along with her sister ships *Superb* and *Temeraire*. *Bellerophon* herself was laid down on the day *Dreadnought* was completed and her design was very similar. There were some changes in the design of the hull and her displacement was greater by about 400 tons.

The St Vincent class battleships (*St Vincent*, *Collingwood* and *Vanguard*) were laid down in May 1908 and all were complete by April 1910. Again, the displacement was increased to 19,560 tons, and the main armament was increased to 50 calibre. The guns were longer, the hull being extended to allow clearance for the longer guns, and the ships were also wider in the beam to compensate.

The next class was HMS *Neptune*, which is not ranked with the similar ships *Colossus* and *Hercules* due to differences in the thickness of armour. *Neptune* was an example of the efforts made to produce a ten-gun broadside and, to facilitate this, the wing turrets were staggered to allow cross-deck firing. The displacement was increased over previous versions and the length was increased by about 10 feet. The design, however, was not a happy one as, in order to achieve the notional ten-gun broadside, some of the guns would have had to fire across deck, which would have caused damage to the ship.

In the succeeding Colossus class, HMS *Colossus* and *Hercules* were fitted with thicker armour and there was some redesign of the staggered wing turrets to allow more room.

Up to this point, the successive design changes and improvements had been relatively modest. With the introduction in 1909 of the first 'super-Dreadnoughts' of the Orion class, however, the changes were more significant. These were the first ships in the Royal Navy to carry all their guns in the centre line. The main armament was changed to a 13.5in Mk 5 gun, which overcame some of the problems in the previous 12in gun.

In 1911, the King George V (1911) battleship class was launched, with an increased displacement over the previous Orions. The ships in the class were HMS *King George V* (launched 9 October 1911), HMS *Centurion* (launched 18 November 1911), HMS *Audacious* (launched 14 September 1912) and HMS *Ajax* (launched 21 March 1912). Sensibly, the main mast containing sighting facilities was positioned ahead of the forward funnel, which reduced the likelihood of smoke obscuring the view. Changes to the armour distribution provided better protection from torpedo threats.

The next class of battleship, the Iron Duke class, was essentially an improved version of the King George V (1911) class, with improved armour and improved secondary armament. The new ships (HMS *Iron Duke*, HMS *Benbow*, HMS *Emperor of India* and HMS *Marlborough*) were distinguished by a torpedo bulkhead. The new ships carried twelve 6in guns as secondary armament. There was some discussion as to the relative merits of the secondary armament, which was included due to a perceived increased threat from destroyers. Others argued that the secondary armament made the ship more vulnerable in other ways by increasing the likelihood of enemy shell penetration, and even the intake of water.

The Queen Elizabeth class of battleship, which followed the Iron Duke class, was to be one of the most successful. The ships in this class were HMS *Barham*, HMS *Malaya* (sponsored by the Federation of Malay States), HMS *Queen Elizabeth*, HMS *Valiant* and, the most famous of all, HMS *Warspite*. The new class was about 23 feet longer than the previous class and 2,500 tons heavier. Despite the greater weight, the Queen Elizabeth class battleships could do 24 knots compared to the maximum 21 for the Iron Duke class. All of these advantages were topped by four twin Mk1 15in guns, backed up by twelve 6in guns. The ships' steam turbines were fuelled by oil, as opposed to coal, which had significant implications in itself as coal could be easily sourced from British mainland reserves, whereas oil would have to be shipped from abroad. Oil was a more efficient fuel than coal, was much easier to load and emitted less smoke. The era of the modern battleship had arrived.

The success of this class of battleship is evidenced by the service histories of the ships themselves. Although launched just before or during the First World War, many saw distinguished service in the Second World War. HMS *Warspite* was the flagship of Admiral Cunningham in the Mediterranean during the Second World War and the effectiveness and accuracy of her 15in guns was such that she landed a hit on the Italian battleship *Giulio Cesare* at a range of 26,000 yards – the longest-range artillery hit between moving targets ever recorded.

In 1913 the building programme began that was to result in the last of the line of British First World War battleships and also the last surface ship named *Revenge* at the time of writing. The Revenge class battleships numbered five and included HMS *Ramillies* (launched 12 June 1916), HMS *Resolution* (launched 14 January 1915), HMS *Revenge* herself (launched 29 May 1915), HMS *Royal Oak* (launched 17 November 1914), and HMS *Royal Sovereign* (launched 29 April 1915).

HMS *Revenge* was laid down on 22 December 1913 at the Vickers shipyard, Barrow-in-Furness in Cumbria. Barrow had been a small fishing village until the Industrial Revolution and the Furness railway brought iron ore to the area. The iron ore had been discovered, not by industrialists of the nineteenth century, but by medieval monks of the nearby Abbey of St Mary of Furness. The monks extracted the iron ore in open-cast mines and smelted it in early furnaces. Hundreds of years later, with the establishment of the Furness railway in 1846, it became possible to construct a steel work and by 1852 shipbuilding became established with the building of the first steamship in the area. The Barrow shipbuilding company was in due course taken over by Vickers in 1897. Barrow-in-Furness would also be the location of the building of the future *Revenge* nuclear submarine.

Whereas the Queen Elizabeth class battleships had been designed to run on oil, which had potential supply problems in time of war, the *Revenge* class battleships were designed to run on either oil or coal, plenty of coal being available in the British Isles. The oil- or coal-powered, reaction-type, direct-drive steam turbines were located in three engine rooms. The Babcock and Wilcox oil- or coal-fired boilers carried either 3,400 tons of oil or 160 tons of coal, allowing the ship a range of 7,500 nautical miles at 12.5 knots and 2,400 nautical miles at 21 knots. The Revenge class ships were slower than the Queen Elizabeth class ships, with a maximum speed of about 21 knots as compared with 24 knots. The Revenge class were also shorter (624 feet against 639 feet 5in). By modern standards, however, the *Revenge* was a giant.

Although in many ways the Revenge class battleships were a disappointing step back from the Queen Elizabeth class battleships, they did retain the excellent C42 Mk 1 15in gun, located in four turrets, each of which weighed about 770 tons. The guns themselves were 54 feet long and weighed about 100 tons each. The tube of the gun was rifled and about 185 miles of flat section wire was wound round this. An outer jacket was shrunk onto this layer. The turrets were manufactured by Sir W.G. Armstrong Whitworth & Co. Ltd, which had been set up in 1847 at Elswick near Newcastle. The company was soon producing artillery for the British Army and then diversified into manufacturing steam locomotives, cars and ships. One branch of the organization became the Elswick Ordnance Company. Apart from Armstrong Whitworth, guns were also manufactured by: William Beardmore & Company in Parkhead, Glasgow; Coventry Ordnance Works; the Royal Arsenal at Woolwich; and by Vickers Ltd in Sheffield.

The gun turrets were in themselves an extraordinary testament to advances in engineering. The barrel was 42 calibres long and could fire a 1,920lb (871kg) shell at a maximum range of 32,500 yards (29,720m) at 30 degrees of elevation. The gun was loaded and fired by an automatic hydraulic mechanism which was powered by four steam engines. The projectile, weighing almost a ton, was lifted from a stack by a grab and taken to a bogey before being transferred into a hoisting cradle. Above the shell room was the magazine, which was sealed off from the turret tube. Here four quarter charges were loaded into a scuttle which revolved, maintaining a permanent seal, so that no flash effects could be transmitted from an enemy shell hitting the turret above.

With both the shell and the charge loaded, the cage passed on up to the next level, which was the working chamber. Here shell and charge were pushed through to the gun-loading cage. This travelled up to the gun house where they were loaded into the gun itself. The shell was then fired by a gunnery officer director up in the mast.

Guns that could throw a shell distances of about 16 miles required sophisticated gunnery control mechanisms. A leading proponent of modern computer-controlled systems was Arthur Joseph Hungerford Pollen (1866–1937). The first computer of this type was known as the Argo Clock. Pollen devised a system that included a gyroscope to identify position and relative movement of a target. Unfortunately for Pollen, his relationship with the Royal Navy was moderated to some degree by Frederick Dreyer. Dreyer was developing his own system, the Dreyer Fire Control Table, which was less complex than Pollen's system and involved more manual correction. Dreyer's system was chosen by the Royal Navy.

One problem that these highly sophisticated early computers experienced was that the information fed into them was often patchy, depending on weather conditions and the fog of war. Range-finding, for example, could be of dubious accuracy and the target's bearing could be misread. Other pieces of information, such as sighting the fall of shot, could be more accurate, but this was not enough in itself to make a sophisticated computational system work.

The weakness of the Dreyer system when tested in action – its most famous public showing being the Battle of Jutland – was not so much in the system itself, which was highly sophisticated and advanced for its time, as in the potential for error resulting in insufficient accurate data being fed into it. This may seem obvious but it should be remembered that this was a system designed for war and it was only in war conditions that it could be effectively judged.

The coincidence-type rangefinder, for example, relied on data the accuracy of which decreased according to the square of the range being estimated. A series of time plots were marked by a typewriter, but the final estimate of the range versus time curve was made by the human eye.

The bearing on the target was calculated by amalgamating the readings from a rifle sight with those from a gyrocompass repeater, which would adjust the readings according to the course of the mother ship. From this information, the rate of change or bearing was calculated.

A Dumaresq device was used to relate range rate and speed across to the enemy speed and heading. A range clock fed into a spotting corrector, which was linked in turn to a range screw with a pencil attachment to mark a line on paper scrolled underneath it. The spotting corrector was also linked to a cyclometric digital display which indicated the gun range.

This is only a brief summary of the scientific complexities of the Dreyer table. It represented the cutting edge of computational maths at the time but, despite this, was limited in its ability to produce accurate target information for ships that were defying traditional standards of naval tactics, and changing course and speed in order to deliberately confuse their potential assailants. Arthur Pollen's invention – the inventor also had the disadvantage of being seen as 'too clever by half', and a Catholic – had been a step too far for a twentieth-century Admiralty with a nineteenth-century mindset, but it would probably have been a better match for the sophistication of modern naval shipping and manoeuvres.

Gunnery training in the Royal Navy had taken place from 1830 on HMS Excellent, which was originally the name of a real ship – a 74-gun Third Rate launched in 1787. From about 1874, Percy Scott joined HMS Excellent and, after leaving her for a period, rejoined her in September 1877, where he remained until 1880. Again, Scott left Excellent to serve on *Inconstant*, with which he served during the Egyptian campaign, before returning to HMS Excellent to serve with one Captain Arbuthnot Fisher, who would later become his sponsor. After a stint in the Mediterranean, he returned once again to HMS Excellent, this time to set up the onshore gunnery school on Whale Island. While commanding the cruiser *Scylla*, he developed some key methods for improving the rate and accuracy of naval gunfire. His ingenuity extended to creating mountings so that naval guns could be used onshore. Some of these were used in the defence of Ladysmith when HMS *Terrible*, commanded by Scott, was detained in South Africa. HMS *Terrible* was to feature in both the Second Boer War and the Boxer Revolution, and her 12pdr gun carriages were inscribed with the motto: 'Ladysmith to Peking – Immediate'. Scott created a field carriage improvised from two wagon wheels and a large piece of timber.

In 1903, Scott was made captain of HMS Excellent and focused on developing accuracy through target practice. He also helped the Navy to develop long-range effective gunnery which was to be fundamental to the concept of the new Dreadnought big-gun battle-ships. From about 1910 Scott concentrated on the development of the gunnery director firing system, the purpose of which was to direct all the guns on a ship at the same target.

The secondary armament of HMS *Revenge* comprised fourteen 6in C45 Mk 12 guns mounted in single casemates. The 6in guns were fitted with director firing, though the director system itself was not fitted to *Revenge* until the end of the First World War. The guns were designed primarily to combat torpedo boats which meant that their limited elevation could not double as anti-aircraft guns. For this purpose she was fitted with two 3in guns in single mountings. She also had four 47mm guns in single mountings and four 21in submerged torpedo tubes.

All of this armament and the technology to direct it was having a marked effect on fleet tactics and manoeuvres. Long-range guns made tactics that were appropriate in the age of Nelson suicidal. All manoeuvres now had to be conducted at much greater ranges and the composition of fleets also provided food for thought. The day of the battleship was not yet over but smaller vessels were taking on roles of increasing importance.

Chapter 13

Jutland

As tension mounted in 1914, the Grand Fleet, under the command of Admiral Jellicoe, moved to its war station at Scapa Flow in the Orkney Islands, with little to entertain those members of the crew who were not avid ornithologists. The Grand Fleet had twenty-four battleships, including HMS *Revenge* which was part of the 1st Division of the 1st Battle Squadron, along with HMS *Iron Duke* (Captain Frederic Dreyer; Admiral Sir John Jellicoe), HMS *Hercules* (Captain Bernard) and HMS *Agincourt* (Captain Doughty). The Battlecruiser Fleet, under Admiral David Beatty, was based further south at Rosyth. This consisted of six battle-cruisers and four fast battleships of the Queen Elizabeth class, including HMS *Warspite*, fourteen light cruisers and twenty-seven destroyers.

The total British Grand Fleet numbered 150 warships, including Dreadnoughts, pre-Dreadnoughts, battlecruisers, armoured cruisers, light cruisers, destroyers, seaplane carriers and minelayers. The German High Seas Fleet numbered eighty-nine warships, including Dreadnoughts, pre-Dreadnoughts, battlecruisers, light cruisers and destroyers. Knowing that they were unlikely to defeat the British *en masse*, the Germans devised a plan to attack the Grand Fleet piecemeal, their first target being the battlecruiser fleet under Admiral Beatty. The plan was to lure Beatty out of port by sending five fast German battlecruisers to trail their coats near the British coast. Once Beatty emerged to chase them, he would be met by a line of waiting German submarines and the whole force of the German High Seas Fleet would descend upon him.

157

The plan had every chance of success and Beatty, like Prince Rupert centuries before, had the sort of temperament that might have made such a chase more likely. That the plan failed, however, was partly due to good fortune for the British and partly due to the work of British Naval Intelligence. The cryptographic branch of the Admiralty, known as Room 40, decoded intercepts, aided by captured German naval codebooks. The *Signalbuch der kaiserlichen Marine* (SKM) had been passed to the British by the Russians, who had taken it from the captured German cruiser *Madgeburg*; the *Handelsschiffsverkehrbuch* (HVB) had been taken from a German steamer by a Royal Australian Navy vessel; and the *Verkehrsbuch*, which contained codes used by naval attachés and embassies, was said to have been dredged up by a British trawler from a sunken German destroyer.

The tempting excursion by the German battlecruisers was planned for 31 May 1914 but, unknown to the Germans, Room 40 had already decoded the initial sailing orders by 30 May. That same day, the signal was being read by Admiral Sir John Jellicoe. By 5.30 p.m. the entire British Grand Fleet, including Beatty's detachment at Rosyth, and Vice Admiral Sir Martyn Jerram's 2nd Battlecruiser Squadron at Invergordon, up the Scottish coast, was making ready to sail. The German quest for a piecemeal battle had been denied. Rather than entice some of the British fleet out for a partial battle, the entire British Grand Fleet was at sea before any German vessels could set their trap.

At the point of sailing, when the ship had been closed down for action, the sound of a side drum was heard on HMS *Revenge*. This may not appear strange in ordinary circumstances – surely some marine drummer was practising or someone was bidding an eccentric farewell from the shore – but no explanation could be found. At this point a possible solution was suggested, not from within the bounds of reason but from the treasure trove of legend. Sir Francis Drake, once master of *Revenge* at the time of the Armada, had taken a snare drum with him on his voyages round the world. When he returned, he ordered that the drum should be kept at his home in Buckland Abbey, Devon, and that at any time that England should be in dire peril it should be sounded so that he could return to defend his country. The sentiment was recorded in poetry by Sir Henry Newbolt:

Drake's Drum

Drake he's in his hammock an' a thousand mile away,
(Capten, art tha sleepin' there below?)
Slung atween the round shot in Nombre Dios Bay,
An' dreamin' arl the time o' Plymouth Hoe.
Yarnder lumes the island, yarnder lie the ships,   5
Wi' sailor lads a-dancin' heel-an'-toe,
An' the shore-lights flashin', an' the night-tide dashin'
He sees et arl so plainly as he saw et long ago.

Drake he was a Devon man, an' ruled the Devon seas,
(Capten, art tha sleepin' there below?),   10
Rovin' tho' his death fell, he went wi' heart at ease,
An' dreamin' arl the time o' Plymouth Hoe.
'Take my drum to England, hang et by the shore,
Strike et when your powder's runnin' low;
If the Dons sight Devon, I'll quit the port o' Heaven,   15
An' drum them up the Channel as we drummed them long ago.'

Drake he's in his hammock till the great Armadas come,
(Capten, art tha sleepin' there below?),
Slung atween the round shot, listenin' for the drum,
An' dreamin' arl the time o' Plymouth Hoe.   20
Call him on the deep sea, call him up the Sound,
Call him when ye sail to meet the foe;
Where the old trade's plyin' an' the old flag flyin',
They shall find him, ware an' wakin', as they found him long ago.[1]

If any body of people was entitled to hear the sound of Drake's drum it was the crew of the ninth successor of Drake's *Revenge* as they set out for a battle that would indeed decide the fate of England in the biggest ship-to-ship battle of all time.

British signals intelligence had served the British well up to this point, but a mistake was made when an officer misunderstood a message given to him by Room 40 pertaining to Admiral Hipper's callsign, DK. The German Admiral only used this callsign in port – when he was at sea it was altered. The message received by the British fleet was that Admiral Hipper was still in port, though he had in fact set sail. At 2.00 p.m. on 31 May, far from being in port, Admiral Hipper was about 50 miles due east of the approaching Admiral Beatty. By 2.20 p.m., Beatty's scouts had reported enemy ships. A neutral Danish steamer had become the focus of interest of light units from both sides and soon shots were being exchanged. The British fired at the German destroyers in the area while the Germans managed to hits HMS *Galatea*.

Beatty changed course in an attempt to cut the German forces off from their base but his speed and failures to signal changes in direction meant that his heavy forces, the potent 5th Battle Squadron, comprising the Queen Elizabeth class battleships, were left behind. Beatty therefore went into battle without the use initially of some of the most powerful battleships then at sea, namely HMS *Barham* (Captain Craig; Rear Admiral Evan Thomas), HMS *Valiant* (Captain Woollcombe), HMS *Warspite* (Captain Philpotts) and HMS *Malaya* (Captain Boyle). As a result either of poor signalling or failure to read signals correctly, the 5th Battle Squadron was about 10 miles behind Beatty at the vital moment of initial engagement with German forces.

Admiral Hipper turned south-east to lead Admiral Beatty towards Admiral Scheer who was approaching about 50 miles away with the main German force. Despite the surprise encounter, the initial German plan of piecemeal destruction still seemed possible.

Beatty appears to have compounded the error – even if it was not entirely his own – whereby the most powerful element of his force was out of range, by delaying the order to fire upon the retreating Germans for a period of about ten minutes when they were within range.

The British and German ships began to engage. Beatty's flagship *Lion* took a hit on her 'Q' turret but a quick-thinking Royal Marines officer, Major Francis Harvey, though mortally wounded, ordered the magazine doors to be shut and the magazine itself to be flooded. This postponed the day that the rest of the crew would join him in the next life. HMS *Indefatigable* was not so lucky and was sunk by a series of piercingly accurate shells. Hipper continued to run for the south, luring the British towards the approaching Scheer. HMS *Queen Mary* was hit and exploded, sinking with the loss of almost all hands.

Hipper's ploy of leading the British towards more powerful German forces was working but now the 5th Battle Squadron, mounting 15in guns, was coming into range and it meant business.

The Germans regarded these super-battleships with understandable trepidation. These were vessels that could almost match the speed of their fast cruisers and yet fire shells twice the size. Now these 15in shells began to hit home. *Seydlitz, Moltke* and *van der Tann* took direct hits. The Germans weaved to avoid more. The question was whether they could find refuge among the advancing German main fleet or be wiped out. A German account described the experience of being on the receiving end of 15in shells from the 5th Battle Squadron as 'highly depressing, nerve-racking and exasperating'[2], sentiments with which it is possible to sympathize.

At 4.30 p.m. the German High Seas Fleet was spotted. The tables had turned and, having already lost two of his cruisers, Admiral Beatty was in no way inclined to take on the full might of the German Kriegsmarine – now it was his turn to lead the Germans towards British forces equipped to deal with them. He ordered the naval equivalent of an about turn – 180° – to head north towards Admiral Jellicoe and the Grand Fleet. If the Germans could play the game of chase me until you meet my big brother, the British could play it too.

Bad signalling meant that the 5th Battle Squadron was again delayed in manoeuvring, exposing it dangerously to enemy fire from the advancing German main fleet. Ships began to take hits, though they gave as good as they got.

Despite their formidable rearguard, Admiral Beatty's cruisers were now not unlike the Scots Greys at Waterloo, chased by Polish lancers. They knew they could not afford to miss a single step or slow down one jot, lest they be skewered by their pursuers. The more the German fleet chased, however, the closer they were drawn towards their nemesis – the British Grand Fleet.

As Admiral Jellicoe got wind of his approaching adversary, he attempted to piece together various bits of information that would enable him to make the right decisions at the right time about the use of his formidable force. The security of the British Isles ultimately rested on its naval forces and should the wrong move be made with a force as powerful as this the result could have been cataclysmic. Winston Churchill was well aware that Jellicoe held the fate of Britain in his hands. HMS *Revenge*, which had fought at that other critical moment in British history in the presence of the Armada, was once again a leading player in a battle where Britain's fortunes hung in the balance.

The order Jellicoe would have to give would be to change the formation of the force from its cruising deployment to a battle line. The critical element in this order would be the choice of course set for the battle line. If Jellicoe got this wrong, the German fleet might gain a tactical advantage that would enable them to severely damage and perhaps defeat the superior British force.

Unfortunately for Jellicoe, the information on which to base this monumental decision was sparse. Admiral Beatty took some time to relay the precise position of the German fleet in answer to a direct question from Admiral Jellicoe. The position was confused further by a variety of factors, including the presence of skirmishing advance forces and the fact that Admiral Scheer had made a turn back towards the main German fleet once he realized he was heading into troubled waters. Accurate positions were not sent by British forces closest to the enemy, namely the 5th Battle Squadron, probably because they were at a critical stage in their manoeuvring away from the German High Seas fleet. HMS *Malaya* had sustained significant damage and was almost lost. Despite his failures in communications, however, Beatty was in fact doing Jellicoe a favour by continuing to engage the German fleet.

At about 6.00 p.m., Beatty's cruisers were in sight of Jellicoe's battle fleet and continued to hold a course to cut in front of them, firing all the while at German units. This continued arc held by the British Battle Cruiser Squadron forced the Germans into a favourable aspect relative to Jellicoe's oncoming force.

As the different elements of the British forces combined, a series of breathtaking manoeuvres took place reminiscent of Italian racing drivers meeting at a roundabout. In the midst of this, the rudder on HMS *Warspite* jammed and she performed a death-defying turn which at one point took her straight towards the German fleet, which concentrated fire on her. *Warspite* took at least six direct hits at this time but continued to fire back and, once she had regained control, was ordered back to Rosyth for repairs, bloody but unbowed.

Like Wellington at Waterloo in 1815, as the French Old Guard breasted the ridge, Jellicoe could cry his own version of 'Now Maitland; now's your chance', and at 6.15 he gave the order for the British Grand Fleet to deploy to the south-east.

One by one, the great ships turned to port, their physical presence awe-inspiring to those who watched, their names echoing down the centuries of past naval and military glories: *King George V – Orion – Iron Duke – Benbow – Colossus – Marlborough – Ajax – Monarch – Royal Oak – Bellerophon – Collingwood – Revenge – Centurion – Conqueror – Superb – Temeraire – Neptune – Hercules – Erin – Thunderer – Canada – Vanguard – St Vincent – Agincourt.*

Despite the paucity of information about the enemy's whereabouts, Jellicoe had made a prescient and accurate deployment that would not only place his fleet in a favourable position with regard to the remaining daylight, but which gave him the key tactical advantage of crossing the T of the advancing German column. This simply meant that whereas all the British guns could be brought to bear on the enemy, only a few of the German guns could be fired in return.

There has been much discussion about the Battle of Jutland and opinions aired as to who won the battle. Suffice it to say that, once Jellicoe had correctly deployed his fleet into battle order, the advancing German fleet ran into the iron walls of England. This fleet was the most powerful ever to put to sea in the history of the Royal Navy. It was in an optimum disposition and bearing, give or take a few degrees, with all guns bearing on the enemy. At this juncture Admiral Scheer knew precisely what his options were. There were only two: retreat to Wilhelmshaven or be annihilated.

Admiral Scheer also knew, however, that headlong retreat posed its own dangers in view of the proximity of British forces, so to cover his retreat he devised an ingenious series of counter-attacks and other ploys designed to disconcert and confuse his pursuers. It is a testimony to Scheer's skills that these tactics and ploys largely worked and prevented the British from wreaking the heavy defeat upon the Germans at sea that they otherwise might have done.

Despite the fact that the cruiser *Invincible* had blown up, the Germans knew that there was no competition against the might of the Grand Fleet and Scheer ordered a turn of 16 points to starboard together – an emergency escape move that had been rehearsed for just such a contingency. The Germans created a smokescreen to cover their departure and, fearing an attack by torpedoes, Jellico did not give chase.

With the shelter of night still too far away for comfort, Scheer ordered a surprise turn back towards the British. Like a limping old dog pursued by baying wolves, he turned to bare his teeth to keep the enemy at bay. The move, though startling to the British, did not

163

have the desired effect and they doggedly shadowed him as he once again turned south-east.

German torpedo boats were sent into the attack but the withering weight of fire from the British forced Scheer to repeat his battle about-turn, which he achieved by 7.20. The attack by cruisers to cover the retreat was led by the cruiser *Derflinger*, which had already inflicted considerable damage on the British. HMS *Revenge* had the range of *Derflinger* at 7.11 and began to straddle her with shells before scoring at least five direct hits. When *Derflinger* moved out of sight, *Revenge* concentrated on the German destroyers which were making a torpedo attack and made an emergency turn at 7.35 to avoid torpedoes fired directly at her.

The Germans' fierce counter-attack to cover their retreat seems to have had the desired effect as from now on the major engagements between heavy ships on both sides were over.

The skill shown by HMS *Revenge* and others in dodging the torpedoes desperately launched at them by the German destroyers suggests that Jellicoe need not have ordered the entire fleet to turn away 45° as this gave the Germans the time they needed to put distance between themselves and the pursuing British. With the wisdom of hindsight, one could surmise that a Nelson would have allowed his commanders more initiative to take individual avoiding action as they deemed fit, and as *Revenge* had demonstrated, they were quite capable of doing so.

Although the Germans had succeeded in placing a useful distance between themselves and the British, the battle was by no means over. Jellicoe decided not to commit heavy forces to a night attack and had a course set to the south-west, designed to cut Scheer off. By 9.30 p.m., the German fleet turned to the south-east and was now following the British fleet, which still did not fully engage them. A series of fierce encounters took place during the night between cruisers, destroyers and battleships which were to prove costly to the British. The destroyers *Tipperary, Ardent, Fortune, Sparrowhawk* and *Turbulent* were sunk as well as the cruiser *Black Prince*.

Despite the British advantage in signals intelligence, some vital reports of the German positions were not passed on soon enough and Jellicoe was suspicious of some that were. Had these messages carried more authority, Jellicoe might have taken more decisive action with his heavy forces.

As it was, Scheer managed to reach the Horn Reef relatively unscathed and at 3.54 a.m. he ordered all his battle-scarred ships into port. The British had missed their chance to destroy the German fleet at sea but the Germans knew they had had a lucky escape and the High Seas Fleet would never set sail again to challenge the Royal Navy.

Following the main action at Jutland, HMS *Revenge*, along with other elements of the fleet, conducted a series of sweeps in the North Sea to ensure that the Kriegsmarine had not decided to try their luck again. By now, however, the Germans had realized that they could not alter the strategic position so far as surface forces were concerned. The British were prepared to sacrifice other commitments around the world in order to ensure that they had an overwhelming advantage over the German High Seas Fleet. In view of this, the Germans embarked on a submarine warfare strategy that would be sustained through the remainder of the First World War and into the Second World War. Submarines, for obvious reasons, did not have the dignity and physical presence of surface warships, nor could they show the flag in quite the same way. The switch of strategy was therefore emblematic of the failure of the Kaiser's ambition to match his British Royal cousins in sea power, and the failure of his naval strategy would mark the end of his rule in Germany.

Despite the fact that they did not sail out of port, the High Seas Fleet remained a fleet in being and, as German fortunes waned on land, the temptation rose to use these floating titans in a last attempt to break British power. Without troubling his superiors with the details, Admiral Scheer devised a plan to sail out to meet the British. The British naval stranglehold, however, had caused dire shortages of food and other essential supplies in Germany. There had been a communist revolution already in Russia and communist notions were spreading among disenchanted servicemen. Admiral Scheer's plan failed and the repercussions would topple the Kaiser himself.

The High Seas Fleet would sail from Wilhelmshaven again but not cleared for action. Under the terms of the Armistice of 11 November 1918, the fleet sailed under British escort for internment at Scapa Flow. The plan was that the German ships would eventually be shared out among the victorious powers as prizes. Although the German ships were ordered to haul down their ensign by Admiral

Beatty as a mark of their defeat, the Germans maintained enough pride in their fleet not to want it handed out piecemeal to their former foes. On 21 June 1919, as the 1st British Battle Squadron under Admiral Fremantle, flying his flag in HMS *Revenge*, set sail for an exercise, Admiral Reuter gave the order for the entire German fleet to be scuttled. Although the British tried desperately to stop it, there was little they could do and almost every ship sank.

The question remains, was it worth it? The First World War has not been viewed with the clarity afforded to its successor. The Second World War would rightly be seen as a just war against one of the most evil regimes in the history of humanity that would perpetrate an unparalleled crime against the Jewish people by murdering about six million of them – men, women and children – in concentration camps and through other forms of murder. Other 'undesirables' would also be removed as well, including Christians, Communists, the disabled, gypsies and whoever else got in the way. The First World War by contrast was painted in retrospect in various shades and mostly came to be seen as an unnecessary war foisted upon the working class by unthinking toffs. Close analysis of the facts would prove otherwise. British command structures proved to be adaptable and in due course open to new technology. Artillery methods were perfected and ground-breaking inventions such as the tank were introduced by the British along with tactics to match.

The underlying issue was one that was familiar to England and to Britain: once again she was faced with an attempt at European hegemony by one of the Continental powers, in this case Germany. She had either to fight or wait to be invaded.

Chapter 14

Between the Wars

HMS *Revenge* emerged from the First World War as part of what was still by far the most dominant navy in the world. The bulk of the German High Seas Fleet was lying at the bottom of Scapa Flow and, although the United States had every intention of catching up, it was still a long way behind Britain in naval strength. The comparative line-up between the two nations in 1918 was as follows:

	UK	USA
Battleships	61	39
Battlecruisers	9	0
Cruisers	30	16
Light cruisers	90	19
Destroyers	443	131
Submarines	147	86
Aircraft carriers and seaplane carriers	4	0

Naval power, however, is largely a visible symbol of economic power and the First World War had had a devastating effect on the British economy. Moreover, a whole generation of highly gifted young men had been lost in the war, with incalculable implications for the inter-war period. In addition to loss of life, cutbacks in naval manning, particularly those instituted by Sir Eric Geddes, would have effects reminiscent of the French pruning of the officer class after the Revolution.

As the American economy grew, it became clear that Britain was unlikely to maintain her naval predominance for long. The status quo was, however, to some extent extenuated by the Washington Conference of 1921–2. The balance of power in the Pacific had previously been maintained by the Anglo-Japanese alliance of 1911. Many Japanese naval officers, moreover, were trained in the tradition of Nelson. The Washington Conference demolished this arrangement and replaced it with a vague consultation agreement which gave the United States more elbow room.

The Five-Power Limitation Treaty involved the scrapping of twenty-six US, twenty-four British and sixteen Japanese ships, and fixed ratios of major ships as five for both the United States and Britain, and three for Japan. The Japanese were disenchanted with this arrangement and by 1936 had pulled out of the agreement.

In view of the relative size of the US and British economies, the treaty maintained British naval power as far as the outbreak of the Second World War. Even though Britain could no longer claim to be the predominant naval power, its strength relative to its nearest rivals was not as diminished as it might have been in an unhindered naval race.

While powers such as the United States, Germany, France and Japan had ambitions and responsibilities that were relatively local, Britain had sole responsibility for an empire that comprised about a quarter of the world's land surface. In 1924, the British Empire was larger than ever before, partly due to the accretion of territories from the defeated powers of the First World War. The Royal Navy had to perform a balancing act of maintaining security in home waters, though the German surface-fleet threat was now much diminished; a presence in the Mediterranean focused on Gibraltar and Malta; and a deterrent influence in the Far East, where there was an incipient threat from Japan. Due to overstretch, the Far East would have to rely on reinforcements from the Mediterranean. The failings of this policy would be revealed in the Second World War, as both Singapore and the naval Force Z succumbed to Japanese attack.

In 1922, *Revenge* was in the Mediterranean when King Constantine I of Greece, who was brother-in-law of the German Kaiser William II, abdicated. Constantine had been pro-German through the First World War and after the war conducted an unsuccessful anti-Turkish policy which resulted in a war in Anatolia in 1922.

HMS *Revenge*, flagship of Rear Admiral Duff, left Malta on the evening of 25 September to sail to the area. Other vessels deployed to the region included the battleships HMS *Centurion* and HMS *Malaya*, the cruisers *Ceres*, *Caledon* and *Carysfort* and the Third Destroyer Flotilla. Britain also deployed military units in the form of the 3rd Battalion Coldstream Guards, the 2nd Battalion Royal Fusiliers and the 2nd Battalion the Rifle Brigade. By 29 September, the First Destroyer Flotilla of the Atlantic Fleet had left Gibraltar to join the growing British forces in the Dardanelles. With such forces in place, the British soon had control of the narrow straits between Chanak and Kara Bournou. The presence of the British in force meant that the local Armenian population could discard the fezes that they had been wearing in expectation of a Turkish takeover. The Christian population in the area also altered their plans to evacuate. Any remaining doubts were dispelled by a fly-over by the RAF. The Greek battleship *Averoff*, which was in the service of the revolutionaries, thought it wise to lower her colours and play God Save the King when sailing past the British naval force.

The crisis had been temporarily contained by the ingenuity of local military officers and the Navy provided critical support for both Allied forces on shore and relief for refugees who were fleeing the fighting. While the crew of HMS *Revenge* and other ships dealt with the immediate problem, the British Cabinet came close to a declaration of war when Turkish forces, which had defeated the Greeks, moved on to threaten British and French forces based at Chanak. A formal declaration of war was expected and the Navy cleared for action. A somewhat breathless report published in the *New York Times* tells us that, notwithstanding the fact that the British ground forces would hold their ground if attacked, it was the presence of the Navy that tipped the balance. The Turkish forces were within range of the 15in guns of HMS *Revenge*, and they would certainly think twice before taking any rash action:

Constantinople, Sept. 28. Events are surely approaching a climax.

The Turks have occupied the entire neutral zone on the Adriatic side of the Dardanelles, with the exception of the Chanak area, around which they have established infantry units in a semi-circle, virtually investing the British lines.

The Turkish cavalry squadrons are retiring, and the British troops, who are in strong force at Chanak, are ready for what may happen ...

Yussuf Kemal Pasha, the Nationalist Foreign Minister, is understood to have gone to Angora to submit the allied joint note to the Nationalist Assembly, but in the meantime Turkish concentrations are being pushed with the greatest speed.

British Reinforcements Arriving

British reinforcements are reaching here and the threatened area. The super-dreadnoughts *Revenge* and *Resolute*, the most powerful fighting machines afloat, have arrived in the Dardanelles, while a battalion of North Staffordshires and 3,000 men of the British air forces landed today and marched through Constantinople with bands playing. Their presence has helped to bring about a reassuring effect.

The Turkish instructions to the men in the Chanak sector are to advance the farthest possible without meeting resistance. They are now practically against the British entrenchments, and obviously the situation cannot be indefinitely prolonged.

Notwithstanding the Kemalist concentrations around Chanak, however, the British are confident of holding their own against all odds. They declare that their flanks are well protected by the fleet. The battleships with their 16-in [sic.] guns can sweep the whole area around Chanak for a distance of twenty miles and it is possible for the British to dismount some of their giant naval guns and use them for shore batteries.[1]

In a message to the Turkish Nationalist leader Mustafa Kemal, the British force commander, General Harington, described elsewhere in the *New York Times* as a man 'not to be trifled with', reminded Kemal of the presence of the reinforcements, including naval units:

I take the opportunity to tell you on behalf of England that the reinforcements which have been sent me are solely in the interests of peace, as I was careful to state in the communiqué I published recently. It is therefore an immense relief to me to hear that you have no aggressive intentions against my troops.[2]

Harington knew, as did Kemal, that the British naval guns could have made short work of the lightly armed Turkish forces, including cavalry, massed in the area. Without the presence of the Navy, however, things would have been somewhat different.

General Sir Charles Harington (1897–1972) had distinguished himself in the First World War with a successful assault on the Messines Ridge in June 1917. He earned a reputation for meticulous attention to detail matched by concern for his men. His diplomatic skills and wisdom were such that, although ordered by the British Government to fire on the Turks, which by September 1922 amounted to about 50,000 men under General Mustafa Kemal, if they did not leave the vicinity of Chanak, he avoided a bloody battle and probably a war by achieving the same ends with tact and diplomacy. Although in the event an armistice was agreed on time, the incident resulted directly in the fall of the Prime Minister, David Lloyd-George.

Meanwhile, HMS *Revenge* moved to the Black Sea via the Dardanelles in view of the ongoing tension created by the Russian Civil War. The defeated White Army was largely evacuated on British ships, though desperate scenes took place as the Red Army did their best to slaughter their escaping enemies. HMS *Revenge* then returned to the Atlantic Fleet.

By March 1923, HMS *Revenge* had rejoined the Atlantic fleet and in November 1924 she became Fleet Flag, Atlantic Fleet when the Queen Elizabeth class ships were deployed to the Mediterranean. HMS *Revenge* would now pursue an important, though routine, series of exercises, designed to keep her crew at the ready for any eventualities. On 30 September she was in Scottish waters carrying out exercises to test the gun crews. At night star shells broke over the waters and searchlights scanned the darkness to pick out the mammoth shapes of ships such as HMS *Hood*. During the day, the big guns were let loose in live firing, the whole ship shuddering with the impact.

In October 1927 HMS *Revenge* was relieved by HMS *Nelson*, which represented the latest thinking in battleship design and was distinguished by her revolutionary design. *The Times* indicated that if another Washington Conference were to further delimit battleship development, HMS *Nelson* might prove to be the last British battleship.

The design of HMS *Nelson* broke the rules, such as they were, and she looked rather more like an oil tanker than a battleship, with the bridge and boilers aft and the guns forward.

	HMS *Nelson*	HMS *Revenge*
Length	660ft	580ft
Breadth	106ft	88½ft
Displacement	35,000 tons	25,750 tons
Armour	14in	13in
Main armament	9 × 16in guns in 3 turrets	8 × 15in guns in 4 turrets
Secondary armament	12 × 6in guns	14 × 6in guns
Anti-aircraft guns	6 × 4.7in guns	2 × 3in guns
Pom-poms & machine guns	4 × 3pd 8 × 2pdr MGs	4 × 3pdr & MGs
Speed	23 knots	23 knots

Nelson could achieve the same nominal speed as *Revenge*, despite the fact that she was considerably heavier, with only a marginal increase in horsepower. She was powered by geared turbines whereas those of *Revenge* were oil-fired. Where *Revenge* retained an advantage over *Nelson* was in comparative costs. Whereas the cost of one 15in gun for *Revenge* was £17,000, the equivalent gun for *Nelson* was £45,000. Another essential difference was in the quantity of rum aboard: 1,600 gallons for *Nelson* and 1,000 gallons for *Revenge*.

During her refit, one of the most marked disparities in armament between *Revenge* and *Nelson* was rectified to some degree. She was fitted with 4in AA guns and two of her 6in guns gave way to a High Angle Control Station Mk1, which would provide improved gun control in the event of an aerial attack.

When *Revenge* was recommissioned in January 1929, it was for the Mediterranean Fleet, where she became flagship of the 1st Battle Squadron. In June 1929 she was made 2nd Flagship of the 1st Battle Squadron.

HMS *Revenge* was to remain part of the Mediterranean Fleet until February 1936, coming back to home waters for the Jubilee Review at Spithead on 16 July 1935. Here she was positioned in 'E' line, with HMS *Resolution*, HMS *Iron Duke*, HMS *Hood*, HMS *Renown* and HMS *Courageous* consecutively to the front of her, and HMS *Ramillies*, HMS *Royal Sovereign*, HMS *Queen Elizabeth* and HMS *Victoria and Albert* consecutively behind her. Although the assembly of ships was impressive by any stretch of the imagination and would have caused the admirals of many a foreign fleet to turn green with envy, there was a marked difference between this and the fleet assembled at Spithead on 18 July 1914. Then there had been over sixty battleships and battlecruisers, and another fifty-five cruisers of different types. In 1935 there were merely eleven heavy vessels and eighteen cruisers, of which only eight could be described as modern.[3] HMS *Revenge* herself, although as sleek and purposeful as ever, was by now an elderly veteran.

By 1935 there were stirrings again in the Mediterranean region with Italy the centre of attention. The Mediterranean fleet was reinforced in order to impose sanctions on Italy but ultimately the gesture proved futile. The stand-off between Britain and Italy presaged battles ahead, when the Mediterranean fleet under Admiral Cunningham ran a series of running battles against the formidable Italian Navy.

Mussolini had vowed to create a new Roman Empire that would allow Italy to break out of the confines of the Mediterranean, which, with the British controlling major ports at Gibraltar, Malta and Alexandria, was effectively a British lake. He also wanted to marginalize both the monarchy and the Church, and he calculated that a full-blown war would enable him to do so.

Large imperial powers such as Britain, France and Germany had possessions in Africa, so it seemed natural for Il Duce to acquire more African territory to bolster Italy's international standing. When the Italian Army invaded, sanctions were applied by the League of Nations but, like many initiatives of the League, the sanctions were half-hearted and did not include an embargo on oil. Germany was not part of the League and therefore not involved in imposing the sanctions, which had the effect of bringing the two fascist regimes closer together. The Hoare-Laval plan, designed effectively to appease Mussolini and hand over part of the captured territory in return for a truce, revealed the underlying weakness of the League.

The reinforcement of the Mediterranean fleet was such that ships were moved to Alexandria and overflowed into Haifa, but many current and potential problems were highlighted, not least the vulnerability of large warships to air attack. Malta was thought to be particularly vulnerable and a large proportion of the fleet was therefore moved to Alexandria. Despite the failings of the fleet and its ports, it was clear that Mussolini was uncomfortable with its presence and requested that the British should reduce the fleet, which they refused to do. A positive effect of the deployment was that it acted like a form of dress rehearsal for the real war that was to follow. One of the greatest threats was perceived to be air power. This was to have implications for the future of capital ships such as HMS *Revenge* and also for ports such as Malta. Although the Mediterranean naval commander Admiral Fisher called for better anti-aircraft defences for Malta, the British Government was unwilling to find the money for the improvements.

As it was, the Mediterranean would no longer be a theatre that would directly concern HMS *Revenge*. In February 1936, she was paid off at Portsmouth for a refit, after which she was recommissioned in June 1937 for the 2nd Battle Squadron of the Home Fleet. For a period she was used to train boys and Royal Naval Reserve officers, and on 9 August 1939 she was present at a review of the fleet at Portland by the King. The presence of *Revenge*, along with HMS *Ramillies* and HMS *Iron Duke*, added a comforting aura of power, despite their age, as Britain stood on the very brink of the Second World War. The King's review took place against the background of practice raids on various counties in south-east England and London.

Apart from the three battleships in Weymouth Bay, there were two aircraft carriers, nine submarines, sixteen cruisers, fifteen destroyers and a variety of other vessels, including motor torpedo boats and patrol craft, amounting to about 130 ships.[4] Meanwhile, the Home Fleet was gathered at Invergordon and Rosyth, including the battleships *Rodney*, *Resolution*, *Royal Oak* and *Royal Sovereign*, and the battlecruiser *Repulse*.

Chapter 15

The Second World War

On 23 and 24 August 1939, Adolf Hitler signed a non-aggression pact with the Soviet Union in which they agreed to divide Poland between them. On 25 August, Britain and Poland signed a treaty of mutual assistance. Despite this, Britain's pusillanimous appeasement policy gave Hitler some reassurance that he could move his forces into yet another neighbouring country without real action being taken against him. This time, however, he had gone too far and on 3 September 1939, at 11.00 a.m., Britain declared war on Germany. At 5.00 p.m. the same day, France followed suit.

At the start of the war, Germany had a preponderance in almost every area apart from surface warships. Britain remained the dominant naval power, with the United States not far behind:

	British Commonwealth	United States	Germany
Battleships	12	15	2 + 2 pocket battleships
Battlecruisers	3	0	2
Cruisers	62	32	6
Aircraft carriers	7	5	0
Submarines	54	87	57

With regard to surface warships, the Germans knew that they had no choice other than to conduct daring commerce raids with their battleships and pocket battleships, as long as they could evade the British fleets. They also made good use of their U-boats to harass merchant ships as well as warships. To match their lightning assault strategy on land, the Germans carried out high-profile raids against British naval vessels, which had an effect on morale disproportionate to their military impact.

The first U-boat attack was against one of HMS *Revenge*'s companion ships in the Home Fleet, the converted aircraft carrier HMS *Courageous*. On 17 September 1939, while carrying out an anti-submarine patrol off the coast of Ireland, she was stalked by U-29, commanded by Kapitanleutnant Otto Schuhart. In order to launch her aircraft, *Courageous* had to turn into the wind, a manoeuvre which unfortunately put her across the bows of the German submarine. Having been hit by two torpedoes, she sank with the loss of over 500 of her crew.

The next target that would loom large in the German U-boat periscope was HMS *Royal Oak*, a Revenge-class battleship, which was anchored at Scapa Flow in the Orkney Islands. These were familiar waters for *Royal Oak* as, with her sister ship HMS *Revenge*, she had sailed from here to do battle with the German High Seas Fleet at Jutland. More recently, *Royal Oak* had been sent out to intercept the German battleship *Gneisenau* which was loose in the North Sea, but the foray had done little more than show her age. She was too slow to catch the faster German ship and took a battering from bad weather. She returned to Scapa Flow and remained there while other ships were moved to safer harbours.

It is not difficult to guess why a German attack on a British ship at Scapa Flow would be of particular significance for it was at the bottom of Scapa Flow that the scuttled German High Seas fleet of the First World War lay.

Kriegsmarine commander Karl Donitz chose U-boat commander Kapitanleutnant Gunther Prien to carry out the daring raid. Having entered Scapa Flow on a moonless night, Prien spotted *Royal Oak* and at 00.58 fired three torpedoes, one of which struck home. The first torpedo strike caused barely enough impact to get the crew out of their bunks and certainly not enough to cause *Royal Oak* to take evasive action, but the U-boat had time to reposition itself for a second attack and this time all three torpedoes found their target.

Within thirteen minutes, HMS *Royal Oak* had capsized and sunk, taking 833 men with her. Those that managed to get away from the ship found themselves swimming around in the cold sea mixed with oil and faced with an 800-metre swim to shore. A Royal Naval Reserve tender, which had been alongside *Royal Oak*, managed to rescue 386 men from the water.

HMS *Revenge*, meanwhile, had received orders to intercept another German threat, the 'pocket' battleship *Admiral Graf Spee*. The 'pocket' referred to the restrictions imposed on her build by the Treaty of Versailles. With typical ingenuity, however, the Germans found their way round the restrictions by using such methods as advanced welding techniques to save weight. The result was a battleship with the proportions and speed of a cruiser. *Graf Spee*, like her sister ship, *Deutschland*, carried 11in guns and had a maximum speed of 28.5 knots. She was also fitted with radar and two seaplanes for reconnaissance. Tactically, her orders were to steer clear of major engagements with enemy forces and to pick off individual ships when the opportunity arose. One such was the British steamer SS *Clement* which was stopped and sunk off the coast of Brazil on 30 September 1939. As with many of *Graf Spee*'s operations, the crews of her various victims were removed to safety before the ship herself was sunk.

On 1 October, *Revenge* received orders to sail for British South Atlantic Command based at Freetown, but the order was rescinded as the *Graf Spee* moved towards her fateful encounter with Commodore Henry Harwood's raider-hunting Group 'G'.

On 5 October, *Revenge* was assigned to the vital role of convoy duty in the North Atlantic. As part of the recently set up North Atlantic Escort Force, based on Halifax in Canada, her first duty was to carry a proportion of Britain's gold reserves for safe keeping in Canada. She would repeat this role in 1940, when she carried £40 million of gold bullion.

Britain was highly dependent on maritime trade and the convoys were literally a lifeline. No one knew this better than Vice Admiral Karl Donitz, commander of German U-boats. At the start of the U-boat campaign designed to sink merchantmen and to cut off the Allied supply line, the U-boats that were available tended to operate singly. Even so, their low profile on the surface and the obvious difficulty in detecting them when they were submerged meant that they could wreak heavy damage. The presence of heavy battleships like HMS *Revenge* not only acted as a deterrent against U-boats, but particularly against the German surface raiders. Although the German pocket battleships were fast and powerful, they would think twice before coming within range of the 15in guns of a Revenge-class battleship.

On 22 June 1940, the French and Germans signed an armistice which divided France into two zones. Marshal Pétain took over the Vichy regime governing the nominally independent south-eastern sector of France. The armistice was in contravention of an agreement between Britain and France of 28 March in which both powers undertook not to sign any peace treaty or armistice without the agreement of the other. General Weygand suggested on 13 June that the French fleet should sail to Britain to prevent it falling into enemy hands but the plan never came off and, seeing the writing on the wall, the British decided to take pre-emptive action. In Operation Catapult, on 3 July 1940, the Royal Navy attacked the French fleet at Mers el-Kebir, while other units were rounded up at Dakar and Alexandria. The French battleship *Paris* had escaped to Portsmouth before the French surrender and she was boarded by a contingent from HMS *Revenge*. The French submarine *Surcouf* was also at Portsmouth and was boarded as well. When the French crew resisted the takeover, two Royal Navy officers were mortally wounded and one leading seaman shot dead. A French officer also died. The whole affair somewhat blotted Britain's otherwise clean copybook at the start of the war.

HMS *Revenge* was transferred to Plymouth Command in August 1940 in anticipation of an invasion attempt. On 12 October 1940, *Revenge* was ordered to take part in the bombardment of Cherbourg as part of Operation Medium, which was designed to hold up the German invasion. *Revenge* was accompanied by the destroyers *Jardin*, *Jupiter*, *Jackal*, *Kashmir* and *Kipling*, with cover provided by the cruisers *Newcastle* and *Emerald*, in turn screened by the destroyers *Broke* and *Wanderer*, and the Polish destroyer *Orp Burza*. An RAF squadron commander, who was flying overhead at the time of the bombardment, was amazed at the effect of shells from HMS *Revenge* and other ships as they found their target. Describing it as all hell let loose, even from a range of 100 miles in his initial approach, the pilot saw flares being dropped by aircraft over the target area while ground defences responded with anti-aircraft fire and searchlights beamed into the sky. When the pilot was directly over the target, the Navy, including HMS *Revenge*, opened fire. At this point the pilot becomes almost lost for words and describes it as the equivalent of 500 simultaneous thunderstorms. He says one of his co-pilots told him that tornadoes he had experienced in the Far East came nowhere near it. The effect on the ground defences at Cherbourg was total shock as 15in shells plunged inwards and found their targets. All the anti-aircraft fire stopped instantaneously, while the searchlights waved their beams aimlessly round the sky as if their operators were drunk.[1]

The number of ships available along the south coast of England points to the real challenge the Germans faced in their ambition to invade. Any attempt to move large numbers of troops in barges across the Channel would have been intercepted by the Royal Navy and destroyers. The only hope the Germans had was to defeat the RAF and then attempt the invasion while holding aerial superiority. Once again, however, the walls of England were sound and the RAF made sure between the summer of 1940 and May 1941 that the Luftwaffe never achieved that aerial superiority.

In December 1940, the German cruiser *Admiral Hipper* was at large in the Atlantic, based on Brest. Hipper attacked convoy WS.5A off the Azores but was beaten off by the British cruisers *Berwick*, *Bonaventure* and *Dunedin*. *Berwick* and *Hipper* both sustained damage in the exchange of fire and *Hipper* escaped into the mist before returning to Brest. *Revenge* was among several ships in the Home Fleet, in addition to Force H from Gibraltar, that were tasked to intercept the *Hipper*, but to no avail. *Hipper* would be back with a vengeance in February 1941 to sink seven merchant ships of convoy SLS-64.

Too late to catch *Hipper*, HMS *Revenge* continued with her other convoy duties and there is little doubt that she was a major deterrent to similar disasters. Between 25 November and 11 December 1940 she escorted Convoy HX91 of about twenty-nine ships and the Commodore of the convoy is recorded as saying that 'HMS *Revenge* was of the greatest assistance in every way.'

On 23 May 1941, HMS *Revenge* was ordered to provide additional cover for Convoy HX128 as Germany's most powerful battleship, the *Bismarck*, was on the loose.

179

	HMS *Revenge*	*Bismarck*
Length	580ft	823.5ft
Breadth	88½ft	118.1ft
Displacement	25,750 tons	41,700 tons
Armour	13in	145–320mm
Main armament	8 × 15in guns in 4 turrets	8 × 15in
Secondary armament	14 × 6in guns; 2 × 3in guns; 4 × 3pdr & MGs	12 × 15mm; 16 × 105mm; 16 × 37mm; 12 × 20mm; 8 × 20mm
Speed	23 knots	30.1 knots

Bismarck was one of the most formidable battleships ever built and well able to deal with any ship the Royal Navy could throw at her. She could not, however, take on the entire British Home Fleet, plus reinforcements from Gibraltar, which was what fate had in store for her.

The purpose of Operation Rheinubung was to maximize the disruption already being caused to Allied convoys in the Atlantic and to force the British to divert naval assets to deal with the fast-moving and deadly raiders. With her speed and formidable array of gunnery, *Bismarck* could make short work of a convoy and do severe damage to any escorts that might take her on. Between January and March 1941, the *Scharnhorst* and *Gneisenau* had already sunk twenty-two Allied ships and there was little doubt that *Bismarck* could sink several more.

Although the German force was originally intended to be larger, including *Bismarck*'s recently completed sister the *Tirpitz*, restrictions meant that it would be *Bismarck* and the heavy cruiser *Prinz Eugen* that would attempt the secret breakout, accompanied by three destroyers (*Z-23*, *Z-16* and *Z-10*). Having left Gotenhafen near Danzig on Sunday, 18 May before turning north towards the Kattegat, the force was sighted by the Swedish cruiser *Gotland* at 1.00 p.m. on 20 May. British reconnaissance and intercepts were picking up ship movements as well, though as yet there had been no definite identification of *Bismarck*. Once they entered the Norwegian fjords, Lutjens decided to anchor the two ships in separate harbours: *Bismarck* at Grimstadfjord and *Prinz Eugen* at Kalvanes. During this break, *Prinz Eugen* was refuelled, though curiously *Bismarck* was not, despite the fact that it was an operational issue that her engines burned fuel at a comparatively high rate. It was while she was in Grimstadfjord that an RAF reconnaissance Spitfire took an aerial photo of the *Bismarck*. RAF Bomber Command was duly alerted but by the time they could run a bombing mission the weather had closed in and the birds had flown.

The commander of the Royal Navy Home Fleet, Admiral Tovey, also took immediate action. The heavy cruisers *Norfolk* and *Suffolk*, which were both fitted with advanced radar, were designated to watch the Denmark Straits for a possible breakout attempt. The Iceland-Faeroes gap was watched by the two light cruisers, *Birmingham* and *Manchester*, while the battlecruiser *Hood*, battleship *Prince of Wales* and six destroyers were sent to Hvalfjord in Iceland. If Admiral Lutjens considered he could either take or escape any of these, Admiral Tovey had in reserve the battleship *King George V*, five cruisers and five destroyers. As if this was not enough, the Admiralty also assigned him the aircraft carrier *Victorious* and the battlecruiser *Repulse*.

Admiral Lutjens had decided to take the long way round to the north of Iceland and through the Denmark Strait, and on Thursday, 22 May, the accompanying destroyers fell back to leave the two battleships on their lonely mission. Due to the dense cloud and mist, Admiral Tovey could not tell whether the German ships had sailed from their fjord harbours, let alone in which direction.

When it was finally confirmed that *Bismarck* and *Prinz Eugen* were no longer at anchor, extra measures were taken to protect convoys either already en route or about to sail. *Revenge* was ordered to boost the protection for convoy HX128, consisting of about forty-three ships. If the *Bismarck* were to get through into the Atlantic unscathed, there was every possibility that *Revenge* would have to engage her.

The cruisers *Suffolk* and *Norfolk* were positioned to the west of Iceland in the Denmark Strait which was about 40 miles wide, taking into account variations in the amount of pack ice. HMS *Hood* and HMS *Prince of Wales* were positioned further south. In view of the presence of minefields, the German task force would be forced into an even narrower passage which, despite the impenetrable weather, substantially increased the chance that they would be sighted by the British.

Sure enough, at 7.22 p.m. on 23 May, a lookout on HMS *Suffolk* caught a fleeting sight of a gigantic shape emerging from a squall of snow before disappearing again. It was then followed by another huge shape which disappeared like the first. The instant the message was relayed to the bridge of the *Suffolk*, action stations were sounded and the ship turned away to conceal herself in the mist. The *Suffolk* had herself been glimpsed from the *Bismarck*, which continued to pick up signals of her presence. The Germans then detected another ship, which was the *Norfolk* joining *Suffolk* in the shadowing operation. When *Norfolk* briefly emerged from the mist, *Bismarck* engaged her but missed. The effects of her own firing, however, damaged the *Bismarck*'s forward radar and *Prinz Eugen* was ordered to take station ahead. The race was on to get to the Atlantic before the British could concentrate their strength.

Like a bull elephant trailed by a couple of jackals, *Bismarck* once turned on its pursuers but they both scampered away into the gloom, only to resume their shadowing operation when the immediate danger had passed. There was nothing that the two British cruisers could do other than record the position of the German task force. Unknown to the Germans, two ships were steaming towards them at high speed with every intention of taking them on: the newest battleship in the Royal Navy, HMS *Prince of Wales*, and the icon of British naval power for the last two decades, the mighty HMS *Hood*.

HMS *Hood* was officially designated a battlecruiser but was in fact longer than any battleship in the British fleet and heavier than most. She carried the heaviest guns available (15in) and was capable of considerable speed (up to 29 knots). Her speed probably explains her designation. Despite these considerable assets, which made her the pride of the British fleet, HMS *Hood* had a fundamental flaw that had caused the sinking of some of the battlecruisers at Jutland, namely the siting of the cordite magazines. Although in the forward part of the ship the magazines had been moved further down to reduce the likelihood of primary or secondary explosions; the rear magazine was close to the upper deck. Although the deck armour on *Hood* was heavier than that with which she had been originally designed, it was at least 4 inches less thick than the armour on the *Bismarck*.

HMS *Prince of Wales*, a King George V-class battleship, was better equipped to tackle the new German battleships but she was not fully worked up and still had civilian contractors on board trying to sort out problems with her turret rotation machinery and other issues.

When *Hood* and *Prince of Wales* intercepted *Bismarck* and *Prinz Eugen*, *Hood* opened fire on *Prinz Eugen* (mistaking her for the *Bismarck*) at 5.53 a.m. at 26,500 yards. The British were taking on one of the most powerful battleships in the world with an inadequately armoured veteran of the First World War and a young pup of a battleship with teething problems. Poorly positioned with regard to the German force, they could only use their forward guns in the initial salvo. In view of the odds against them, they needed to get their shooting right from the start but the first salvo from *Hood* was aimed at the wrong ship.

When *Bismarck* responded, her first three salvoes were dangerously close to *Hood*. The fourth salvo, which hit *Hood* just as she was turning to bring her aft guns to bear, tore through the upper decks and exploded a magazine in her depths. The whole ship erupted and broke in two before sinking. Of her crew of 1,419, only three survived.

Barely able to get over the shock of their own success, the Germans switched fire to HMS *Prince of Wales* and a shell soon killed all but the captain and yeoman of signals on the compass bridge. *Prince of Wales*'s guns were not fully operational so she turned away and escaped under cover of smoke. If the Germans had known her identity (they thought she was *King George V*) and her state of unreadiness, they may well have given chase and finished her off. As it was, Admiral Lutjens decided to continue his course towards the south.

The young pup *Prince of Wales* had, however, proved to have sharp teeth. Three of her 14in shells had hit *Bismarck*, one of them rupturing two of her fuel tanks. The bull elephant, despite its victory, was now limping. In view of his failure to take on more fuel during the stop in the Norwegian fjord, or to meet with an oiler later on, Lutjens had little choice other than to head for St Nazaire to refuel and carry out repairs.

Prince of Wales needed to get out of the area, but she had inflicted critical damage upon *Bismarck,* and her sister ship *King George V*, with her accompanying force of *Repulse*, the aircraft carrier *Victorious* and five cruisers, HMS *Renown* and the air-craft carrier HMS *Ark Royal* of Force H, were steaming up from the south-east. Both HMS *Ramillies* and HMS *Revenge* were instructed to intercept *Bismarck* as she headed south.

Meanwhile the two dogged county cruisers, *Norfolk* and *Suffolk*, continued to track the footsteps of the two German titans. *Suffolk* had been well out of range for most of the battle but now came closer to loose off several broadsides against *Prinz Eugen*.

The *Bismarck* and *Prinz Eugen* separated on the evening of 24 May so that *Prinz Eugen* could operate unhindered. *Bismarck* turned back towards the pursuing cruisers to keep them at bay but by now there were even more pursuers converging on her in the form of Admiral Tovey's task force. The aircraft carrier *Victorious* launched a flight of torpedo-carrying Swordfish aircraft and during this attack one torpedo hit the *Bismarck* but did not penetrate her armour belt.

Bismarck fooled her pursuers for a while by taking a clockwise sweep round behind them, but through a mixture of chance sightings and radio intercept, the position of *Bismarck* was eventually replotted. One aircraft that spotted her was an RAF Catalina seaplane, which was subjected to fierce anti-aircraft fire from the *Bismarck*. The Catalina encountered *Bismarck* in misty and hazy weather conditions and managed to conceal itself temporarily in cloud. Unfortunately the cloud ran out and the aircraft found itself directly over *Bismarck* at a range of about 400 yards with no cover. *Bismarck* let loose with all her anti-aircraft armament and the Catalina crew found themselves on the receiving end of the most powerful barrage they had ever experienced from one of the most powerful ships then afloat. *Bismarck* also took avoiding action, turning 90 degrees, clearly thinking that the Catalina was going to attempt to bomb her. More by luck than design, the Catalina escaped with just a few holes in the fuselage and was thus able to report back the *Bismarck*'s position.[2]

On the basis of this new intelligence, the aircraft carrier *Ark Royal*, approaching from the south, was ordered to send aircraft against *Bismarck*. On 26 May, at about 3.00 p.m., fifteen Swordfish were launched from the heaving deck of *Ark Royal*. In the murk, the flight of Swordfish attacked the first ship they saw, which turned out to be the British cruiser *Sheffield*, which was on the lookout for the *Bismarck* and fortunately managed to evade the torpedoes.

The Swordfish returned to *Ark Royal* to rearm and set off again into the murky night. If their mission were to fail again, it would be almost certain that *Bismarck* would be able to get under safe aerial cover from Luftwaffe units in France before the British heavy units could catch up with her. However, one of the Swordfish torpedoes hit the stern of *Bismarck*, locking the rudders and damaging the steering gear; this was to prove fatal as *Bismarck* would now be unable to escape the fast-approaching battleships. Apart from the *Sheffield*, a group of destroyers were first on the scene to harass *Bismarck* with torpedo attacks. The next morning HMS *King George V* and HMS *Rodney* arrived and split up to divide *Bismarck*'s fire. They began to pound *Bismarck* from ever closer range and gradually her fire-control systems were destroyed. The cruiser *Dorsetshire* finished the job with torpedoes and the crew of *Bismarck* scuttled their own ship.

After this momentous event, when the balance of naval power in the Atlantic see-sawed perilously, the British firmly re-established their dominance so far as surface warships were concerned. As if to underline the point, several armed merchant raiders were rounded up and sunk. *Bismarck*'s sister ship, *Tirpitz*, was compromised in her movements for the rest of the war and several bombing missions were sent against her.

HMS *Revenge* continued her convoy duties in the Atlantic in November 1941 when she accompanied a troop convoy to Durban in South Africa. After a refit she was sent to Ceylon to form part of the 3rd Battle Squadron of the Eastern Fleet, along with her sister ships HMS *Ramillies*, HMS *Resolution* and HMS *Royal Sovereign*. The fleet would be commanded by Admiral James Somerville who had his flag in HMS *Warspite*. The role of the ships was to protect the passage of essential supplies which were being brought across the Indian Ocean, including oil, rubber and a variety of other imports from India, New Zealand and Australia. The initial threat to the Eastern Fleet in 1941 came from Italian submarines, destroyers and other forces. HMS *Royal Sovereign* narrowly escaped an attack by the Italian submarine *Gauleo Ferraras* while en route to Aden and there were several other clashes between Italian and British forces against a backdrop of the East African campaign, which would eventually lead to the fall of Italian East Africa.

Apart from the battles being waged against the Italians in Africa, the other major event was the attack on Pearl Harbor by Japanese forces on 7 December 1941. On 15 February, they attacked Singapore. On 19 February, they ravaged Port Darwin in Australia. The Japanese then rolled on to attack Burma. Rangoon fell on 8 March, followed by Java on 9 March. The Japanese occupied the Andaman Islands on 23 March. Admiral Somerville assembled his forces at the British base at Colombo and received notice that a Japanese carrier attack, similar to the one perpetrated upon Pearl Harbor, was planned for Ceylon on 1 April. The Japanese strike force under Admiral Nagumo comprised the aircraft carriers *Akagi, Zuikaku, Kirishima, Hiei, Haruna* and *Kongo*, carrying between them about 300 aircraft, the heavy cruisers *Tone* and *Chikuma* and the light cruiser *Akuhuma*, as well as eight destroyers. Somerville's force initially consisted of the Revenge-class battleships *Ramillies* and *Royal Sovereign*. Not surprisingly, he asked for urgent reinforcements and a more balanced force to deal with the Japanese aerial threat. The force was supplemented by two more Revenge-class battleships, HMS *Revenge* herself and HMS *Resolution*, as well as two heavy and five light cruisers, sixteen destroyers, seven submarines and three aircraft carriers, carrying between them fifty-seven strike aircraft and thirty-six fighters.

Admiral Somerville duly tasked his forces to search the area, particularly towards the south-east, in order to pre-empt the Japanese attack, and although the search continued for three days and two nights, no Japanese ships were seen. The British force then headed for the secret base at Addu Atoll, about 600 miles south-west of Ceylon, to replenish their water supplies and refuel.

On 4 April, the force received word of an aerial sighting by an RAF Catalina of the Japanese carrier force at 0° 4′ N, long. 83° 10′ E, on course for Ceylon. The harbour at Colombo was cleared of as many ships as possible before the Japanese storm hit on Sunday, 5 April, destroying many of the port facilities but damaging only two ships in port. Admiral Geoffrey Layton was upbeat about the extent of damage and the quality of the response in an official statement in which he said the damage from the raid at 8 o'clock in the morning was relatively slight and that only a small number of civilians had been killed or wounded. The figures he gave for the number of enemy fighters shot down (twenty-five for certain and probably five more) gave the impression that the aerial defence had been more effective than it actually was, given the limited resources available.[3]

A later announcement continued in a similar morale-boosting vein, laying emphasis on the effective preparations for the attack and the spirit of the Blitz which kept panic at bay.[4]

Admiral Sir Geoffrey Layton (1884–1964) was a decisive and somewhat blunt naval officer who was able to take difficult decisions and to see them through. In this respect he was probably exactly the right person for the job of preparing Colombo and other naval harbours for attack, as any wavering or half-measures would have been severely punished by the fast-moving Japanese. Although he did not have many resources with which to hit back at the Japanese, his experiences at Singapore enabled him to limit drastically the destructive power of the Japanese onslaught.

Like a swarm of wasps, the Japanese planes went off in search of British ships at sea and found the heavy cruisers *Dorsetshire* and *Cornwall* sailing to join Somerville's force. Both were sunk.

After this tragedy, Admiral Somerville decided not to risk his forces by day, especially in view of the fact that the battleships in the Revenge class offered substantial targets to aerial bombers while carrying barely adequate anti-aircraft armament. Somerville divided his forces according to their speed. Force A consisted of HMS *Warspite*, the aircraft carriers HMS *Indomitable* and HMS *Formidable* and the cruisers HMS *Cornwall*, HMS *Emerald* and HMS *Enterprise*; Force B consisted of the four Revenge-class battleships and the aircraft carrier HMS *Hermes*. He planned to close with the enemy at night to attempt a torpedo attack but failed to make contact.

On 9 April, the Japanese paid a visit to the British base at Trincomalee, where there was a similar pattern to Colombo. The port had been mostly cleared but the Japanese later found the aircraft carrier HMS *Hermes* and destroyer HMS *Vampire* at sea. Both were sunk. *Hermes* was the first fully fledged, as opposed to converted, aircraft carrier in the world.

Having bombed the naval bases at Colombo and Trincomalee to no great effect, the Japanese were eager to find the main British Eastern Fleet. The building of the secret base at Adu Attol, the existence of which the Japanese never suspected, was an act of fortuitous foresight not dissimilar to the construction of the lines of Torres Vedras in the Peninsular War.

Admiral Sir James Somerville (1882–1949) was an able naval officer who had made a significant contribution to naval wireless telegraphy and played a key role in ship-to-ship communications during the Gallipoli landings. Somerville had sound judgement of tactics and ship handling and if he thought it was wise to keep the

Eastern Fleet out of the way of the Japanese carrier attack as far as possible, and to probe cautiously at night for the chance to launch a carrier-launched torpedo response, it was probably the right course of action in the circumstances. It was Somerville who, of all Royal Navy officers, appreciated the advantages of carrier-borne air power and it was the *Ark Royal*, under his jurisdiction, that had succeeded in crippling the *Bismarck* with torpedoes.

Second-in-command to Admiral Somerville was Rear Admiral Algernon Willis (1889–1976), with his flag on HMS *Resolution*, who was a torpedo expert and had gained valuable experience with Admiral Cunningham in the Mediterranean.

The Japanese swarm disappeared as quickly as it had come, this time to regroup before taking on American forces in the Pacific. The Revenge-class battleships and their old friend HMS *Warspite*, all of which had fought at Jutland and which represented a substantial naval ancestry, remained unscathed, which was of considerable comfort to the British at a turning point in the Second World War.

Despite the fact that the Eastern Fleet had survived the attacks and that it still flew the White Ensign in a key operational area for the British, it was clear that HMS *Revenge* and her sister ships were unsuited to the new, fast, carrier-based warfare. Admiral Somerville was keen for them to be replaced by the newer battleships HMS *Rodney* and HMS *Nelson*, and was even more keen for supplementary aircraft carriers.

Since Addu Attoll had no anti-aircraft protection, Somerville decided to move the Revenge-class battleships to Kilindini at Mombasa in East Africa. Here they could still carry out their convoy duties while keeping out of range of any Japanese resurgence. The harbour at Kilindini was a deep-water port and torpedo nets were strung across the harbour to deter intruders. Each of the battleships took it in turn to send out a pinnace at regular intervals which would drop a minor depth charge to deter any enemy divers.

HMS *Revenge* had sailed from the northern Atlantic, where the appearance of the *Bismarck* and *Prinz Eugen* had marked the high point of the German raider threat to the Atlantic convoys. The *Bismarck* had eventually been seen off by the new battleships of the fleet, HMS *Prince of Wales*, HMS *King George V* and HMS *Rodney*, and by carrier-borne aircraft.

In the Indian Ocean the balance of power had been severely threatened by the appearance of the Japanese carrier-borne strike force, and it had become evident that to repulse such a force what was needed was not venerable battleships but fast aircraft carriers, with plenty of good-quality aircraft. In addition, the fleet required well-resourced bases from which to operate with proper anti-aircraft protection and ground-based fighter protection. This would be a huge commitment for a country still fighting a world war effectively on its own and covering home waters, the entire Atlantic, the Mediterranean and the Indian Oceans.

As the Japanese became fully engaged with the Americans in the Pacific and as priorities became more urgent in Europe, the Eastern fleet was depleted even of the small reinforcements it had received, including the aircraft carrier HMS *Illustrious*. HMS *Revenge* and her sister ships, however, continued to fulfil a useful role, escorting convoys and in January 1943 she moved back to base in Trincomalee, Ceylon, which by now had been repaired after the Japanese assault. In February, she escorted the troop convoy carrying the Australian Division back to their homeland.

Ironically, the Japanese aircraft-carrier operations had not been created by themselves but learned from the British. The British had invented and developed many of the first aircraft carriers and had demonstrated the effectiveness of carrier-borne aircraft, both in their strikes against the *Bismarck* and on the Italian fleet at Taranto, where they had disabled three battleships, among other vessels. The Japanese would prove highly adept at perfecting other people's creations and it was the inventors who were now paying a heavy price.

In March 1943, HMS *Revenge* was given orders to return to England, ostensibly for a refit. By October of the same year, however, she had been withdrawn from operational service and placed in the reserve. It certainly looked like the glory days were over and that, like a retired racehorse, *Revenge* would have nothing to do other than remember the great days of the past when her mere presence would sent shivers of pride down the spines of her countrymen and shivers of apprehension down the spines of her enemies. The days when *Revenge* was the newest battleship in the fleet and her enemies sailed in trepidation of being on the receiving end of her 15in shells were over. Although her guns had roared in defiance at the German occupants of Cherbourg only two years before, causing dumbfounded amazement to both friend and foe, her excursion to the Indian Ocean had shown that the days of the big battleship were numbered. It was not right for the descendant of ships that had fought the Armada and at Trafalgar, and one that had herself fought at Jutland, to be shepherded about and protected by other ships and by aircraft lest she be bombed and sent to the bottom.

In January 1944, *Revenge* was transferred to the Portsmouth Command at Southampton and in May 1944 she began to be dismantled to provide spares for other ships, the most important items of which were her guns. *Revenge* was still used for training purposes and in the final months of the Second World War she was attached to the Imperieuse Training Establishment at Devonport. She was finally scrapped in September 1948.

The battleship HMS *Revenge* was the last surface ship to bear the name at the time of writing. With her paint barely dry and her engines barely run in, she had fought in the largest naval battle of all time at Jutland, but by the Second World War she was long in the tooth and, although still a formidable presence and enough of a deterrent to German surface raiders, she was too slow to keep up with more modern battleships and their escorts. Her contemporary, the Queen Elizabeth-class battleship HMS *Warspite*, proved to be a more successful design, primarily because she had a better balance of speed and hitting power. At the point, where a German invasion of England, Operation Sea Lion, was both planned by the Germans and expected by the British, however, it was the old *Revenge* which was brought to Plymouth to back up the Home Fleet and stand, as her ancestors of old had done, as one of the walls of England.

Winston Churchill wrote of that event:

> In Britain, whatever our shortcomings, we understood the sea affair very thoroughly. For centuries it has been in our blood, and its traditions stir not only our sailors but the whole race. It was this above all things which enabled us to regard the menace of invasion with a steady gaze ... Had the Germans possessed in 1940 well-trained amphibious forces equipped with all the apparatus of modern amphibious war their task would still have been a forlorn hope in the face of our sea- and air-power.[5]

The Royal Navy had accomplished a great deal in the Second World War and had adapted itself to overcome serious challenges.

Despite its surface dominance in the Atlantic, the elusive German battleship and battlecruiser raiders had proved to be a constant menace and the battle against the U-boats had required huge resources of patience, determination and ingenuity before they were finally defeated. In the Mediterranean the Navy had largely managed to keep the Italian fleet at bay and pioneered successful carrier-borne raids, but it also suffered grievously from Italian and German airborne and submarine attacks. In the Indian Ocean the Navy had experienced what Winston Churchill described as the most dangerous moment of the war. The overstretched Eastern Fleet narrowly missed decimation at the hands of a much more powerful Japanese carrier raiding group, whose previous work had been seen at Pearl Harbor. Good leadership, both at sea and on land, had mitigated the effects of the attack. In home waters, the Royal Navy proved invincible.

Chapter 16

Nuclear Option

The Royal Navy came out of the Second World War in many respects stronger than it had ever been, despite the tragic losses of about 1,525 warships and the death of about 50,000 personnel. In order to cope with the demands of war, the Navy had more than doubled the number of its vessels and it had about six times the number of personnel. The somewhat constrained tactics of the First World War had given way to a more adaptable style where lessons were quickly learned, new concepts tried and individual initiative rewarded. Despite its success and strength, however, the post-war era and the cold war would demand a very different navy.

The new reality was that the United States was now the dominant naval power, with an economy capable of maintaining that status. Britain's economy, by contrast, would need plenty of time to recover. There was no immediate mass scrapping of ships, however, as Britain still had massive imperial responsibilities.

HMS *Vanguard*, launched in 1944, would be the last British battleship whose star role would be to carry a princess to South Africa and bring a queen back. The aircraft carrier had by now asserted its dominance well into the twentieth century.

The Defence White Paper of 1957 set the tone for the new era. It banished conscription, raised the profile of nuclear weapons and placed a question mark over the future role of the Navy in war. The interest in a British nuclear submarine was fostered in particular by the First Sea Lord at the time, Earl Mountbatten. Although the original idea had been to produce an all-British nuclear submarine, the Americans had taken the technological lead in this area and it seemed a good idea to use their knowledge. The first nuclear-powered submarine was the USS *Nautilus*, but in the early days

[handwritten margin notes:] ≠ Rubbish! Vanguard took King George VI to S A in 1947. Princess Elizabeth flew to SA in 1952, and flew back as Q.E. II.

192

Admiral Rickover, who was in charge of the US programme, would not even allow Mountbatten to inspect *Nautilus*. Mountbatten had good relations with the US Chief of Naval Operations, Arleigh Burke, and, after a visit to the United States, Mountbatten managed to forge a productive relationship with Rickover as well. In due course, the Americans provided not only technological information but the entire power system from a US Skipjack-class submarine which was fitted into a hull designed by the British. HMS *Dreadnought*, the first British nuclear submarine, was launched on 21 October 1960.

In the meantime, Rolls-Royce and the United Kingdom Atomic Energy Authority developed an all-British nuclear power system for submarines which was subsequently fitted to HMS *Valiant*, heralding a new class of submarine which would include herself, HMS *Dreadnought* and HMS *Warspite*. This was all well and good but the British nuclear deterrent still rested on the shoulders of the Royal Air Force, whose fleet of V-bombers carried the aerial ballistic missile that would deliver unacceptable damage to an aggressor, namely the Soviet Union. The Vickers Valiant, Handley Page Victor and Avro Vulcan were each in their own way extraordinary achievements. These bombers were capable, such as in the case of the Victor, of carrying the Blue Steel stand-off nuclear missile at a loaded weight of 165,000lb (75,000kg) at 650mph (1,050kph) with a range of 2,500 miles (4,000km) and a service ceiling of 56,000 feet (17,000m). These amazing bombers could leave many fighter aircraft standing as they roared into the sky.

The problem with the aerial deterrent was the rapid development of Soviet ground-to-air defences which made aerial approaches to enemy territory ever more hazardous. Another problem arose with the development of the US Skybolt missile, a stand-off nuclear missile that would obviate overflight or even near proximity to enemy territory. The incoming Kennedy administration doubted the wisdom of placing this weapon technology in independent British hands and it raised the whole question of the viability of the aerial deterrent. The British Prime Minister Harold Macmillan resisted American efforts to impose a 'dual-key' arrangement on the British, whereby the Americans could retain a measure of control. Negotiations eventually led in the direction of the Polaris system, which would require a submarine platform. The days of the V-bombers were numbered.

There was some significance in the name of the new nuclear submarines. *Dreadnought* signified the passing of the mantle from the battleships to the nuclear submarine. The aircraft carriers would continue to play their particular vital role but the big punch that major naval forces had traditionally possessed had now passed from 15in guns to missiles of stupendous destructive power.

The Valiant class submarines proved successful and HMS *Valiant* herself would take part in the Falklands War, decades hence. The carriers of the nuclear deterrent, however, would be a new Resolution-class submarine. The first was HMS *Resolution* herself in February 1966, followed by *Repulse*, built at Vickers Armstrong in Barrow-in-Furness; later came *Renown* and *Revenge*, built by Cammell Laird in Birkenhead. Originally five boats had been planned but the incoming Labour administration saw fit to cut costs by cancelling the fifth, HMS *Ramillies*.

HMS *Revenge* was constructed in separate parts, including the bow, stern and the American-designed missile-launch system in between. The submarine carried sixteen Polaris A3 missiles and it also had six torpedo tubes to fire Tigerfish wire-guided homing torpedoes.

HMS *Revenge*

Length: 130m
Width: 10.1m
Height: 9m
Displacement: 8,500 tons submerged; 7,700 tons surfaced
Speed: 25 knots
Dive depth: 275 metres (900 feet)
Crew: 143

UGM-27 Polaris missile

The British version of the Polaris missile was based on the A-3 version of the missile, which was bigger and heavier than the previous A-1 and A-2 versions, and had a longer range. The A-3 version incorporated three multiple re-entry vehicles (MRVs) which were spread around a common target. With the development of Soviet anti-ballistic missile systems, research was done in both the United States and the United Kingdom to develop the MRV concept.

The US programme was called Antelope and the UK programme was called Chevaline.

The Chevaline project involved an immensely complex co-ordination of MRVs which proved to be correspondingly expensive. The programme had begun in 1969 and it was only in 1980 that the costs of the project were placed before Parliament, amounting to about £1 billion. There was some consternation at the cost and it sparked a debate about the viability of the independent British nuclear deterrent.

The Chevaline concept comprised two live warheads and four decoy warheads along with a set of decoy balloons, the aim being to confuse the defence system. The Chevaline system was first deployed on HMS *Renown* in 1982 and was withdrawn in 1987.

In view of the very high costs of these systems and, in the case of Chevaline, the comparatively short period of deployment, it is not surprising that the issue of a nuclear deterrent has sparked such lively debate. The reason the British pressed ahead with Chevaline was because the credibility of the independent nuclear deterrent depended on upgrading the weapon system. The Soviets deployed about 100 anti-ballistic missiles around Moscow, whereas the current British system could only place forty-eight warheads over the target, derived from sixteen Polaris missiles. The Soviets could be pretty confident that they could defeat this. One way round the problem would have been to increase the number of submarines on deployment and therefore double the number of missiles and warheads over the target, but this option was obviated by the cancellation of the fifth submarine.

The solution recommended by the British Chiefs of Staff was to purchase the new American Poseidon missile, which would allow a submarine like HMS *Revenge* to put 208 warheads over the target. With their great wisdom, the Conservative Government of the time decided to push ahead with the mysteriously named Chevaline system, which was opposed by those who were responsible for implementing it. As the Chevaline system was developed, moreover, it became apparent that its range would not be as great as the original version of the A-3 Polaris missile. This raised serious tactical and strategic concerns for, by having to operate substantially closer to their targets, the Resolution-class submarines would also be more exposed to counter-attack by enemy hunter-killer submarines and would be outside the fold of the main NATO protection forces.

In 2009, at the time of writing, the issue of the British nuclear deterrent blew up again as MPs were given the opportunity to discuss the pros and cons and to vote whether to replace the existing Trident system and therefore to continue with the nuclear deterrent or to discontinue it. The replacement for the Vanguard-class submarines was estimated at £20 billion and these would be deployed by 2020 with an estimated completion date of 2050. The critical part of the debate, in the view of the House of Commons Defence Select Committee, was not so much the missile as the submarine platform. The submarines HMS *Vanguard*, HMS *Victorious*, HMS *Vigilant* and HMS *Vengeance* were due to be withdrawn from service in 2019, 2020, 2023 and 2026 respectively. Advance planning for their replacement and allocation of costs was the crucial point.

After lively debate, 409 MPs supported the proposals and 161 opposed, leaving a majority of 248. The Labour Government of the day was supported by the Conservatives, whose leader David Cameron said, 'Replacing Britain's independent nuclear deterrent is clearly in the national interest.' With the end of the cold war and with Britain's armed forces overstretched in war theatres such as Iraq and Afghanistan, many both military and non-military people took the view that the money would be better spent on conventional equipment to deal with real and present threats. Supporters of the nuclear deterrent argued that nuclear weapons were available to a wide number of nations and that it would be a mistake for Britain to forego her nuclear guarantee. Like any insurance scheme, the problem with the nuclear deterrent was that it soaked up very large sums of money without ever being used. On the other hand, the consequences of being on the receiving end of what it was designed to deter were unthinkable.

Vice Admiral Sir Hugh Mackenzie was put in charge of the Polaris programme, which was to prove a very steep learning curve for the Royal Navy. Mackenzie received his first orders for the programme from the First Sea Lord, Admiral Sir Caspar John, in December 1962. The first British Polaris submarine, HMS *Resolution*, successfully completed its first test firing off Cape Canaveral at 11.15 Eastern Standard Time on 15 February 1968. In view of the fact that the British, within the space of six years, had to produce the appropriate platforms for the missiles and learn how to use them, this was a considerable achievement.

Despite having put the submarine in place at the test-firing range, there were a few last-minute hitches which put some nerves on edge. A US destroyer on station failed to inform HMS *Resolution* of her movements and as a result there was a minor collision in which *Resolution*'s telemetry mast was bent. The incident could have been far worse as the fin on *Resolution* could have ripped a hole in the destroyer and sunk her. A replacement mast was rapidly flown in by the US Navy and the test firing was a success.

The Resolution-class submarines introduced a new level of sophistication into the submarine world and the days of flying by the seat of your pants were gone. Navigation systems which are now familiar on most submarines and surface vessels were introduced, some of them predating the global positioning system, such as the Ship's Inertial Navigation System (SINS). This system continuously updated the submarine's position after basic navigational details had been fed into the system, such as initial latitude, longitude, heading and orientation. The SINS system computed a form of dead reckoning by sensing acceleration.

The advantage of the SINS system for a nuclear submarine like HMS *Revenge*, which was carrying the national nuclear deterrent, was that the submarine's navigation system was completely self-contained and therefore the submarine did not need to risk giving its position away by plotting its position against stars, as Drake's crew would have done, or by using detectable radio navigation. The system was entirely self-contained, did not radiate energy, was not detectable from the outside, could not be jammed and was unaffected by outside weather conditions. It comprised an extraordinary device made up of accelerometers, gyroscopes and servo systems feeding information to computers which then calculated the submarine's position to within a few yards.

In order to make the systems work and to carry out the other multitude of high-tech tasks aboard a nuclear submarine, the crew were of a very high calibre and there was a disproportionate number of senior officers and ratings. Due to the long periods spent at sea, HMS *Revenge* had two complete sets of crew changing over on a three-monthly cycle. While one crew worked on board to prepare for sailing, carry out training and perform the live deterrent patrol for a period of sixty days, the spare crew would go on leave, attend on-shore training and carry out any other support duties.

Due to the high demand on personnel, not all those serving in nuclear submarines were necessarily volunteers. Experts with skills such as electronics would be co-opted from other parts of the Navy and had to learn to adapt to the very particular demands and lifestyle of a submarine. For those who might consider this a dubious privilege, the space available on board at least made it more bearable than in the old days when crews had to share bunks in stages, usually six hours on, six hours off. To while away any spare time, there was a cinema and a library, and the crew could take part in correspondence courses to learn new skills. There was also a daily newspaper.

The submarine was steered 'blind' by a planesman who had a co-pilot standing by at all times to take over on a duplicate control. The appearance of the planesman in his seat holding a semi-circular wheel was similar to that of a bomber pilot. The planesman had to negotiate an underwater world which had rifts and valleys and mountains just like the world above water. As there was no visual sight, all movements were calculated by reference to instruments, including depth gauges, while sonar picked up all that was going on around the submarine. Sophisticated equipment was designed to distinguish between the 'noise' of sea life and any potential threats. The only visual information on patrol was derived from the occasional surfacing to periscope depth in order to receive radio signals and to take visual sightings and photographs of any vessels that happened to be about.

While there is plenty of room for manoeuvre in the depths of the ocean, great care has to be taken when returning to port as the ocean shelf slopes upwards and there is considerably less depth of water to remain concealed in. Apart from geographical features, the crew also have to be aware of man-made hazards such as shipwrecks.

The firing of the Polaris missiles aboard HMS *Revenge* would require a sophisticated procedure of confirmations and counter-checks to avoid accidental or misguided firing. The system involved the presence of several people at the moment of firing, multiple consent and a series of key combinations.

The presence of both a nuclear power plant and sixteen nuclear missiles in a comparatively confined and sealed space, with no diluting outer atmosphere, would conjure up dangers of radiation for most people. This was apparently not the case and on HMS *Revenge* there was considerably greater danger from the gasses emitted by the fridge than any side effects from the nuclear power plant or war-heads. If worn, a wristwatch with luminous hands might trigger the radiation alarm.

Typical menu for the crew of a nuclear submarine in the 1980s

	Breakfast	Lunch	Supper
Monday	Standard choice Eggs to order Bacon, sausage, baked beans, tomatoes plus extra black pudding	Steak and vegetable pie. Omelettes to order Salad selection Chipped and boiled potatoes Choice of vegetables Fruit flan & custard	Roast lamb and mint sauce Liver & bacon Cottage pie Fondant and creamed potatoes Cabbage, butter beans and peas Cheese and biscuits
Tuesday	Standard choice plus extra fish cakes	Cheesy Hammy Eggy Omelette to order Salad selection Chipped and boiled potatoes Choice of vegetables Sultana roll and custard	Boiled silverside and dumplings Sweet and sour pork Rabbit pie Boiled and creamed potatoes Turnips, green beans, broccoli Cheese and biscuits Fresh fruit
Wednesday	Standard choice plus extra sautéd kidney	Choice of fish dishes Omelettes to order Salad selection Chipped and boiled potatoes Choice of vegetables Chocolate pudding and custard	Roast chicken and stuffing Shepherd's pie Pork chops and apple sauce Roast and marquis potatoes Cabbage, carrots and brussel sprouts Cheese and biscuits
Thursday	Standard choice plus extra kippers	Pizza pie Omelettes to order Salad selection Chipped and boiled potatoes Choice of vegetables Apple crumble and custard	Baked gammon and peach sauce Braised liver and onions Lamb chop and vegetables Lyonnaise and baked potatoes BITS, peas and carrots Cheese and biscuits Fresh fruit

	Breakfast	Lunch	Supper
Friday	Standard choice plus extra pork luncheon meat fritters	Brown stew and dumplings Omelettes to order Salad selection Chipped and boiled potatoes Choice of vegetables Fruit and ice cream	Grilled and fried steak Cod portions Spaghetti bolognaise Chipped and creamed potatoes Fried onions, sweetcorn and peas Cheese and biscuits
Saturday	Standard choice plus extra smoked haddock	Cottage pie Omelettes to order Salad selection Sautéd and boiled potatoes Choice of vegetables Rice pudding and jam sauce	Chicken pie Savoury mince Gammon steak and pineapple Scallop and creamed potatoes Swede, tomatoes and green beans Cheese and biscuits Fresh fruit
Sunday	Standard choice plus extra grapefruit segments and mushrooms	Roast beef and Yorkshire pudding Roast turkey and stuffing Roast pork and apple sauce Roast and braised potatoes Cabbage, carrots and cauliflower Jelly, fruits and cream	100% salad Baked potatoes Cheese and biscuits

When HMS *Revenge* departed port on patrol, she would be accompanied in the initial phase by either a helicopter or a hunter-killer submarine to ensure that she was not being trailed by a potential aggressor. From then on the submarine would not transmit any messages – she would only receive them. Apart from any operational aspects, this meant the crew could not send any messages to their families while on patrol, which put them in a similar position to the early sailing versions of HMS *Revenge*. Radio signals sent in ultra-low frequency were received from base by an aerial towed behind the submarine.

Although, at 25 knots, HMS *Revenge* could travel faster under water than her battleship predecessor, speed was not of the essence for a nuclear submarine unless she should need to remove herself quickly from a potential danger zone. Her security lay in the fact that her massive bulk was imperceptible in the vastness of the oceans, where she would be a lurking menace to Britain's enemies and a comfort to her own country.

HMS *Revenge* continued with her secret patrols for twenty-three years, finally being paid off in May 1992 after carrying out fifty-six patrols. She was laid up at Rosyth while her sister ships ran through the final months of their operations, gradually being replaced by the new Vanguard-class submarines carrying the Trident nuclear deterrent (HMS *Vanguard*, HMS *Vigilant*, HMS *Victorious* and HMS *Vengeance*).

At the time of writing, there is no HMS *Revenge* in the Royal Navy but perhaps when there is the sound of a distant drum the old *Revenge* will appear once again to do her duty for England:

> *Drake he's in his hammock till the great Armadas come,*
> *(Capten, art tha sleepin' there below?),*
> *Slung atween the round shot, listenin' for the drum,*
> *An' dreamin' arl the time o' Plymouth Hoe.*
> *Call him on the deep sea, call him up the Sound,*
> *Call him when ye sail to meet the foe;*
> *Where the old trade's plyin' an' the old flag flyin',*
> *They shall find him, ware an' wakin', as they found him long ago.*

Notes

Chapter 1

1. Rodger, N.A.M., *The Safeguard of the Sea: A Naval History of Britain*, vol. 1, 1660–1649, London, HarperCollins, 1997, p. 28.
2. Loades, David, 'From the King's Ships to the Royal Navy', in Hill, J.R. (ed.), *Illustrated History of the Royal Navy*, Oxford, OUP, 1995, p. 42.
3. 'The shape of the ships that defeated the Spanish Armada', Glasgow, Tom, *Mariner's Mirror*, vol. 50, 1964.
4. Loades, op. cit.
5. Moorhouse, E. Hallam, *Letters of the English Seamen 1587–1808*, London, Chapman & Hall, 1910.
6. Chaucer, Geoffrey, *A Treatise on the Astrolabe*, 1391.
7. Moorhouse, op. cit.
8. Moorhouse, op. cit.
9. Mattingly, Garrett, *The Armada*, Boston, Houghton Mifflin, 1959.
10. Moorhouse, op. cit.
11. Cobbett, William, *A History of the Protestant Reformation in England and Ireland*, Illinois, Tan Books and Publishers Inc., 1988.
12. Moorhouse, op. cit.
13. Moorhouse, op. cit.
14. van Meteeren, Emanuel, *History of the Low Countries*, quoted in Hakluyt, *Voyages and Discoveries*, Penguin Books, 1972.
15. Loades, David, *The Tudor Navy: An Administrative, Political and Military History*, Studies in Naval History, Aldershot, Ashgate Publishing, 1992.
16. Ibid.
17. Williamson, James A., *Hawkins of Plymouth*, London, A&C Black, 1949.
18. Lewis, Michael, *Armada Guns*, London, George Allen & Unwin, 1961, p. 10.
19. Lewis, op. cit.
20. Andrews, Kenneth R., *Drake's Voyages*, Weidenfeld & Nicolson, 1967.
21. Ribadeneyra, Pedro de, S.I., *Historias de la Contrareforma*, Biblioteca de Autores Cristianos, Madrid, 1945, pp. 1331 & 1333.
22. Javier Zamora, J.M. and López-Córdon, M V., 'La Imagen de Europa y el pensamiento político-internacional' in Menendez Pidal, R. and Javier Zamora, M.M. (eds), *Historia de España XXVI (El siglo del Quijote) (1580–1680)*, Madrid, 1986, p. 363.

23. Jiménez, Carlos Gómez-Centurión, *England, Spain and the Gran Armada 1585–1604: The New Crusade, Essays from the Anglo-Spanish Conferences*, London and Madrid 1988, Rodríguez-Salgado, M.J. and Adams, Simon (eds), Edinburgh, John Donald Publishers Ltd, 1991, p. 268.
24. Waugh, Evelyn, *Edmund Campion*, London, 1935.
25. Haydon, Alexander, *Edmund Campion*, London, Catholic Truth Society, 2003.
26. Ibid.
27. Ibid.
28. Roper, William and Harpsfield, Nicholas, *Lives of Saint Thomas More*, Reynolds, E.E. (ed.), London, Dent, 1963.
29. Stapleton, Thomas and Reynolds, E.E. (eds), *The Life of Sir Thomas More*, London, Burns & Oates, 1966, p. 178.
30. Ibid.
31. Sultana De Maria, Fiorella, *Robert Southwell: Priest, Poet and Martyr*, London, Catholic Truth Society, 2003.
32. Gerard, John, *The Autobiography of an Elizabethan*, London, 1951, pp. 108–9.

Chapter 2

1. Moorhouse, op. cit.
2. Mattingly, Garrett, *The 'Invincible' Armada and Elizabethan England*, Cornell University Press, 1963, p. 16.
3. Loades, op. cit., pp. 249–50.
4. Loades, op. cit., p. 252.
5. Moorhouse, op. cit.
6. Moorhouse, op. cit.
7. Moorhouse, op. cit.
8. Moorhouse, op. cit.

Chapter 3

1. Moorhouse, op. cit.
2. Loades, op. cit., p. 259.
3. Linschoten, Jan van Huyghen.
4. Rowse, A.L., *Sir Richard Grenville of the Revenge*, London, Jonathan Cape, 1940.
5. Letters of Philip Gawdy, Roxburghe Club, 1906, p. 53.
6. Gawdy, op. cit.
7. Gawdy, op. cit.
8. Gawdy, op. cit.
9. Raleigh, Sir Walter, *A report of the truth of the fight about the iles of Acores, this last sommer* [sic] *betwixt the Revenge, one Her Majesties shippes, and an Armada of the King of Spaine*, Lisboa, Imprensa Nacional, 1915.
10. Rowse, op. cit.
11. Raleigh, op. cit.
12. Rowse, op. cit.
13. Rowse, op. cit.

14. Bacon, Francis, 'Considerations touching a war with Spain', *Letters and Life*, Spedding (ed.).
15. Babington, Thomas, 'Horatius', *Lays of Ancient Rome*, 1881.
16. Rowse, op. cit.
17. Rowse, op. cit.
18. Linschoten, op. cit.
19. Tennyson, Alfred Lord, 'The Revenge: A Ballad of the Fleet'.

Chapter 4

1. Cowburn, Philip, *The Warship in History*, London, Macmillan, 1966.
2. Powell, J.R. and Timing, E.K. (eds), *The Rupert and Monck Letter Book, 1666*, Navy Records Society, vol. 112, 1969, pp. 274–5.
3. Ibid.
4. Ibid.

Chapter 5

1. Pool, Bernard, *Navy Board Contracts 1660–183: Contract Administration under the Navy Board*
2. *Samuel Pepys and the Second Dutch War, Pepys Navy White Book and Brook House Papers*, Navy Records Society, Vol. 133.
3. Samuel Pepys, op. cit.
4. Pool, op. cit.
5. Pool, op. cit.
6. Albion, Robert Greenhalgh, *Forests and Sea Power: The Timber Problem of the Royal Navy 1652–1862*, Cambridge, Harvard University Press, 1926.
7. Albion, op. cit.
8. Pool, op. cit.
9. Samuel Pepys and the Second Dutch War, op. cit.
10. Pool, op. cit.
11. *The Journal of Sir George Rooke*, Admiral of the Fleet, 1700–1702, Navy Records Society, vol. 9.
12. Rooke, op. cit.
13. Stenuit, Robert, *Les Epaves de L'Or: des pêcheurs de trésor a la recherche des galions espagnols de la baie de Vigo*, Paris, Editions Gallimard, 1976.

Chapter 6

1. Harris, Simon, *Sir Cloudesley Shovell: Stuart Admiral*, Spellmount, 2001, p. 256.
2. Owen, J.H., *War at Sea Under Queen Anne 1702–1708*, Cambridge University Press, 1938.
3. Captain's Log, HMS *Revenge*.

Chapter 7

1. Corbet, Julian S., *England in the Mediterranean 1603–1713: A Study of the Rise and Influence of British Power within the Straits*, vol. II, London, Longmans, Green & Co., 1904.

2. Idid., p. 301.
3. Ibid., p. 301.
4. Ibid., p. 301.
5. Lavery, Brian, *The Ship of the Line: Development of the Battlefleet 1650–1850*, vol. 1, London, Conway Maritime Press, 1983.
6. Ibid.
7. Ibid.
8. 'Papers Relating to the Loss of Minorca in 1756', Richmond, Captain H.W., RN, (ed.), Navy Records Society, vol. XLII.
9. 'The trial of the Hon. Admiral John Byng at a Court Marshal', in the 'Papers Relating to the Loss of Minorca in 1756', op. cit.
10. Pajol, Charles Pierre Victor, *'La Guerre Sous Louis XV'*, vol. vi, p. 4, in 'Papers relating to the Loss of Minorca', op. cit., p. xii.
11. 'Papers relating to the Loss of Minorca', op. cit.
12. Ibid.
13. Ibid.
14. Ibid.
15. Ibid.
16. Ibid.

Chapter 8

1. Baugh, Daniel, 'The Eighteenth-Century Navy as a National Institution, 1690–1815', in *The Oxford Illustrated History of the Royal Navy*, Oxford, OUP, 1995.
2. Lavery, op. cit.
3. Falconer, William, *An Universal Dictionary of the Marine*, London, T. Cadell, 1780.
4. Falconer, op. cit.
5. Robinson, William, *Jack Nastyface: Memoirs of a Seaman*, Warner, Oliver (ed.), Annapolis, Naval Institute Press, 1973.

Chapter 9

1. Adams, Max, *Admiral Collingwood: Nelson's Own Hero*, London, Weidenfeld & Nicolson, 2005.
2. Burke, Edmund, *Reflections on the Revolution in France: And on the Proceeding in Certain Societies in London Relative to that Event*, O'Brien, Conor Cruise (ed.), London, Penguin Books, 1986.
3. Burke, op. cit.
4. Ibid.
5. Thatcher, Margaret, 'The Bruges Speech', Bruges Belfry, Bruges, 20 September 1988.
6. Fraser, E., *The Enemy at Trafalgar: An Account of the Battle from Eye-Witnesses' Narratives and Letters and Despatches from the French and Spanish Fleets*, London, Hodder & Stoughton, 1906.
7. Fraser, op. cit.
8. Fraser, op. cit.

9. Robinson, op. cit.
10. Ibid.
11. Ibid.
12. Fraser, op. cit.
13. Fraser, op. cit.
14. Southey, Robert, *The Life of Nelson*, London, Constable, 1999.
15. Robinson, op. cit.
16. Fraser, op. cit.
17. Robinson, op. cit.

Chapter 10

1. Gambier to Pole, 26 March 1809, 'Autobiography', in Cordingly, David, *Cochrane the Dauntless: The Life and Adventures of Thomas Cochrane*, London, Bloomsbury, 2007, pp. 211–12.
2. James, William, *The Naval History of Great Britain: From the Declaration of War by France in 1793 to the Accession of George IV*, Lambert, Andrew (ed.), London, Conway Maritime Press, 2002.
3. James, op. cit.

Chapter 11

1. Kincaid, John, *Adventures in the Rifle Brigade in the Peninsula, France and the Netherlands from 1809 to 1815*, Staplehurst, Spellmount, 1998.
2. Kincaid, John, *Random Shots from a Rifleman*, Staplehurst, Spellmount, 1998.
3. Rodger, Nicholas, *The Command of the Ocean: A Naval History of Britain*, vol. 2, 1649–1815, London, Allen Lane, 2004.
4. James, op. cit.

Chapter 13

1. Newbolt, Henry, 'Drake's Drum', *Admirals All*, 1897.
2. Hase, Georg von, *Kiel and Jutland*, New York, E.P. Dutton, 1922.

Chapter 14

1. *Associated Press*, 29 September 1922.
2. Ibid.
3. *The Times*, 16 July 1935.
4. *The Times*, 9 August 1939.

Chapter 15

1. *The Times*, 12 October 1940.
2. *The Times*, 28 May 1941.
3. *The Times*, 6 April 1942.
4. *The Times*, 6 April 1942.
5. Churchill, Winston, *The Second World War*, Penguin Books, 1989.

Bibliography

Adams, Max, *Admiral Collingwood: Nelson's Own Hero*, London, Weidenfeld & Nicolson, 2005.

Adams, Simon, *The Armada Campaign of 1588*, Historical Association, *c.*1988.

Adkins, Roy, *Trafalgar: The Biography of a Battle*, London, Little, Brown, 2005.

Albion, Robert Greenhalgh, *Forests and Seapower: The Timber Problem of the Royal Navy 1652–1862*, Cambridge, Harvard University Press, 1926.

Anderson, R.C. (ed.), *The Journal of Edward Montagu First Earl of Sandwich Admiral and General at Sea 1659–1665*, The Navy Records Society, 1928.

Arantegne y Sanz, *Artillería Española*.

Arber, Edward (ed.), *The last fight of the Revenge at Sea: under the command of Sir Richard Grenville, on the 10–11 September 1591, described by Sir Walter Raleigh, 1591, Gervase Markham, 1595 and Jan Huygen van Linschoten*, London, Arber, 1871.

'Armada Guns: The Guns of the Spanish Fleet, 1588', *The Mariner's Mirror*, vol. 29, No. 1, January 1943.

Barrington, Michael, 'Sir Richard Grenville's Last Fight', *Mariner's Mirror*, vol. 36, 1950.

Baumber, Michael, *General-at-Sea, Robert Blake and the Seventeenth Century Revolution in Naval Warfare*, London, John Murray, 1989.

Castellanos, Juan de, *Discurso de el Capitán Francisco Draque*, Madrid, Instituto de Valencia de D. Juan, 1921.

Chambers, R.W., *Thomas More*, Brighton, Harvester Press, 1982.

Childs, D.J., 'The Little Revenge – I', *The Naval Review*, vol. 79, No. 3, July 1991; 'The Little Revenge – II', vol. 79, No. 4, October 1991.

Churchill, Winston, *The Second World War*, London, Penguin Books, 1989.

Clowes, William Laird, *The Royal Navy: A History*, 7 vols, London, 1897–1903.

Corbett, Julian (ed.), *Fighting Instructions 1530–1816*, London, Navy Records Society, 1905.

Corbett, Julian S., *Drake and the Tudor Navy, with a History of the Rise of England as a Maritime Power*, vols I and II, London, Longmans Green and Co., 1898; republished Aldershot, Gower Publishing, 1988.

Corbett, Julian Stafford (ed.), *Papers relating to the navy during the Spanish War, 1585–1587*, London, printed for the Navy Records Society, 1897.

Corbett, Julian Stafford, with an introduction by R.B. Wernham, *Drake and the Tudor Navy: with a history of the rise of England as a maritime power*, Aldershot, Temple Smith, 1988.

Corbett, Julian Stafford, *England in the Mediterranean 1603–1713: A Study of the Rise and Influence of British Power within the Straits*, vol. II, London, Longmans, Green & Co., 1904.

Corbett, Julian Stafford, *Sir Francis Drake*, London, Macmillan, 1898.

Cordingly, David, *Cochrane the Dauntless: The Life and Adventures of Thomas Cochrane*, London, Bloomsbury, 2007.

Davies, J.D., *Gentlemen and Tarpaulins: The Officers and Men of the Restoration Navy*, Oxford, Clarendon Press, 1991.

De Mel-o de Matos, Gastão, *Notícias do terço da armada real*, Imprensa da Armada, 1932.

Dolley, Michael, 'The Historical Background to the 1580 Map of Smerwick', *The Mariner's Mirror*, vol. 53, No. 1, February 1967.

Elliott, J.H., *Imperial Spain 1469–1716*, London, Penguin Books, 1990.

Falconer, William, *An Universal Dictionary of the Marine: or A copious explanation of the technical terms and phrases employed in the construction, equipment, furniture, machinery, movements and military operations of a ship*, London, T. Caddell, MDCCLXXX.

Fernandez Duro, Capitán Cesario, *La Armada Invencible*, Madrid, Sucesores de Rivadeneyra, 1884–1885.

Fraser, Edward, 'The Revenge (The Battle Honours of the British Fleet)', *The Navy and Army Illustrated*, 21 October 1896.

Fraser, E., *The Enemy at Trafalgar: An Account of the Battle from Eye-Witnesses' Narratives and Letters and Despatches from the French and Spanish Fleets*, London, Hodder & Stoughton, 1906.

Froude, James Anthony, *English seamen in the sixteenth century*, London, Longmans, Green, 1895.

Gardiner, Samuel Rawson, and Atkinson, C.T. (eds), 'Letters and papers relating to the First Dutch War', 6 vols, London, Navy Records Society, 1652–4.

Glasgow, Tom, 'Elizabethan Ships pictured on the Smerwick Map, 1580, Background, Authentication and Evaluation', with Salisbury, W., 'The Ships', *The Mariner's Mirror*, vol. 52, No. 2, May 1966.

Glasgow, Tom, 'The Shape of the Ships that defeated the Spanish Armada', *The Mariner's Mirror*, vol. 50, No. 3, August 1964.

Goodman, David, *Spanish Naval Power: Reconstruction and Defeat, 1589–1665*, Cambridge, Cambridge University Press, 1997.

Gordon, Andrew, *The Rules of the Game: Jutland and British Naval Command*, London, John Murray, 1996.

Hakluyt, Richard and Beeching, Jack (ed.), *Voyages and Discoveries: The Principal Navigations Voyages, Traffiques and Discoveries of the English Nation*, London, Penguin Books, 1985.

Harris, Simon, *Sir Cloudesley Shovell: Stuart Admiral*, Staplehurst, Spellmount, 2001.

Hase, Georg von, *Kiel and Jutland*, New York, E.P. Dutton, 1922.

Hattendorf, Professor John, B.; Padfield, Peter; Vincent, Edgar; Monaque, Admiral Remi; Tracy, Dr Nicholas; Goodwin, Peter; Callo, Rear Admiral Joseph; Lambert, Professor Andrew, *The Trafalgar Companion*, Oxford, Osprey, 2005.

Haydon, Alexander, *Edmund Campion*, London, Catholic Truth Society, 2003.

Hayward, J.F., *The Art of the Gunmaker, 1550–1660*, London, Barrie & Rockliffe, 1962.

Hill, J.R. (ed.), *The Oxford Illustrated History of the Royal Navy*, Oxford, OUP, 1995.

James, William, *The Naval History of Great Britain: From the Declaration of War by France in 1793 to the Accession of George IV*, Lambert, Andrew (ed.), London, Conway Maritime Press, 2002.

Kemp, P.K., *Nine Vanguards*, London, Hutchinson & Co., 1951.

Kincaid, John, *Adventures in the Rifle Brigade in the Peninsula, France and the Netherlands from 1809 to 1815*, Staplehurst, Spellmount, 1998.

Kincaid, John, *Random Shots from a Rifleman*, Staplehurst, Spellmount, 1998.

Knighton, C.S. and Loades, D.M., *The Anthony Roll of Henry VIII's Navy*, Aldershot, Ashgate/Navy Records Society, 2000.

Knox, John (ed.), *State Papers Relating to the defeat of the Spanish Armada, anno 1588*, London, Navy Records Society, 1894.

Latham, Agnes M.C., *Sir Walter Raleigh: Selected Prose and Poetry, The Last Fight of the Revenge*, The Athlone Press, University of London, 1965.

Laughton, John Knox (ed.), *From Howard to Nelson: twelve sailors*, London, Lawrence and Bullen, 1899.

Lavery, Brian, *The Ship of the Line: Development of the Battlefleet 1650–1850*, vol. 1, London, Conway Maritime Press, 1983.

Lavery, Brian, *Nelson's Fleet at Trafalgar*, London, National Maritime Musuem, 2004.

Lewis, Michael, *Armada Guns: A Comparative Study of English and Spanish Armaments*, London, Allen & Unwin, 1961.

Lewis, Michael, *The Spanish Armada*, London, Batsford, 1960.

Loades, David, *The Tudor Navy: An Administrative, Political and Military History* (Studies in Naval History), Aldershot, Ashgate Publishing, 1992.

Lopes de Mendonça, Henrique, *Estudos sobre navios portugueses nos seculos XV e XVI*, Academia Real das Sciencias, 1892.

Martin, Colin and Parker, Geoffrey, *The Spanish Armada*, London, Penguin, 1992.

Mattingly, Garrett, *The 'Invincible' Armada and Elizabethan England*, New York, Ithaca, 1963.

Mattingly, Garrett, *The Armada*, Boston, Houghton Mifflin, 1959.

Mattingly, Garrett, *The Defeat of the Spanish Armada*, London, Jonathan Cape, 1959.

McFee, William, *Sir Martin Frobisher*, London, The Bodley Head, 1928.

Moorhouse, E. Hallam (ed.), *Letters of the English Seamen: 1587–1808, Drake's Letter from Revenge*, London, Chapman & Hall, 1910.

Oppenheim, M., *A History of the Administration of the Royal Navy and of Merchant Shipping in relation to the Navy from 1509 to 1660 with an Introduction treating of the preceding period*, London, The Bodley Head, 1896; reprinted Aldershot, Temple Smith, 1988.

Owen, J.H., *War at Sea under Queen Anne, 1702–1708*, Cambridge, Cambridge University Press, 1938

Papers Relating to the Spanish War 1585–1587, The Navy Records Society, MDCCCCXCVIII.

Peebles, Hugh B., *Warship Building on the Clyde: Naval Orders and the Prosperity of the Clyde Shipbuilding Industry, 1889–1939*, Edinburgh, Donald, c.1987.

Pool, Bernard, 'Some notes on warship-building by contract in the eighteenth century', *Mariner's Mirror*, vol. 49, 1963.

Pool, Bernard, *Navy Board Contracts 1660–1833: Contract Administration under the Navy Board*, London, Longman, 1966.

Powell, John Roland, *Robert Blake: General at Sea*, London, Collins, 1972.

Powell, J.R. and Timing, E.K. (eds), *The Rupert and Monck Letter Book, 1666*, Navy Records Society, vol. 112, 1969.

Quirino da Fonseca, Henrique, *A caravela portuguesa e a prioridade tecnica das navegacões henriquinas*, Coimbra, Imprensa da Universidade, 1934.

Raleigh, Sir Walter, *A report of the truth of the fight about the iles of Acores, this last sommer [sic] betwixt the Revenge, one Her Majesties shippes, and an Armada of the King of Spaine*, Lisboa, Imprensa Nacional, 1915.

Robinson, Gregory, 'The Loss of HMS Revenge, 1591', *The Mariner's Mirror*, vol. 38, No. 2, May 1952.

Robinson, William, *Jack Nastyface: Memoirs of a Seaman*, Warner, Oliver (ed.), Annapolis, Naval Institute Press, 1973.

Rodger, N.A.M, *The Safeguard of the Sea: A Naval History of Britain*, vol. 1, 1660–1649, London, HarperCollins, 1997

Rodger, N.A.M., *The Command of the Ocean: A Naval History of Britain*, vol. 2, 1649–1815, London, Allen Lane, 2004.

Rodriguez-Salgado, M.J. and Adams, Simon (eds), *England, Spain and the Grand Armada, 1585–1604: Essays from the Anglo-Spanish Conferences*, London and Madrid 1988, Edinburgh, Donald, c.1991.

Roper, William and Harpsfield, Nicholas, *Lives of Saint Thomas More*, Reynolds, E.E. (ed.), London, Dent, 1963.

Roskill, S.W., *HMS Warspite*, London, William Collins & Sons Ltd, 1957.

Roskill, S.W., *The Navy at War 1939–1945*, London, Collins, 1960.

Rowse, A.L., *Sir Richard Grenville of the Revenge*, London, Jonathan Cape, 1940.

Samuel Pepys and the Second Dutch War, Pepys Navy White Book and Brook House Papers, Latham, Robert (ed.), Navy Records Society, vol.133, 1995.

Smith, Edgar Charles, *A Short History of Naval and Marine Engineering*, Cambridge, Cambridge University Press, 1937.

Southey, Robert, *The Life of Nelson*, London, Constable, 1999.

Stapleton, Thomas, *The Life of Sir Thomas More*, E.E. Reynolds (ed.), London, Burns & Oates, 1966.

Sugden, John, *Sir Francis Drake*, London, Barrie & Jenkins, 1990; New York, Henry Holt, 1991.

Sultana De Maria, Fiorella, *Robert Southwell: Priest, Poet and Martyr*, London, Catholic Truth Society, 2003.

The Log of HMS Renown

The Mariners' Mirror, various volumes.

Thomas, David A., *The Illustrated Armada Handbook*, London, Harrap, 1988.

Thomson, George Malcolm, *Sir Francis Drake*, London, Secker & Warburg, 1972.

Waters, Lt Cdr D.W., 'The Elizabethan Navy and the Armada Campaign', *Mariner's Mirror*, vol. 35, No. 2, April 1949.

Williamson, James A., *Hawkins of Plymouth*, London, A&C Black, 1949.

Williamson, James A., *Sir Francis Drake*, London, Collins, 1951.

Williamson, James A., *Sir John Hawkins: The Time and the Man*, Oxford, Clarendon Press, 1927.

Williamson, James, *Hawkins of Plymouth: a new history of Sir John Hawkins and of the other members of his family prominent in Tudor England*, London, Black, 1949.

Winton, John, *The Submariners: Life in British Submarines 1901–1999*, London, Constable, 1999.

World-Wide-Web

http://archive.timesonline.co.uk/tol/archive/

http://en.wikipedia.org/wiki/HMS_Revenge_(06)

http://en.wikipedia.org/wiki/Revenge_class_battleship

http://en.wikipedia.org/wiki/Battle_of_Jutland

http://en.wikipedia.org/wiki/Trafalgar_order_of_battle_and_casualties

http://www.oxforddnb.com

http://www.pdavis.nl

http://www.shipsnostalgia.com/guides/Revenge_Class_Battleship_HMS_Revenge?cruise_forum

Index